Millennium
Eyewitness

Millennium Eyewitness

A thousand years of history
written by those who were there

Compiled by
Brian Stone

PIATKUS

In memory of my parents, William Edward and Dora Stone

Copyright © 1997 by Brian Stone

First published in 1997 by
Judy Piatkus (Publishers) Ltd of
5 Windmill Street, London W1P 1HF

First published in paperback in 1998

**The moral right of the author has
been asserted.**

*A catalogue record for this book
is available from the British Library*

ISBN 0 7499 1883 7

Designed by Paul Saunders
Typeset by Butler & Tanner Ltd, Frome and London
Printed and bound in Great Britain by
Butler & Tanner Ltd, Frome and London

CONTENTS

INTRODUCTION

WITHOUT EYEWITNESS accounts, recorded history simply ceases to exist. Everything we know about the past originated in someone relating what they had seen or experienced, either to someone else who recorded it, or by speaking directly to posterity in the form of a journal, letter or memoir. Historians, therefore, always try to get back to the original source when seeking to understand an historical event.

That does not mean, however, that we have to accept uncritically everything that was recorded at first-hand. There are many compelling reasons why eyewitness evidence should be treated with caution: the account may have been written many years after the event and may suffer from the author's defective memory; he or she may have had a personal or political axe to grind and may, consciously or not, distort the truth; or they may simply have witnessed only part of the event and have an erroneous view; lastly, the eyewitness may have seen everything and yet have drawn a wholly misleading view. Still, first-hand accounts are, ultimately, the only evidence we have, and the historian must do the best with them that he or she can.

The value of the eyewitness account, however, goes far beyond this. It brings history alive for the ordinary person in a way that nothing else can; it enables us to feel, at least to a degree, what it must have been like to have lived at the time, and this is the main reason why I have used them so extensively, and I hope with some degree of success, over twelve years of teaching history to adult education classes. In a very real sense, this book is a response to the requests of many of my students to make historical eyewitness accounts accessible in a single volume, and this is what I have tried to do with *Millennium Eyewitness*. It is a tribute to the interest and enthusiasm of many of my class-members, and I hope it will also find a wider audience which will discover in these extracts the drama, excitement, brutality, humour and tenderness that make up the human condition – humans are always the same, only the context changes.

Faced with a period of 1000 years from which to draw sources, the anthologist faces an almost impossible task. I had to decide not only which geographical area should be covered, but also whether I should limit the subject matter to a particular language and particular themes. With some misgivings, I have decided that this anthology will cover the world, but that it will be limited to accounts published in English or English translation. This has enabled me to include many fascinating insights into history which a narrower definition would have excluded. If, for example, I had limited the scope just to Britain or Europe, and only to accounts *originally* published in English, I could not have included Spanish accounts of the conquest of Mexico and Peru, Italian accounts of the Black Death, a French account of the Battle of Agincourt or an American-Indian version of the Battle of the Little Big Horn.

Inevitably, this book has a European bias, but I hope that it is not, taken as a whole, unduly ethno-centric or exclusive. I have also tried to ensure that it covers each century as well as the sources allow. This has, I admit, been extremely difficult. The anthologist of the millennium faces some acute problems — not enough material for the first 300 years and far too much for the nineteenth and twentieth centuries — indeed an embarrassment of riches. I hope I will be forgiven, therefore, if the reader notices that some of the earlier accounts are not, strictly speaking, eyewitness accounts. The Battle of Hastings, for example, has no eyewitness accounts, but could not properly have been left out. Where this is the case, I have used the very best source available, which is usually based on eyewitness testimony given to the chronicler at the time or shortly afterwards. Likewise, for the last 150 years of the period there is such a huge quantity of material that, inevitably, some important events have had to be ignored. Like every anthology it is largely a reflection of my own interests, pre-occupations and prejudices. As a friend commented to me, 'It all sounds a bit of a rag-bag.' Well if it is, I can only hope that it proves to be at least an interesting, instructive and entertaining one!

Finally it is my very pleasant duty to record a debt of gratitude to the many friends and family who have helped me in this enjoyable but sometimes onerous task by allowing me access to their libraries, lending books, suggesting suitable extracts and generally keeping up my (sometimes flagging) enthusiasm, and in particular the following: Peter Astley, Lindsay Brydson, Ann Dodd, Bernard Hawcroft, Pete Jermy, Val Spotswoode, Barbara Stirrup, Liam Tomlinson and Bis Whatling. Special thanks to my son William and to Karen Proudler of Advanced Typing Services who between them typed my hideously illegible manuscript, to my wife Sue and my daughter Penelope for putting up with this project for so long, to my editor Rachel Bond, and last but not least, to my conscientious and hard-working researcher Jeremy Ellis who has wrenched many lively and interesting accounts from the bowels of the Bodleian Library.

Vikings Reach North America   ANON

The Norse explorer Leif Ericsson, son of Eric the Red, was probably the first European to set foot on the continent of North America. The Vikings at this time had settlements on Greenland, and the 'Vinland' referred to in this extract is now generally accepted to be Newfoundland, where a Norse settlement was discovered in the 1960s.

ONE EVENING it turned out that a man of their company was missing. This was Tyrkir the German. Leif was greatly put out by this, for Tyrkir had lived a long while with him and his father, and had shown great affection for Leif as a child. He gave his shipmates the rough edge of his tongue, then turned out to go and look for him, taking a dozen men with him. But when they had got only a short way from the hall there was Tyrkir coming to meet them. His welcome was a joyous one: Leif could see at once that his foster-father was in fine fettle. He was a man with a bulging forehead, rolling eyes, and an insignificant little face, short and not much to look at, but handy at all sorts of crafts.

'Why are you so late, foster-father,' Leif asked him, 'and parted this way from your companions?'

By way of a start Tyrkir held forth a long while in German, rolling his eyes all ways, and pulling faces. They had no notion what he was talking about. Then after

A Viking
long-ship reaches
North America

a while he spoke in Norse. 'I went no great way further than you, yet I have a real novelty to report. I have found vines and grapes.'

'Is that the truth, foster-father?' Leif asked.

'Of course it's the truth,' he replied. 'I was born where wine and grapes are no rarity.'

They slept overnight, then in the morning Leif made this announcement to his crew. 'We now have two jobs to get on with, and on alternate days must gather grapes or cut vines and fell timber, so as to provide a cargo of such things for my ship.' They acted upon these orders, and report has it that their towboat was filled with grapes. A full ship's cargo was cut, and in the spring they made ready and sailed away. Leif gave the land a name in accordance with the good things they found in it, calling it Vinland, Wineland; after which they sailed out to sea and had a good wind till they sighted Greenland and the mountains under the glaciers.

Thorfinn Karlsefni Encounters Native Americans, North America ANON

c.1010

Thorfinn Karlsefni, Leif Ericsson's brother-in-law and an Icelandic merchant, was the first European to attempt to establish a permanent settlement in North America, though by this stage confrontations with Native Americans were becoming increasingly frequent. The following description is taken from Eirik's Saga *(c. 1260).*

KARLSEFNI'S men saw a huge number of boats coming from the south, pouring in like a torrent. This time all the sticks were being waved anti-clockwise and all the Skrælings were howling loudly. Karlsefni and his men now hoisted red shields and advanced towards them.

When they clashed there was a fierce battle and a hail of missiles came flying over, for the Skrælings were using catapults. Karlsefni and Snorri saw them hoist a large sphere on a pole; it was dark blue in colour. It came flying in over the heads of Karlsefni's men and made an ugly din when it struck the ground. This terrified Karlsefni and his men so much that their only thought was to flee, and they retreated farther up the river. They did not halt until they reached some cliffs, where they prepared to make a resolute stand.

Freydis came out and saw the retreat. She shouted, 'Why do you flee from such pitiful wretches, brave men like you? You should be able to slaughter them like cattle. If I had weapons, I am sure I could fight better than any of you.'

The men paid no attention to what she was saying. Freydis tried to join them but she could not keep up with them because she was pregnant. She was follow-ing them into the woods when the Skrælings closed in on her. In front of her lay a dead man, Thorbrand Snorrason, with a flintstone buried in his head, and his sword beside him. She snatched up the sword and prepared to defend herself. When the Skrælings came rushing towards her she pulled one of her breasts out of her bodice and slapped it with the sword. The Skrælings were terrified at the sight of this and fled back to their boats and hastened away.

Karlsefni and his men came over to her and praised her courage. Two of their men had been killed, and four of the Skrælings, even though Karlsefni and his men had been fighting against heavy odds.

They returned to their houses and pondered what force it was that had attacked them from inland; they then realised that the only attackers had been those who had come in the boats, and that the other force had just been a delusion.

Demoniacal Fate of a Witch, Berkeley, Gloucestershire, England

1065

WILLIAM OF MALMESBURY

The following extract from William of Malmesbury's Chronicle of the Kings of England *illustrates the interest of contemporary writers in supernatural and magical happenings as much as in the worldly affairs of kings and popes. It relates the curious fate of a witch on the eve of the Norman Conquest. William of Malmesbury was a Benedictine monk and historian.*

THERE RESIDED at Berkeley a woman addicted to witchcraft, as it afterwards appeared, and skilled in ancient augury: she was excessively gluttonous, perfectly lascivious, setting no bounds to her debaucheries, as she was not old, though fast declining in life. On a certain day, as she was regaling, a jack-daw, which was a very great favourite, chattered a little more loudly than usual. On hearing which the woman's knife fell from her hand, her countenance grew pale, and deeply groaning, 'This day,' said she, 'my plough has completed its last furrow; to-day I shall hear of, and suffer, some dreadful calamity.' While yet speaking, the messenger of her misfortunes arrived; and being asked why he approached with so distressed an air, 'I bring news,' said he, 'from the village,' naming the place, 'of the death of your son, and of the whole family, by a sudden accident.' At this intelligence, the woman, sorely afflicted, immediately took to her bed, and perceiving the disorder rapidly approaching the vitals, she summoned her surviving children, a monk, and a nun, by hasty letters; and, when they arrived, with faltering voice, addressed them thus: 'Formerly, my children, I constantly administered to my wretched circumstances by demoniacal arts: I have been the sink of every vice, the teacher of every allurement: yet, while practising these crimes, I was accustomed to soothe my hapless soul with the hope of your piety. Despairing of myself, I rested my expectations on you; I advanced you as my defenders against evil spirits, my safeguards against my strongest foes. Now, since I have approached the end of my life, and shall have those eager to punish, who lured me to sin, I entreat you by your mother's breasts, if you have any regard, any affection, at least to endeavour to alleviate my torments; and, although you cannot revoke the sentence already passed upon my soul, yet you may, perhaps, rescue my body, by these means: sew up my corpse in the skin of a stag; lay it on its back in a stone coffin; fasten down the lid with lead and iron; on this lay a stone, bound round with three iron chains of enormous weight; let there be psalms sung for fifty nights, and masses said for an equal number of days, to allay the ferocious attacks of my adversaries. If I lie thus secure for three nights, on the fourth day bury your mother in the ground.'

The Battle of Hastings, England

1066

WILLIAM OF POITIERS

There were, in fact, no eyewitness accounts of this crucial event in English history. But the author of this account wrote it within a few years of the event, and had access to many of the participants. From their accounts he pieced together what is generally regarded as the most reliable narrative of the battle, fought on Senlac Hill, Sussex, when Norman cavalry overcame the resolute defence of the Anglo-Saxon army fighting on foot.

THE TERRIBLE sound of trumpets on both sides announced the opening of the battle. The eager courage of the Normans gave them the first strike, just as when contenders meet in a trial for theft the prosecution speaks first. So the Norman foot, coming in close, challenged the English, raining wounds and death upon them with their missiles. They, on the other hand, valiantly resisted, each according to his ability. They threw spears and weapons of every kind, murderous axes and stones tied to sticks. By these means you would have thought to see our

William's invasion as shown in the Bayeux Tapestry

CASTELLVM·AT·HESTENGA CEASTRA HIC·NVNTIATVM·EST WILLELM DEhAROLD hIC

men overwhelmed as though by a deadly mass. And so the knights (*equites*) came up in support, and those who were last became first. Spurning to fight at long range, they challenged the event with their swords. Even the war-cries of the Normans on the one side and the barbarians on the other were drowned by the clash of arms and the groans of the dying. Thus for some time the fight was waged with the utmost vigour on both sides. The Normans now believed their duke and leader had fallen. Their retreat was not thus an occasion of shameful flight but of grief, for he was their whole support.

The duke therefore, seeing a large part of the enemy line launching itself forward in pursuit of his retreating troops, galloped up in front of them, shouting and brandishing his lance. Removing his helmet to bare his head, he cried: 'Look at me. I am alive, and, by God's help, I shall win. What madness puts you to flight? Where do you think you can go? Those you could slaughter like cattle are driving and killing you. You are deserting victory and everlasting honour; you are running away to destruction and everlasting shame. And by flight not one of you will avoid death.' At this they recovered their morale. He himself was the first to charge forward, sword flashing, cutting down the foe who deserved death as rebels to him, their king. The Normans, enflamed, surrounded some thousands of those who had pursued them and annihilated them in an instant, not one of them surviving.

Henry IV's Penance at Canossa, Tuscany, Italy

GREGORY VII

1077

The efforts of Pope Gregory VII to increase the powers of the papacy created a deep enmity between himself and Henry IV, Emperor of the Germans. Gregory challenged Henry's right to elect his own bishops, who at that time were effectively princes of the realm with considerable wealth and influence at court. In a bitter confrontation, Henry was excommunicated. However, under pressure from a league of German princes, he was forced to seek humbling absolution from Gregory VII at the Tuscan castle of Canossa.

WE LEARNED for certain that the king was approaching. He also, before entering Italy, sent on to us suppliant legates, offering in all things to render satisfaction to God, to St Peter and to us. And he renewed his promise that, besides amending his life, he would observe all obedience if only he might merit to obtain from us the favour of absolution and the apostolic benediction. When, after long deferring this and holding frequent consultations, we had, through all the envoys who passed, severely taken him to task for his excesses: he came at length of his own accord, with a few followers, showing nothing of hostility or boldness, to the town of Canossa where we were tarrying. And there, having laid aside all the belongings of royalty, wretchedly, with bare feet and clad in wool, he continued for three days to stand before the gate of the castle. Nor did he desist from imploring with many tears the aid and consolation of the apostolic mercy until he had moved all of those who were present there, and whom the report of it reached, to such pity and depth of compassion that, interceding for him with many prayers and tears, all wondered indeed at the unaccustomed hardness of our heart, while some actually cried out that we were exercising, not the gravity of apostolic severity, but the cruelty, as it were, of a tyrannical ferocity.

Finally, conquered by the persistency of his compunction and by the constant supplications of all those who were present we loosed the chain of the anathema and at length received him into the favour of communion and into the lap of the holy mother church.

1096–7 · Arrival of the Crusaders, Syria IBN AL-QALANIST

Ibn Al-Qalanist, whose surname meant literally 'the Hatter', had a distinguished career of public service in Damascus. His chronicle of the Crusaders was based on information often taken down from the lips of actual participants. The First Crusade owed its success largely to Syria's fragmented political situation, which weakened Muslim opposition.

I N THIS year there began to arrive a succession of reports that the armies of the Franks had appeared from the direction of the Sea of Constantinople with forces not to be reckoned for multitude. As these reports followed one upon the other, and spread from mouth to mouth far and wide, the people grew anxious and disturbed in mind. The king, Dā'ud b. Sulaimān b. Qutulmish, whose dominions lay nearest to them, having received confirmation of these statements, set about collecting forces, raising levies, and carrying out the obligation of Holy War. He also summoned as many of the Turkmens as he could to give him assistance and support against them, and a large number of them joined him along with the 'askar of his brother. His confidence having been strengthened thereby, and his offensive power rendered formidable, he marched out to the fords, tracks, and roads by which the Franks must pass, and showed no mercy to all of them who fell into his hands. When he had thus killed a great number, they turned their forces against him, defeated him, and scattered his army, killing many and taking many captive, and plundered and enslaved. The Turkmens, having lost most of their horses, took to flight. The King of the Greeks bought a great many of those whom they had enslaved, and had them transported to Constantinople. When the news was received of this shameful calamity to the cause of Islām, the anxiety of the people became acute and their fear and alarm increased. The date of this battle was the 20th of Rajab (4th July, 1097).

In the middle of Sha'bān (end of July) the amīr Yāghī Siyān, lord of Antioch, accompanied by the amīr Sukmān b. Ortuq and the amīr Karbuqā [lord of Mosul], set out with his 'askar towards Antioch, on receipt of news that the Franks were approaching it and had occupied al-Balāna. Yāghī Siyān therefore hastened to Antioch, and dispatched his son to al-Malik Duqāq at Damascus, to

Janāh al-Dawla at Hims, and to all the other cities and districts, appealing for aid and support, and inciting them to hasten to the Holy War, while he set about fortifying Antioch and expelling its Christian population. On the 2nd of Shawwāl (12th September) the Frankish armies descended on Baghrās and developed their attack upon the territories of Antioch, whereupon those who were in the castles and forts adjacent to Antioch revolted and killed their garrisons except for a few who were able to escape from them. The people of Artāh did likewise, and called for reinforcements from the Franks. During Sha 'bān a comet appeared in the West; it continued to rise for a space of about twenty days, and then disappeared.

Death of William Rufus, New Forest, England

1100

WILLIAM OF MALMESBURY

The death of William Rufus, son of William the Conqueror, has always remained a mystery. It could have been a simple hunting accident; but it has been suggested that it might have been an assassination, or even a ritual killing for occult purposes. William of Malmesbury almost certainly obtained his information for this account from those present at the time.

AFTER DINNER he went into the forest, attended by a few persons; of whom the most intimate with him was Walter, surnamed Tirel, who had been induced to come from France by the liberality of the king. This man alone had remained with him, while the others, employed in the chase, were dispersed as chance directed. The sun was now declining, when the king, drawing his bow and letting fly an arrow, slightly wounded a stag which passed before him; and, keenly gazing, followed it still running, a long time with his eyes, holding up his hand to keep off the power of the sun's rays. At this instant Walter conceiving a noble exploit, which was while the king's attention was otherwise occupied to transfix another stag which by chance came near him, unknowingly, and without power to prevent it, Oh, gracious God! pierced his breast with a fatal arrow. On receiving the wound the king uttered not a word; but breaking off the shaft of the weapon where it projected from his body, fell upon the wound, by which he accelerated his death. Walter immediately ran up, but as he found him senseless and speechless, he leapt swiftly upon his horse, and escaped by spurring him to his utmost speed. Indeed there was none to pursue him: some connived at his flight; others pitied him; and all were intent on other matters. Some began to fortify their dwellings; others to plunder; and the rest to look out for a new king.

A few countrymen conveyed the body, placed on a cart, to the cathedral at Winchester; the blood dripping from it all the way. Here it was committed to the ground within the tower, attended by many of the nobility, though lamented by few.

1106

The Battle of Tinchebrai, Normandy, France

ANON

William the Conqueror, William Rufus and Henry Beauclerc (Henry I) had each, in turn, to face the question of whether the kingship of England necessitated conceding power in Normandy. In the case of Henry I, his brother Robert Curthose had ruled Normandy from 1100 and attempted to oust him and reunite their father's inheritance. However, Henry was able to take possession of Normandy until his death in 1135, after laying siege to the castle of Tinchebrai and crushing Curthose's troops in September 1106.

To HIS LORD, the priest of Séez, the priest of Fécamp, sends greeting and prayers. I bring you good news, my lord, inasmuch as I realise you are eager for tidings in this matter. Our lord king fought with his brother at Tinchebrai on 28 September [1106] at the third hour. Thus was the battle disposed. In the first line were the men of the Bessin, the Avranchin and the Cotentin, and these were all on foot. In the second line was the king with his very numerous barons and these likewise were on foot. Seven hundred mounted knights were placed with each line; and besides these the count of Maine, and Alan Fergaunt, count of Brittany, flanked the army with about a thousand mounted knights. All the camp followers and servants were removed far to the rear of the battle. The whole army of the king may be reckoned as having consisted of about forty thousand men. When the battle had lasted only an hour, Robert of Bellême turned and fled, and all his men were dispersed. The count himself was captured, and the count of Mortain with his barons, and my friend, Robert of Estouteville. The rest all disappeared in flight. Wherefore the land became subject to the king. Nor must I fail to tell you about this marvel: that the king in the battle lost only two men; and only one was wounded, namely Robert of Bonnebosc. When I came to the king, he received me very graciously at Caen, and he willingly granted all those things which he had exacted from our land. And now, thank God, peace is restored in the land.

c.1110

Customs and Manners of the Cistercians, England WILLIAM OF MALMESBURY

The strict, secluded order of Cistercian monks rose to prominence in the early 12th century as an offshoot of the Benedictine monastic rule. They sought to return to what they considered to be its original simplicity of life, as demonstrated in this contemporary description.

CERTAINLY many of their regulations seem severe, and more particularly these: they wear nothing made with furs or linen, nor even that finely spun linen garment, which we call Staminium; neither breeches, unless when sent on a journey, which at their return they wash and restore. They have two tunics with cowls, but no additional garment in winter, though, if they think fit, in summer they may lighten their garb. They sleep clad and girded, and never after matins return to their beds: but they so order the time of matins that it shall be light ere the lauds begin; so intent are they on their rule, that they think no jot or tittle of it should be disregarded. Directly after these hymns they sing the prime, after which they go out to work for stated hours. They complete whatever labour of service they have to perform by day without any other light. No one is ever absent from the daily services, or from complines, except the sick. The cellarer and hospitaller, after complines, wait upon the guests, yet observing the strictest silence. The abbot allows himself no indulgence beyond the others – everywhere present – everywhere attending to his flock; except that he does not eat with the rest, because his table is with the strangers and the poor. Nevertheless, be he where he may, he is equally sparing of food and of speech; for never more than two dishes are served either to him or to his company; lard and meat never but to the sick. From the Ides of September till Easter, through regard for whatever festival, they do not take more than one meal a day, except on Sunday. They never leave the cloister but for the purpose of labour, nor do they ever speak, either there or elsewhere, save only to the abbot or prior. They pay unwearied attention to the canonical services, making no addition to them except the vigil for the defunct. They use in their divine service the Ambrosian chants and hymns, as far as they were able to learn them at Milan. While they bestow care on the stranger and the sick, they inflict intolerable mortifications on their own bodies, for the health of their souls.

The Crusades, Warfare Against the Franks, Syria USAMAH IBN-MUNQIDH

1119

The memoirs of Usamah Ibn-Munqidh – gentleman, warrior, man of letters and later friend to the great Saladin – are representative of Arab–Syrian chivalry as it flourished during the early crusading period. Many of Usamah's military efforts were taken up defending the ancient Syrian town of Shayzar.

M Y UNCLE had instructed my father to send me against Afāmiyah at the head of the men who were with me in Shayzar, and to call out the people, together with the Arabs, for the pillage of the crops of Afāmiyah. A great number of the Arabs had recently joined us.

A few days after the departure of my uncle, the public announcer called us to arms, and I started at the head of a small band, hardly amounting to twenty horsemen, with full conviction that Afāmiyah had no cavalry in it. Accompanying me was a great body of pillagers and Bedouins. As soon as we arrived in the Valley of Bohemond, and while the pillagers and the Arabs were scattered all over the planted fields, a large army of the Franks set out against us. They had been reinforced that very night by sixty horsemen and sixty footmen. They repulsed us from the valley, and we retreated before them until we joined those of our number who were already in the fields, pillaging them. Seeing us, the Franks raised a violent uproar. Death seemed an easy thing to me in comparison with the loss of that crowd [24] in my charge. So I turned against a horseman in their vanguard, who had taken off his coat of mail in order to be light enough to pass before us, and thrust my lance into his chest. He instantly flew off his saddle, dead. I then faced their horsemen as they followed, and they all took to flight. Though a tyro in warfare, and having never before that day taken part in a battle, I, with a mare under me as swift as a bird, went on, now pursuing them and plying them with my lance, now taking cover from them.

In the rear guard of the Franks was a cavalier on a black horse, large as a camel, wearing a coat of mail and the full armour of war. I was afraid of this horseman, lest he should be drawing me further ahead in order to get an opportunity to turn back and attack me. All of a sudden I saw him spur his horse, and as the horse began to wave its tail, I knew that it was already exhausted. So I rushed on the horseman and smote him with my lance, which pierced him through and projected about a cubit in front of him. The lightness of my body, the force of the thrust and the swiftness of my horse made me lose my seat on the saddle. Moving backward a little, I pulled out my lance, fully assuming that I had killed him. I then assembled my comrades and found them all safe and sound.

A skirmish between Saracens and Crusaders

The Battle of Lincoln, England

HENRY OF HUNTINGDON

1141

The following passage is taken from Henry, Archdeacon of Huntingdon's Historia Anglorum. *It describes a siege against King Stephen by the 'disinherited barons', led by Rannulf, Earl of Chester, and Robert, Earl of Gloucester and son of King Henry I. Though the citizens of Lincoln had fought in the battle on the King's side, casualties were small in number – not more than 100 knights were slain.*

AND SO King Stephen was left alone with his infantry in the midst of the enemy. The latter encircled the royal army and attacked it from all sides, as if they were assaulting a castle. Thenceforth the battle was seen to rage horribly around the royal defences, helmets and swords gleamed as they clashed, and the dreadful noise re-echoed from the hills and the walls of the city. The cavalry, furiously charging the royal column, slew some and trampled down others, while yet others were dragged away captive. No respite, no breathing-space was given, except in the quarter where the most valiant king had taken his stand and the foe recoiled from the incomparable ferocity of his counter-strokes. Perceiving this and envious of the king's glory, the Earl of Chester threw himself upon him with the whole weight of his men-at-arms. Even then the lightning strokes of the king were made manifest, and, wielding his great two-handed battle-axe, he slew some and cut down others. Then a fresh shout arose and every man rushed at the king while he in turn thrust back at them all. At length his battle-axe was shattered by repeated blows, whereupon he drew his trusty sword, well worthy of a king, and with this he wrought wonders, until it too was broken. At sight of this William 'de Chesney', a very valiant knight, rushed upon him and, seizing him by the helmet, shouted with a loud voice, 'Hither, all of you, hither, I hold the king.' Everyone flew to his aid and the king was taken prisoner. Until the king was captured his troops continued the struggle, for they were so hemmed in on all sides that flight was impossible. Thus the whole army was either slain or captured. The city in consequence was given over to pillage in accordance with the laws of war, and the king was brought back to it in his wretched plight.

Hunting in Egypt USAMAH IBN-MUNQIDH

When Usamah Ibn-Munqidh was not fighting in the Crusades, he had birds, other animals and wild beasts to fight. He had first-hand experience of hunting practices in Syria, Mesopotamia and Egypt.

c.1150

I HAVE ALSO witnessed the chase in Egypt. Al-Ḥāfiẓ li-Dīn-Allāh 'Abd-al-Majīd abu-al-Maymūn (may Allah's mercy rest upon his soul!) possessed a large number of birds of prey, including falcons, sakers and river [baḥriyyah] shahins. These birds were in charge of a master huntsman who used to take them out twice a week, most of them perching on the hands of falconers on foot. I made it a point on their day of outing to mount my horse and enjoy the sight of them in action.

The master huntsman, noticing me, went to al-Ḥāfiẓ and said to him, 'Thy guest, so and so, goes out regularly with us,' seeking to find out his opinion in the matter. Al-Ḥāfiẓ replied, 'Let him go out with thee and enjoy the sight of the birds.'

One day as we went out together one of the falconers was carrying a red-eyed falcon which was intermewed. We saw cranes. The master said to that falconer, 'Go ahead. Hurl at them the red-eyed falcon.' So he proceeded and hurled it. The cranes took the air. The falcon overtook one of them at some distance and brought it down. I said to one of my attendants on an excellent horse, 'Gallop the horse towards the falcon, dismount and thrust the bill of the crane in the ground.

Hold it thus and keep its legs under thine until we overtake thee.' The man went and did as I commanded. When the falconer arrived, he slew the crane and fed the falcon to the point of satisfaction.

In that country are birds called *al-bujj*, similar to the flamingo, which they also hunt. The waterfowl are easy to hunt at the fords of the Nile. The gazelle is rare in Egypt, but there live in that land the 'cows of the children of Israel'. These are yellow cows whose horns are like those of the ordinary cow, but they are smaller in body than the latter and can run very fast.

The Nile brings forth to the people an animal called hippopotamus, which resembles a small cow and has small eyes. Its skin, however, is hairless, like the skin of the buffalo. In its lower jaw it has long teeth. In its upper jaw it has holes through which the roots of the teeth issue from underneath the eyes. It grunts like a hog, and cannot live except in a pool of water. Its food is bread, grass and barley.

1170

Murder of Thomas à Becket, Canterbury, England EDWARD GRIM

The quarrel between Thomas à Becket, Archbishop of Canterbury, and King Henry II over the position of the Church, led to Becket's murder on 29 December 1170 at the hands of three of Henry's knights who mistakenly thought that this was his wish. It made Becket the most famous saint and martyr of medieval England.

THEN THEY laid sacrilegious hands on him, pulling and dragging him that they might kill him outside the Church, or carry him away a prisoner, as they afterwards confessed. But when he could not be forced away from the pillar, one of them pressed on him and clung to him more closely. Him he pushed off calling him 'pander', and saying, 'Touch me not, Reginald; you owe me fealty and subjection; you and your accomplices act like madmen.' The knight, fired with terrible rage at this severe repulse, waved his sword over the sacred head. 'No faith', he cried, 'nor subjection do I owe you against my fealty to my lord the king.' Then the unconquered martyr seeing the hour at hand which should put an end to this miserable life and give him straightway the crown of immortality promised by the Lord, inclined his neck as one who prays and joining his hands he lifted them up, and commended his cause and that of the Church of God, to S. Mary, and to the blessed martyr Denys. Scarce had he said the words than the wicked knight fearing lest he should be rescued by the people and escape alive, leapt upon him suddenly and wounded this lamb, who was sacrificed to God, on the head, cutting off the top of the crown which the sacred unction of chrism had dedicated to God; and by the same blow he wounded the arm of him who tells this. For he, when the others, both monks and clerks, fled, stuck close to the sainted archbishop and held him in his arms till the one he interposed was almost severed. . . .

Then he received a second blow on the head but still stood firm. At the third blow he fell on his knees and elbows, offering himself a living victim, and saying in a low voice, 'For the Name of Jesus and the protection of the Church I am ready to embrace death.' Then the third knight inflicted a terrible wound as he lay, by which the sword was broken against the pavement, and the crown which was large was separated from the head; so that the blood white with the brain and the brain red with blood, dyed the surface of the virgin mother Church with the life and death of the confessor and martyr in the colours of the lily and the rose. The fourth knight prevented any from interfering so that the others might freely perpetrate the murder. As to the fifth, no knight but that clerk who had entered with the knights, that a fifth blow might not be wanting to the martyr who was in other things like to Christ, he put his foot on the neck of the holy priest and precious martyr, and, horrible to say, scattered his brains and blood over the pavement, calling out to the others, 'Let us away, knights; he will rise no more.'

Beavers on the River Teifi, Wales

GERALD OF WALES

1188

A fascinating description from Gerald of Wales, a well-connected Welsh churchman born at Manorbier (Pembrokeshire). This extract is a reminder that the European beaver could still be found in Wales in the late 12th century, although already a rarity.

THE TEIFI has another remarkable peculiarity. Of all the rivers in Wales, and of those in England south of the Humber, it is the only one where you can find beavers. Beavers build their castle-like lodges in the middle of rivers. They have an extraordinary method of conveying and carting timber from the woods to the water, for they use other beavers as waggons. The beavers of one team gnaw down the branches, and then another group has the instinct to turn over on their backs and to hold this wood tightly against their bellies with their four feet. Each of these last grips a branch in its teeth which sticks out on either side. A third group holds tightly on to this cross-branch with its teeth and pulls the animal in question along backwards together with its load. Anyone who witnesses this manoeuvre cannot fail to be impressed. Badgers use a not dissimilar device when they are cleaning out their sets, which they arrange to their satisfaction by digging into the soil and scraping at it with their paws. It is remarkable that in both species of animal there are to be found slaves which are prepared to accept a debasement of their natural habits and to suffer at the same time a certain wear and tear of the skin on their backs.

There in some deep and tranquil bend of the river the beavers piece together with such skill the logs of wood which form their lodge that no drop of water can easily enter and no storm however violent do harm to it or loosen it. They have no reason to fear any attack, except that of us human beings, and even we must bring our weapons shod with iron. When they are building a lodge, they bind the logs together with willow-wands. The number of storeys placed one above the other varies according to the rise in the water-level which they foresee. They plan their construction so that it just protrudes from the water, with connecting door-ways inside to lead from one storey to another. Whenever they have decided that it is necessary, they can keep a lookout from the top and watch the rising waters when the river is in spate. As the years pass and the willow-wands keep on grow-ing, the lodge is constantly in leaf and becomes, in fact, a grove of willow-trees, looking like a natural bush from the outside, however artificially constructed it may be within.

1192 · The Assassins Kill Conrad of Montferrat, Palestine ANON

The Assassins (indirectly from the Arabic hashshashin, *hashish-eaters) were a secret society of Muslim fanatics established in Persia towards the end of the 11th century. Although often neutral in the Crusades, on this occasion they arranged the murder of the Count of Montferrat fearing that his crusader kingdom on the Lebanese coast around Tyre would be a threat to their own domains in the Bekaa Valley.*

ONE DAY the marquis was returning from an entertainment given by the bishop of Beauvais, at which he had been a guest. He was in a very cheer-ful and pleasant humour and had just reached the custom-house when two young men, without cloaks – Assassins – suddenly rushed upon him with poniards, which had been concealed in their hands. Stabbing him to the heart, they turned and fled away at full speed.

The marquis instantly fell from his horse and rolled dying on the ground; one of the murderers was immediately slain, but the second took shelter in a church. In spite of this sanctuary, he was captured and condemned to be dragged through the city until life should be extinct. Before he expired, he was closely questioned to discover at whose instigation, and for what reason, they had done the deed: he confessed that they had been sent a long time before, and had done it by com-mand of their superior, whom they were bound to obey.

This turned out to be true; for these young men had been some time in the service of the marquis, waiting for a favourable opportunity to complete the deed. The Old Man of Masyād had sent them over to assassinate the marquis within a certain space of time; for every one the Old Man judged deserving of death, he caused to be assassinated in the same manner.

The Old Man of Masyād, according to hereditary custom, brings up a large number of noble boys in his palace, causing them to be taught every kind of learning and accomplishment, and to be instructed in various languages so that they can converse without the aid of an interpreter in any country of the known world. Cruelty of the greatest degree is also inculcated with profound secrecy; and the pupils are carefully and anxiously trained to follow it up. When they reach the age of puberty, the senior calls them to him and enjoins on them, for the remission of their sins, to slay some great man, whom he mentions by name; and for this purpose he gives to each of them a poniard of terrible length and sharpness. From their devoted obedience, they never hesitate to set out as they are commanded; nor do they pause until they have reached the prince, or tyrant, who has been pointed out to them; and they remain in his service until they find a favourable opportunity for accomplishing their purpose, believing that by so doing they shall gain the favour of heaven.

Burning of Constantinople

GEOFFREY DE VILLEHARDOUIN

1204

The Fourth Crusade to the Holy Land started with all good intentions. After the Crusaders sacked Zara on the Dalmatian coast, however, they were excommunicated by the Pope and the situation began to degenerate. By April of 1204 they were heavily involved in the internal politics of Byzantium. This account, by a French crusader, is of the fire that broke out on 9 April during fighting between the crusading army and the Greek inhabitants, and which destroyed most of the city.

WHILE THE Emperor Alexius was away on this progress, there befell a very grievous misadventure; for a conflict arose between the Greeks and the Latins who inhabited Constantinople, and of these last there were many. And certain people – who they were I know not – out of malice, set fire to the city; and the fire waxed so great and horrible that no man could put it out or abate it. And when the barons of the host, who were quartered on the other side of the port, saw this, they were sore grieved and filled with pity – seeing the great churches and the rich palaces melting and falling in, and the great streets filled with merchandise burning in the flames; but they could do nothing.

Thus did the fire prevail, and win across the port, even to the densest part of the city, and to the sea on the other side, quite near to the church of St Sophia. It lasted two days and two nights, nor could it be put out by the hand of man. And the front of the fire, as it went flaming, was well over half a league broad. What was the damage then done, what the possessions and riches swallowed up, could no man tell – nor what the number of men and women and children who perished – for many were burned.

All the Latins, to whatever land they might belong, who were lodged in Constantinople, dared no longer to remain therein; but they took their wives and their children, and such of their possessions as they could save from the fire, and entered into boats and vessels, and passed over the port and came to the camp of the pilgrims.

Satanic Rituals, Stedlingerland, Germany

1232

GREGORY IX

Pope Gregory IX's letter Vox in Rama, *from which the following passage is taken, was addressed to the Emperor of Germany, and written in the context of reports that witchcraft was rife in northern Germany. At this time, witchcraft was still an ecclesiastical, rather than civil, concern, and the Pope's despair at the threat to orthodox belief is evident.*

WHEN A novice is to be initiated and is brought before the assembly of the wicked for the first time, a sort of frog appears to him; a toad according to some. Some bestow a foul kiss on his hind parts, others on his mouth, sucking the animal's tongue and slaver. Sometimes the toad is of a normal size, but at others it is as large as a goose or a duck. Usually it is the size of an oven's mouth. The novice comes forward and stands before a man of fearful pallor. His eyes are black and his body so thin and emaciated that he seems to have no flesh and be only skin and bone. The novice kisses him and he is as cold as ice. After kissing him every remnant of faith in the Catholic Church that lingers in the novice's heart leaves him.

Then all sit down to a banquet and when they rise after it is finished, a black cat emerges from a kind of statue which normally stands in the place where these meetings are held. It is as large as a fair-sized dog, and enters backwards with its tail erect. First the novice kisses its hind parts, then the Master of Ceremonies proceeds to do the same and finally all the others in turn; or rather all those who deserve the honour. The rest, that is those who are not thought worthy of this favour, kiss the Master of Ceremonies. When they have returned to their places they stand in silence for a few minutes with heads turned towards the cat. Then the Master says: 'Forgive us.' The person standing behind him repeats this and a third adds, 'Lord we know it.' A fourth person ends the formula by saying, 'We shall obey.'

When this ceremony is over the lights are put out and those present indulge in the most loathsome sensuality, having no regard to sex. If there are more men than women, men satisfy one another's depraved appetites. Women do the same for one another. When these horrors have taken place the lamps are lit again and everyone regains their places. Then, from a dark corner, the figure of a man emerges. The upper part of his body from the hips upward shines as brightly as the sun but below that his skin is coarse and covered with fur like a cat. The Master of Ceremonies cuts a piece from the novice's vestments and says to the shining figure: 'Master, I have been given this, and I, in my turn, give it to you.' To which the other replies: 'You have served me well and will serve me yet more in the future. I give into your safekeeping what you have given me.' And he disappears as soon as he has spoken these words. Each year at Easter when they receive the body of Christ from the priest, they keep it in their mouths and throw it in the dirt as an outrage against their Saviour. Furthermore, these most miserable of men blaspheme against the Lord of Heaven and in their madness say that the Lord has done evil in casting out Lucifer into the bottomless pit. These most unfortunate people believe in Lucifer and claim that he was the creator of the celestial bodies and will ultimately return to glory when the Lord has fallen from power. Through him and with him they hope to achieve eternal happiness. They confess that they do not believe that one should do God's will but rather what displeases Him.

The Castration of a Knight, England

1248

MATTHEW PARIS

The penalty for adultery in the Middle Ages could sometimes be severe. Then, as now, matters of family honour coupled with sexual jealousy were a potent brew. Matthew Paris, the author of this extract, was a monk and historian. He entered the monastery of St Albans, where he compiled his celebrated Chronicles, *a work of great historical value.*

I MUST NOT omit to mention, even if it seems ridiculous, the disgrace and irreparable harm which happened in this same most unlucky month to the knights. For a certain Norfolk knight of noble birth and accomplished prowess, named Godfrey de Millers, wretchedly led astray, one night secretly entered the house of a knight called John Brito to sleep with his daughter. But he was prevented by some people placed in ambush with the connivance of the whore, who was afraid of being found out. He was seized, savagely thrown to the ground and badly wounded. Then he was suspended from a beam by his feet with his legs stretched apart, so that he was completely at the mercy of his enemies, who disgracefully mutilated him by cutting off his genital organs, though he would have preferred to be beheaded. Thus wounded and castrated, he was thrown out half dead. The noise of complaint reached the king, the authors of this cruelty were arrested, and John Brito was convicted and sentenced to irrecoverable disinheritance and irrevocable exile. The adulteress managed to avoid death by going into hiding so that she could not be found. All who were present at this flagrant deed were dispersed and banished, exiles and fugitives, so that this inhuman and in every way merciless crime involved many nobles in a miserable calamity.

An Incident from the Seventh Crusade, France

1248

JEAN SIRE DE JOINVILLE

Joinville accompanied King Louis IX on his crusade in 1248. This story takes place while the host is assembling. The 'falchion' referred to is a heavy curved sword, much in fashion at the time.

WHILE I was on my way to Paris, I found three men dead upon a cart, whom a clerk had killed; and I was told they were being taken to the king. When I heard this, I sent one of my squires after, to know what befell. And my squire, whom I had sent, told me that the king, when he came out of his chapel, went to the entrance steps to look at the dead, and inquired of the provost of Paris how this thing had happened.

And the provost told him that the dead men were three of his sergeants of the Châtelet, who had gone into unfrequented streets to rob people. 'And they found,' said he to the king, 'this clerk, whom you see here, and robbed him of all his clothes. The clerk, being only in his shirt, went to his lodging, and took his crossbow, and caused a child to bring his falchion. Then when he saw them again, he cried out upon them, and said they should die. So the clerk drew his crossbow, and shot, and pierced one of the men through the heart. The two others made off flying. And the clerk took the falchion which the child handed to him, and followed them in the moonlight, which was fine and clear. The one man thought to pass through a hedge into a garden, and the clerk struck him with his falchion,' said the provost, 'and cut right through his leg, in such sort that it only holds to the boot, as you may see here. The clerk then followed the other, who thought to go down into a strange house, where the people were still awake; but the clerk struck him in the middle of the head with his falchion, so that he clove his head to the teeth, as you may see here,' said the provost to the king. 'Sire,' continued he, 'the clerk showed what he had done to the neighbours in the street, and then came and made himself your prisoner. And now, sire, I have brought him to you, to do with him what you will. Here he is.'

'Sir clerk,' said the king, 'you have forfeited your priesthood by your prowess;

A knight from the time of the Seventh Crusade

and for your prowess I take you into my service, and you shall go with me overseas. And this thing I do for you, because I would have my men to fully understand that I will uphold them in none of their wickednesses.'

Drunken and Lecherous Priests, Normandy, France ARCHBISHOP ODO OF RIGAUD

1248

The scandalous state of his clergy uncovered by the Archbishop's visitation in 1248 strikes certain chords with our own times. Clerical celibacy has never been an easy option.

FEBRUARY 1248. We visited the deanery of Brachi near St Just. We found that the priest of Ruiville was ill-famed with the wife of a certain stonecarver, and by her is said to have a child; also he is said to have many other children; he does not stay in his church, he plays ball, he does not stay in his church, and he rises around in a short coat [the garb of armed men]; we have letters from him [of confession], and they are written on folio 125.

Also, the priest of Gonnetot is ill-famed with two women, and went to the pope on this account, and after he came back he is said to have relapsed; also with a certain woman of Waletot.

Also, the priest of Wanestanville, with a certain one of his parishioners whose husband on this account went beyond the sea, and he kept her for eight years, and she is pregnant; also he plays at dice, and drinks too much, he frequents taverns, he does not stay in his church, he goes hawking in the country as he wishes; we imposed on him a penance which is found on folio 125.

Also, the priest of Brachi, with a certain woman, and because she left the home of that priest, he goes to eat with her, and has his food and flour brought to her house. The chaplain of Brachi frequents taverns. Simon, the priest of St Just, is pugnacious and quarrelsome.

Vision of a Son's Death, England

MATTHEW PARIS

1250

The Battle of Fariskur in April 1250 resulted in the total defeat of the Crusaders by Egyptian forces and the capture of Louis IX of France. The Countess of Salisbury is supposed to have had a vision in a dream of the death of her son, William Longespee.

ON THE night before this battle a vision appeared to his most noble mother the lady countess [of Salisbury] and abbess of Lacock, Ela by name, in which a certain knight, fitted out in full armour, was received into the opened

OPPOSITE PAGE The
Battle of Crecy 1346

heavens. Recognising the device on the shield, she asked in amazement who this was ascending to be received with such glory by the angels, whose arms she recognised. A clearly articulated voice replied, 'William, your son.' She noted which night that was, and afterwards the meaning of the vision became apparent.

Robert Count of Artois being drowned and William Longespee killed, the Saracens, certain of victory, pitiably put the surrounded and helpless Christians to the sword. Out of all that splendid and famous body of knights, only two Templars and a Hospitaller escaped, and one lesser person who swam the river with nothing on and announced this eternally deplorable event to the king of the French and the rest of the army. Others who escaped were so exhausted and wounded and out of breath that they were unable to cross the river but awaited the darkness of night concealed in the sedge. Nor did the anger, or rather fury, of the Lord allow anyone of note to escape.

A Visit to the Great Khan, Mongolia

1253

WILLIAM OF RUBRECK

In 1253 the Franciscan monk Rubreck was sent on a diplomatic mission to the great Khan of the Tartars by King Louis IX of France. This is his description of the Khan, Mangu's, Palace.

THE HOUSE was all covered inside with cloth of gold, and there was a fire of briars and wormwood roots – which grow here to great size – and of cattle dung, in a grate in the centre of the dwelling. He (Mangu) was seated on a couch, and was dressed in a skin spotted and glossy, like a seal's skin. He is a little man, of medium height, aged forty-five years, and a young wife sat beside him; and a very ugly, full-grown girl called Cirina, with other children sat on a couch after them. This dwelling had belonged to a certain Christian lady, whom he had much loved, and of whom he had had this girl. Afterwards he had taken this young wife, but the girl was the mistress of all this *ordu*, which had been her mother's.

He had us asked what we wanted to drink, wine or *terracina*, which is rice wine (*cervisia*), or *caracosmos*, which is clarified mare's milk, or *bal*, which is honey mead. For in winter they make use of these four kinds of drinks. I replied: 'My lord, we are not men who seek to satisfy our fancies about drinks; whatever pleases you will suit us.' So he had us given of the rice drink, which was clear and flavoured like white wine, and of which I tasted a little out of respect for him, but for our misfortune our interpreter was standing by the butlers, who gave him so much to drink, that he was drunk in a short time. After this the Khan had brought some falcons and other birds, which he took on his hand and looked at, and after a long while he bade us speak. Then we had to bend our knees. He had his interpreter, a certain Nestorian, who I did not know was a Christian, and we had our interpreter, such as he was, and already drunk.

Kublai Khan and his Concubines, China

MARCO POLO

At the age of seventeen, Marco Polo travelled with his father, a Venetian trader, to the court of the Great Khan at Shangtu, where he stayed for seventeen years. It has recently been suggested that his bestselling memoirs were a fake – that he never went to China and wrote the entire book whilst in jail in Genoa. Proof of this is probably impossible, and an anthology such as this would not be complete without an extract!

KUBLAI, who is styled grand khan, or lord of lords, is of the middle stature, that is, neither tall nor short; his limbs are well formed, and in his whole figure there is a just proportion. His complexion is fair, and occasionally suffused with red, like the bright tint of the rose, which adds much grace to his countenance. His eyes are black and handsome, his nose is well shaped and prominent. He has four wives of the first rank, who are esteemed legitimate, and the eldest born son of any one of these succeeds to the empire, upon the decease of the grand khan. They bear equally the title of empress, and have their separate courts. None of them have fewer than three hundred young female attendants of great beauty, together with a multitude of youths as pages, and other eunuchs, as well as ladies of the bedchamber; so that the number of persons belonging to each of their respective courts amounts to ten thousand. When his majesty is desirous of the company of one of his empresses, he either sends for her, or goes himself to her palace. Besides these, he has many concubines provided for his use, from a

Kublai Khan (1216–94)

province of Tartary named Ungut, having a city of the same name, the inhabitants of which are distinguished for beauty of features and fairness of complexion. Thither the grand khan sends his officers every second year, or oftener, as it may happen to be his pleasure, who collect for him, to the number of four or five hundred, or more, of the handsomest of the young women, according to the estimation of beauty communicated to them in their instructions.

1333

Handsome Women in Cologne, Germany

PETRARCH

The letters of Petrarch – poet, scholar and one of the initiators of the humanistic revival that became the Renaissance – document his travels and give a flavour of the everyday existence of medieval man.

I THEN went on to Cologne, on the left bank of the Rhine, a city famous for its situation, its river, and its inhabitants. It is remarkable to find in a barbarous country such a fine city, with so much culture, so much dignity of the men and beauty of the women. I arrived, as it happened, on St John's Eve; the sun was near its setting. At the urging of friends – for even there my reputation, rather than my merit, had procured me friends – I was led in all haste from my inn to the river to witness a strange sight. It was well I did so, for the whole bank was lined with a great swarm of handsome women. I was amazed. Good gods, what figures, what fine clothes! Anyone whose heart was not already pledged might there have learned to love. I stood on a little bluff, where I could see what was going on. There was a vast but orderly crowd. Some of the women were girded with fragrant grasses. They took turns washing their white hands and arms in the stream, rolling up their sleeves above the elbow, and talking softly in their strange tongue. I never understood better what Cicero and the old proverb say, that where the language is unknown we are all deaf and dumb. I was so fortunate as to have some very welcome interpreters; for, wonderfully enough, even that clime nourishes Pierian spirits.

Whenever there was anything to be heard, or when I was supposed to answer, I used my companions as my ears and tongue. Wondering at the sight, and ignorant of its meaning, I addressed one friend in Virgil's lines: 'What means this concourse by the river? What seek these souls?' He answered that this was a very ancient rite and that the common people, especially the women, were convinced that every lowering calamity of the coming year could on that day be washed away in the river, thus assuring a happier fate. 'O how happy,' I said, smiling, 'are the dwellers by the Rhine, which purges all their woes! Neither the Po nor the Tiber have ever availed to purge our own! You send your ills to the Britons by way of the Rhine; we should gladly send ours to the Africans or the Illyrians, but our rivers are evidently too lazy.' There was a general laugh at this, and then, as it was getting late, we went home.

Charles IV's Temptation at Lucca, Italy

CHARLES IV

1333

The German emperor Charles IV's personal piety was legendary – he went frequently to the sacraments, both confession and communion, he learnt from his mother a reverence for the ascetic and mystical ideals of Catholicism, and his undoubted chastity was an unusual quality in a medieval prince.

HERE I had a vision at night. An angel appeared to strike me on the left side and say, 'Arise and come with us.' I answered, 'Lord, I know neither whither nor how to go with you.' Taken by my hair through the air, I saw a great force of horsemen drawn up in front of a castle ready to fight. Holding me in the air over them, the angel said, 'Look and see.' Another angel with a flaming sword then appeared, and struck the leader of the host on the thigh. In great agony with the wound he still sat his horse. The angel asked me, 'Do you know who he is who is struck by the angel and wounded to death?' 'Lord,' said I, 'I neither know him nor the place where he is.' 'Know, then,' answered he, 'this is the Dauphin of Vienne, who on account of his sins of impurity is stricken by God. Beware, then, and tell your father that he too should beware of the same sin, or worse will befall him and you.' I was sorry for that Dauphin of Vienne called Bigon [Guiges, 1318–1333], whose grandmother was the sister of our grandfather, and who was the son of the sister of King Charles I of Hungary. I asked the angel, 'Shall he be able to confess before he dies?' so sad was I. 'He will confess and live a few days,' was the answer. Then I saw on my left a group of many in white, men of great reverence and holiness, talking to each other, looking at the horsemen, and I noted them well.

Suddenly I found myself back, and dawn was breaking as I woke. Thomas of Villeneuve, the chamberlain of my father, a knight of Liege, came and woke me, saying: 'Sir, why do you not get up? Your father is up and ready on horseback.' Then I got up, and found I was quite tired out, as though after a great labour. I said to him, 'Where shall I go, for this night I have suffered much, and I do not know what I ought to do?' 'Why, Sir?' said he. I answered, 'The dauphin is dead; now my father wants to gather an army and go to the dauphin's support, who is at war with the Count of Savoy: our aid will not profit him, for he is dead.' But he laughed at me, and when we got to Parma told my father what I had said. Then my father called me and asked if it were true. To whom I answered, 'Yes, sir, I know for sure that the dauphin is dead.' My father upbraided me, saying, 'Never believe in dreams.' To these two I had not told all that I had seen, but only that the dauphin was dead. After some days news arrived that as the dauphin was besieging a castle of the Count of Savoy he was hit by a great arrow in the thigh, and after some time confessed and died. My father was astonished and said so. But no one spoke of my vision to those who brought the news.

Lawlessness and Cruelty in Naples, Italy

c.1343

PETRARCH

Young and violent males are certainly nothing new; medieval Italy suffered particularly from 'machismo' in the form of professional swordsmen and duellists – immortalised by the character Mercutio in Shakespeare's Romeo and Juliet.

THOUGH Naples is very outstanding in many ways, it suffers this one dark, obscene, inveterate evil: the streets by night are as perilous as deep forest ambushes. The streets are the resort of young nobles, armed to the teeth, unrestrained by home training, the authority of the magistrates, or the majesty of king and country. Their wanton boldness under the cover of night, without witnesses, is hardly surprising, since the infamous gladiatorial games are celebrated in this Italian city with worse than barbarian savagery in the full light of day, with royalty and the common people looking on. In these human blood is shed like that of cattle; and often, to the applause of maddened spectators, unhappy sons are massacred under the eyes of their wretched parents. It is regarded as the height of infamy to withdraw one's throat from the sword, as if one were fighting for one's country or for eternal life.

Yesterday, all unwitting, I was taken to a place near the city, called Carbonaria, 'the Furnace'; a very appropriate name, for that smoky smithy of ferocity blackens and befouls the workers at the anvil of death. The Queen and her young consort, Andrea, were present. The whole Neapolitan militia was there, very well accoutred and outfitted; the common people swarmed in. I was impressed by the great concourse and by the intentness of so many eminent men, and I watched closely, expecting to see something grand. Then suddenly an immense outburst of applause rose to heaven, as if at something very delightful. I looked around, and there at my feet lay a very handsome youth transfixed by a sword. I shuddered with horror, and giving my horse the spur, I fled from that evil, hellish spectacle, inveighing against the companions who had tricked me into attending, the cruelty of the spectators, and the players at the game. This plague, my good Father, has been passed on from the elders to the younger, ever growing worse, and has now reached the point where a licence to commit crime bears the name of honour and freedom.

English Archers at Crécy, France

1346

JEAN FROISSART

The longbowmen who won the Battle of Crécy established England as a major power in Europe for nearly 100 years. This was the first of a trilogy of great victories won by the longbow – Poitiers followed in 1356 and Agincourt in 1415. Jean Froissart was a French historian and poet, born at Valenciennes, who at the age of nineteen began to write the history of the wars of his time.

PHILIP came near the place where the English were and saw them, his blood boiled, for he hated them. Nothing could now stop him from giving battle. He said to his Marshals: 'Send forward our Genoese and begin the battle, in the name of God and St Denis.'

He had with him about fifteen thousand Genoese bowmen who would sooner have gone to the devil than fight at that moment, for they had just marched over eighteen miles, in armour and carrying their crossbows. They told their commanders that they were not in a state to fight much of a battle just then. These words came to the ears of the Count of Alençon, who grew very angry and said: 'What is the use of burdening ourselves with this rabble who give up just when they are needed!'

While this argument was going on and the Genoese were hanging back, a heavy storm of rain came on and there were loud claps of thunder, with lightning. Before the rain, huge flocks of crows had flown over both armies, making a deafening noise in the air. Some experienced knights said that this portended a great and murderous battle.

Then the sky began to clear and the sun shone out brightly. But the French had it straight in their eyes and the English at their backs. The Genoese, having been marshalled into proper order and made to advance, began to utter loud whoops to frighten the English. The English waited in silence and did not stir. The Genoese hulloa'd a second time and advanced a little farther, but the English still made no move. Then they raised a third shout, very loud and clear, levelled their crossbows and began to shoot.

At this the English archers took one pace forward and poured out their arrows on the Genoese so thickly and evenly that they fell like snow. When they felt those arrows piercing their arms, their heads, their faces, the Genoese, who had never met such archers before, were thrown into confusion. Many cut their bowstrings and some threw down their crossbows. They began to fall back.

English archers
practising at the butts

1348

The Black Death Reaches Florence, Italy

GIOVANNI BOCCACCIO

The Italian writer Boccaccio based The Decameron *around stories told by a group of people fleeing the plague in Italy. This description is part of the introduction to* The Decameron, *but is based on his own experiences in Florence.*

THIRTEEN HUNDRED and forty-eight years had elapsed since the fruitful Incarnation of the Son of God, when the noble city of Florence, which for its great beauty excels all others in Italy, was visited by the deadly pestilence.

In the face of its onrush, all the wisdom and ingenuity of man were unavailing. Large quantities of refuse were cleared out of the city by officials specially appointed for the purpose, all sick persons were forbidden entry, and numerous instructions were issued for safeguarding the people's health, but all to no avail. Nor were the countless petitions humbly directed to God by the pious, whether by means of formal processions or in any other guise, any less ineffectual. For in the early spring of the year we have mentioned, the plague began, in a terrifying and extraordinary manner, to make its disastrous effects apparent. It did not take the form it had assumed in the East, where if anyone bled from the nose it was an obvious portent of certain death. On the contrary, its earliest symptom, in men and women alike, was the appearance of certain swellings in the groin or the armpit, some of which were egg-shaped whilst others were roughly the size of the common apple. Sometimes the swellings were large, sometimes not so large, and they were referred to by the populace as *gavòccioli*. From the two areas already mentioned, this deadly *gavòcciolo* would begin to spread, and within a short time it would appear at random all over the body. Later on, the symptoms of the disease changed, and many people began to find dark blotches and bruises on their arms, thighs, and other parts of the body, sometimes large and few in number, at other times tiny and closely spaced. These, to anyone unfortunate enough to contract them, were just as infallible a sign that he would die as the *gavòcciolo* had been earlier, and as indeed it still was.

But what made this pestilence even more severe was that whenever those suffering from it mixed with people who were still unaffected, it would rush upon these with the speed of a fire racing through dry or oily substances that happened to be placed within its reach. Nor was this the full extent of its evil, for not only did it infect healthy persons who conversed or had any dealings with the sick, making them ill or visiting an equally horrible death upon them, but it also seemed to transfer the sickness to anyone touching the clothes or other objects which had been handled or used by its victims.

Symptoms of the Plague, Italy

GABRIELE DE MUSSIS

This is one of the most detailed and useful descriptions of the Black Death, which spread from Central Asia into Europe in the late 1340s, by a lawyer living in Piacenza.

THOSE OF both sexes who were in health, and in no fear of death, were struck by four savage blows to the flesh. First, out of the blue, a kind of chilly stiffness troubled their bodies. They felt a tingling sensation, as if they were being pricked by the points of arrows. The next stage was a fearsome attack which took the form of an extremely hard, solid boil. In some people this developed under the armpit and in others in the groin between the scrotum and the body. As it grew more solid, its burning heat caused the patients to fall into an acute and putrid fever, with severe headaches. As it intensified its extreme bitterness could have various effects. In some cases it gave rise to an intolerable stench. In others it brought vomiting of blood, or swellings near the place from which the corrupt humour arose: on the back, across the chest, near the thigh. Some people lay as if in a drunken stupor and could not be roused. Behold the swellings, the warning signs sent by the Lord. All these people were in danger of dying. Some died on the very day the illness took possession of them, others on the next day, others – the majority – between the third and fifth day. There was no known remedy for the vomiting of blood. Those who fell into a coma, or suffered a swelling or the stink of corruption very rarely escaped.

Flagellants in England   ROBERT OF AVESBURY

The Black Death was the most destructive pandemic in history. It killed perhaps a third of the population of Europe, but as much as half of the population of England. Little wonder then that in the aftermath people sought spiritual and psychological comfort from cults such as the one described here.

IN THAT same year of 1349, about Michaelmas [29 September], more than 120 men, for the most part from Zeeland or Holland, arrived in London from Flanders. These went barefoot in procession twice a day in the sight of the people, sometimes in St Paul's church and sometimes elsewhere in the city, their bodies naked except for a linen cloth from loins to ankle. Each wore a hood painted with a red cross at front and back and carried in his right hand a whip with three thongs. Each thong had a knot in it, with something sharp, like a needle, stuck through the middle of the knot so that it stuck out on each side, and as they walked one after the other they struck themselves with these whips on their naked, bloody bodies; four of them singing in their own tongue and the rest answering in the manner of the Christian litany. Three times in each procession they would all prostrate themselves on the ground, with their arms outstretched in the shape of a cross. Still singing, and beginning with the man at the end, each in turn would step over the others, lashing the man beneath him once with his whip, until all of those lying down had gone through the same ritual. Then each one put on his usual clothes and, always with their hoods on their heads and carrying their whips, they departed to their lodgings. It was said that they performed a similar penance every night.

1358

The Peasants' Revolt, France   JEAN FROISSART

At the Battle of Poitiers in 1356, the French army was heavily defeated and King John and many of his nobles held to ransom by the English. The resulting heavy increase in taxation needed to pay the ransoms was the immediate cause of a savage uprising of the French peasantry, suppressed with English help.

NOT LONG after the King of Navarre had been set free, there were very strange and terrible happenings in several parts of the kingdom of France. They occurred in the region of Beauvais, in Brie and on the Marne, in Valois, in Laonnais, in the fief of Coucy and round Soissons. They began when some of the men from the country towns came together in the Beauvais region. They had no leaders and at first they numbered scarcely a hundred. One of them got up and said that the nobility of France, knights and squires, were disgracing and betraying the realm, and that it would be a good thing if they were all destroyed. At this they all shouted: 'He's right! He's right! Shame on any man who saves the gentry from being wiped out!'

They banded together and went off, without further deliberation and unarmed except for pikes and knives, to the house of a knight who lived near by. They broke in and killed the knight, with his lady and his children, big and small, and set fire to the house. Next they went to another castle and did much worse; for, having seized the knight and bound him securely to a post, several of them violated his wife and daughter before his eyes. Then they killed the wife, who was pregnant, and the daughter and all the other children, and finally put the knight to death with great cruelty and burned and razed the castle.

They did similar things in a number of castles and big houses, and their ranks swelled until there were a good six thousand of them. Wherever they went their numbers grew, for all the men of the same sort joined them. The knights and squires fled before them with their families. They took their wives and daughters many miles away to put them in safety, leaving their houses open with their possessions inside. And those evil men, who had come together without leaders or arms, pillaged and burned everything and violated and killed all the ladies and girls without mercy, like mad dogs.

A Mystical Experience of Severe Illness, Norwich, England JULIAN OF NORWICH

1373

Julian of Norwich is believed to have been a contemplative nun. Her spiritual writings are part of the Christian mystical tradition and, in particular, emphasise the mothering role of Christ.

M Y CURATE was sent for to be present at my end; and before he came my eyes were fixed upwards, and I could not speak. He set the cross before my face, and said: I have brought the image of your saviour; look at it and take comfort from it. It seemed to me that I was well, for my eyes were set upwards towards heaven, where I trusted that I by God's mercy was going; but nevertheless I agreed to fix my eyes on the face of the crucifix if I could, and so I did, for it seemed to me that I would hold out longer with my eyes set in front of me rather than upwards. After this my sight began to fail. It grew as dark around me in the room as if it had been night, except that there was ordinary light trained upon the image of the cross, I did not know how. Everything around the cross was ugly and terrifying to me, as if it were occupied by a great crowd of devils.

After this the upper part of my body began to die, until I could scarcely feel anything. My greatest pain was my shortness of breath and the ebbing of my life. Then truly I believed that I was at the point of death. And suddenly at that moment all my pain was taken from me, and I was as sound, particularly in the upper part of my body, as ever I was before. I was astonished by this sudden change, for it seemed to me that it was by God's secret doing and not natural.

The Peasants' Revolt, England

1381

ANON (ANONIMALLE CHRONICLE)

The high rate of poll tax and grievances about the control of wages led to an insurrection of the people in June 1381 led by Watt Tyler and a defrocked priest, John Ball. Clearly the author of this account was an eyewitness of the events that he relates.

P RESENTLY Watt Tighler, in the presence of the king, sent for a flagon of water to rinse his mouth, because of the great heat that he was in, and when it was brought he rinsed his mouth in a very rude and disgusting fashion before the king's face. And then he made them bring him a jug of beer, and drank a great draught, and then, in the presence of the king, climbed on his horse again. At this time a certain valet from Kent, who was among the king's retinue, asked that the said Walter, the chief of the commons, might be pointed out to him. And when he saw him, he said aloud that he knew him for the greatest thief and robber in all Kent. Watt heard these words, and bade him come out to him, wagging his head at him in sign of malice; but the valet refused to approach, for fear that he had of the mob. But at last the lords made him go out to him, to see what he [Watt] would do before the king. And when Watt saw him he ordered one of his followers, who was riding behind him carrying his banner displayed, to dismount and behead the said valet. But the valet answered that he had done nothing worthy of death, for what he had said was true, and he would not deny it, but he could not lawfully make debate in the presence of his liege lord, without leave, except in his own defence: but that he could do without reproof; for if he was struck he would strike back again. And for these words Watt tried to strike him with his dagger, and would have slain him in the king's presence; but because he strove so to do, the mayor of London, William Walworth, reasoned with the said Watt for his violent behaviour and despite, done in the king's presence, and arrested him. And because he arrested him, the said Watt stabbed the mayor with his dagger in the stomach in great wrath.

1392

Charles VI Goes Mad, France JEAN FROISSART

The temporary insanity of the French king, in the middle of a punitive expedition against the Duke of Brittany, caused consternation at the court. The king was cured by Guillaume de Harselly and reigned for another thirty years.

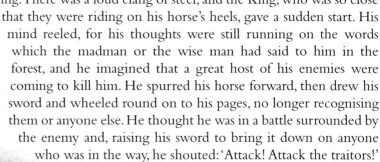

King Charles VI of France (1368–1422)

As THEY were all riding along, the page carrying the lance forgot what he was about or dozed off, as boys and pages do through carelessness, and allowed the blade of the lance to fall forward on to the helmet which the other page was wearing. There was a loud clang of steel, and the King, who was so close that they were riding on his horse's heels, gave a sudden start. His mind reeled, for his thoughts were still running on the words which the madman or the wise man had said to him in the forest, and he imagined that a great host of his enemies were coming to kill him. He spurred his horse forward, then drew his sword and wheeled round on to his pages, no longer recognising them or anyone else. He thought he was in a battle surrounded by the enemy and, raising his sword to bring it down on anyone who was in the way, he shouted: 'Attack! Attack the traitors!'

The Duke of Orléans was not far off. The King rode up to him brandishing his sword. He had lost all recollection of who people were and could not recognise his own brother or his uncles. When he saw him coming at him with drawn sword, the Duke was naturally afraid and spurred hurriedly away, with the King after him. The Duke of Burgundy was riding on the flank when, startled by the cries of the pages and the pounding of the horses' hooves, he looked across and saw the King chasing his brother with the naked sword. He was horror-struck and called out: 'Ho! Disaster has overtaken us! The King's gone out of his mind! After him, in God's name! Catch him!' And then: 'Fly, nephew, fly! The King means to kill you!' It was certain that the Duke of Orléans felt far from reassured and he was fleeing in earnest as fast as his horse could carry him, with knights and squires after them both.

Richard II's Capture and Imprisonment in the Tower of London, England ADAM USK

1399

The alleged 'tyranny' of Richard II, and the consequent seizure of the throne by his cousin, Henry Bolingbroke, crowned Henry IV, is one of the most controversial episodes in English history. Adam Usk had joined Bolingbroke's army in July 1399, and was an eyewitness observer of the capture of Richard II at Flint Castle, as well as of the pathetic figure he cut during his confinement in the Tower.

O N THE eve of the Assumption of the Blessed Virgin (*14 August*), my lord of Canterbury and the Earl of Northumberland went away to the king at the castle of Conway, to treat with him on the duke's behalf; and the king, on condition of saving his dignity, promised to surrender to the duke at the castle of Flint. And so, delivering up to them his two crowns, valued at one hundred thousand marks, with other countless treasure, he straightaway set forth to Flint. There the duke coming to him with twenty thousand chosen men — the rest of his host being left behind to guard his quarters and the country and castle and city of Chester — sought the king within the castle, for he would not come forth [girding it round with his armed men on the one side and with his archers on the other; whereby was fulfilled the prophecy: 'The white king shall array his host in form of a shield']. And he led him away prisoner to Chester castle, where he delivered him into safe keeping. Thus, too, he placed in custody certain lords, taken along with the king, to be kept till the parliament which was to begin on the morrow of Michaelmas-day.

A prison inside the Tower of London

While the duke was then at Chester, three of the twenty-four aldermen of the city of London, on behalf of the same city, together with fifty other citizens, came to the duke, and recommended their city to him, under their common seal, renouncing their fealty to King Richard. And so the duke, having gloriously, within fifty days, conquered both king and kingdom, marched to London; and there he placed the captive king in the Tower, under fitting guard.

On St Matthew's day (*21 September*), just two years after the beheading of the Earl of Arundel, I, the writer of this history, was in the Tower, wherein King Richard was a prisoner, and I was present when he dined, and I marked his mood and bearing, having been taken thither for that very purpose by Sir William Beauchamp. And there and then the king discoursed sorrowfully in these words: 'My God!, a wonderful land is this, and a fickle; which hath exiled, slain, destroyed or ruined so many kings, rulers, and great men, and is ever tainted and toileth with strife and variance and envy'; and then he recounted the histories and names of sufferers from the earliest habitation of the kingdom. Perceiving then the trouble of his mind, and how that none of his own men, nor such as were wont to serve him, but strangers who were but spies upon him, were appointed to his service, and musing on his ancient and wonted glory and on the fickle fortune of the world, I departed thence much moved at heart.

1413

Execution of Pierre des Essarts, Paris

JOURNAL D'UN BOURGEOIS DE PARIS

The traditional enmity of France and England started with the Hundred Years War in 1337 and was pursued vigorously by both sides (with brief intervals of peace) until it finally ended in 1453. This extract demonstrates a typical execution for treason during the Hundred Years War.

THE FIRST day of July, 1413, the said provost [Pierre des Essarts] was seized in the palace, dragged on a litter to the Heaumerie, and then seated on a plank in the tumbril, holding a wooden cross in his hand, clad in a black greatcoat, fringed and furred with marten, white breeches, with black slippers on his feet; in that condition he was taken to the market-place of Paris and there they cut off his head; and it was put higher than the others by more than three feet. And it is true that, from the time he was put on the litter up to his death, he did nothing but laugh, as he did in his great majesty, from which most people thought him mad; for all those who saw him wept so piteously that you would never hear of greater tears for the death of a man; and he alone laughed. And it was his belief that the common people would prevent his death; but he intended, if he had lived, to betray the city and to deliver it into the hands of the enemy, and himself to make great and cruel slaughter, and to pillage and strip the good citizens of the good city of Paris who had loved him so loyally.

Thus was decapitated Pierre des Essarts, and his body taken to the gibbet, and hung the highest. And about two years before, the Duke of Brabant, brother of the Duke of Burgundy, who observed his outrageous government, said to him, in the hotel of the king: 'Provost of Paris, Jehan de Montaigu took twenty-two years to get his head cut off; but truly you will not take more than three'; and he didn't do it, for he took only about two years and a half from this word; and they said for amusement throughout Paris, that the said duke was a prophet speaking the truth.

Battle of Agincourt, Picardy, France

JEHAN DE WAVRIN

1415

This was the last victory of the English longbow – fittingly narrated by a French knight who fought in the battle. It was the culminating event of Henry V's invasion of Normandy.

AFTER THE parley between the two armies was finished, as we have said, and the delegates had returned, each to their own people, the King of England, who had appointed a knight called Sir Thomas Erpingham to place his archers in front in two wings, trusted entirely to him, and Sir Thomas, to do his part, exhorted every one to do well in the name of the king, begging them to fight vigorously against the French in order to secure and save their own lives. And thus the knight, who rode with two others only in front of the battalion, seeing that the hour was come, for all things were well arranged, threw up a baton which he held in his hand, saying 'Nestrocq' ['Now Strike!'], which was the signal for

The Battle of Agincourt

attack; then dismounted and joined the king, who was also on foot in the midst of his men, with his banner before him. Then the English, seeing this signal, began suddenly to march, uttering a very loud cry, which greatly surprised the French. And when the English saw that the French did not approach them, they marched dashingly towards them in very fine order, and again raised a loud cry as they stopped to take breath.

Then the English archers, who, as I have said, were in the wings, saw that they were near enough, and began to send their arrows on the French with great vigour. The said archers were for the most part in their doublets, without armour, their stockings rolled up to their knees, and having hatchets and battle-axes or great swords hanging at their girdles; some were bare-footed and bare-headed, others had caps of boiled leather, and others of osier, covered with harpoy [skins] or leather.

Then the French, seeing the English come towards them in this fashion, placed themselves in order, every one under his banner, their helmets on their heads. The constable, the marshal, the admirals, and the other princes earnestly exhorted their men to fight the English well and bravely; and when it came to the approach the trumpets and clarions resounded everywhere; but the French began to hold down their heads, especially those who had no bucklers, for the impetuosity of the English arrows, which fell so heavily that no one durst uncover or look up.

1439

Wolves in Paris   JOURNAL D'UN BOURGEOIS DE PARIS

A reminder that wolves were still commonplace in 15th-century France – and a danger even in the capital itself.

1439. ALSO, at this time, especially while the king was in Paris, the wolves were so mad to eat the flesh of men, women, or children that, in the last week of September, they strangled and ate fourteen persons, both large and small, between Montmartre and the Porte St Antoine, both in the vineyards and within the swamps; and if they found a flock of animals, they assailed the shepherd and left the beasts. On the Eve of St Martin there was chased a wolf so terrible and horrible that they said that he alone had done more of the aforesaid horrors than all the others. On that day he was taken, and he had no tail, and for this he was named Courtaut [short tail]; and they talked as much about him as one does about a bandit or a cruel soldier, and they said to the people who were going out to the fields: 'Beware of Courtaut!' On that day he was put in a wheelbarrow, his jaws open, and taken within Paris; and the people left everything they were doing, drinking, eating, or any other necessary thing whatsoever, to go to see Courtaut; and in truth, he was worth to them more than ten francs.

Henry VI's Sickness, Greenwich, England

Edmund Clere

In August 1453, shortly after the defeat and death of Shrewsbury at Castillon, Henry VI lapsed into a state of complete mental withdrawal – in modern terminology, catatonic schizophrenia. Incapable of communication with anyone around him, he was thought to be communicating directly with God. He only recovered in 1455, Richard of York having become Protector in March 1454.

BLESSED BE God, the king is well amended, and hath been since Christmas Day; and on Saint John's day commanded his almoner to ride to Canterbury with his offering, and commanded the secretary to offer at Saint Edward's.

And on the Monday afternoon the Queen came to him, and brought my Lord Prince with her, and then he asked what the prince's name was, and the queen told him Edward; and then he held up his hands, and thanked God thereof.

And he said he never knew him till that time; nor wist not what was said to him, nor wist not where he had been, whilst he hath been sick till now; and he asked who were godfathers, and the queen told him, and he was well apaid (*content*).

And she told him that the cardinal was dead; and he said, he knew never thereof till that time; and he said, one of the wisest lords in this land was dead.

And my Lord of Winchester and my lord of Saint John's were with him on the morrow after Twelfthday, and he spake to them as well as ever he did; and when they came out they wept for joy. And he saith he is in charity with all the world, and so he would all the lords were.

And now he saith matins of Our Lady, and evensong, and heareth his mass devoutly

At the Court of King Alfonso V of Portugal, Lisbon Jorg von Ehingen

The hospitality of Alfonso V towards travellers was well known, involving a range of diversions, feasting, jumping, fencing and dancing.

WE INFORMED the King that we had understood that his Majesty was waging war against the infidel King of Fez, and that we were willing to serve in this war by land or sea. The King heard this very graciously, and told us that he would rely on us, and that at the proper time he would make use of our services, but that we must first remain for some time longer with him at court in order to become acquainted with the lords and nobles, and to see something more of his country. He caused us to be escorted back to our inn, and commanded the lords and nobles to lend us their company, which also happened. And such were the honours and merrymakings that the like can never have been seen by any king or prince. We were also introduced frequently into the apartments of the Queen's ladies, where many beautiful dances were held. Then to the chase, with jumping, wrestling, throwing, fencing, and racing with horses and jennets, and there was also much feasting. It was indeed delightful to be there. The King was named Alfonso. He was a handsome, well-grown prince, the most Christian, the worthiest, and most righteous King I have ever known. He kept also a regal court, and had with him two margraves and many counts and lords and knights, as well as beautiful women without number. We exercised ourselves in the same manner with knightly sports, on horseback and on foot, with jousting, and tourneys in full armour, since the King took great pleasure in such pastimes. My companion was the strongest in throwing the stone and iron bar, the latter being not light but very weighty, for he was a tall and powerful man, and no one could surpass him in throwing the great stone or at wrestling on horseback or on foot. I was particularly diligent in the combats in armour, for therein I was more skilful than my companion.

c. 1457

Single Combat with a Mighty Saracen Knight, Ceuta, Morocco   JORG VON EHINGEN

Single combats were at this time quite common, nonetheless the following encounter between a Christian and an infidel knight became a spectacular talking point in Portugal. The Portuguese had captured Ceuta in 1415, a vital strategic blow against the Moors.

WHEN EVENING came on, certain of our men drew near and reported that a mighty man among the infidels desired to engage in combat with a Christian in the plain between the two hills. Then I begged the captain that he would send me, for I was well arrayed and very apt in tilting-armour.

I approached, having my spear at the thigh, but as I drew near I couched my spear and thrust at his shield, and although he struck at me with his spear in the flank and forearm, I was able to give him such a mighty thrust that horse and man fell to the ground. But his spear hung in my armour and hindered me, and I had great difficulty in loosing it and alighting from my horse. By this time he also was dismounted. I had my sword in my hand; he likewise seized his sword, and we advanced and gave each other a mighty blow. The infidel had excellent armour, and although I struck him by the shield he received no injury. Nor did his blows injure me. We then gripped each other and wrestled so long that we fell to the ground side by side. But the infidel was a man of amazing strength. He tore himself from my grasp, and we both raised our bodies until we were kneeling side by side. I then thrust him from me with my left hand in order to be able to strike at him with my sword, and this I was able to do, for with the thrust his body was so far removed that I was able to cut at his face, and although the blow was not wholly successful, I wounded him so that he swayed and was half-blinded. I then struck him a direct blow in the face and hurled him to the ground, and falling upon him I thrust my sword through his throat, after which I rose to my feet, took his sword, and returned to my horse.

The Races at Pienza, Italy   PIUS II

1462

Pius II, who ascended to the papal throne in 1458, wrote his memoirs in the third person, demonstrating little indication of deep spirituality but a genuine enthusiasm for sport and people.

MANY LUSTY, active youths who had often run in the stadium competed in the foot race. There had been a light rain and the track was slippery. They ran naked and now one, now another was ahead and often one or another could be seen to slip and fall and roll on the ground and mud and those who had been last were now ahead. In this way they ran four *stades* as far as the gate with very little space between the victor and the vanquished and they were so befouled with mud as to be unrecognisable. Then a cook from the Pope's kitchen named Trippes, throwing off his boots and clothes except only his cloak, dashed out from a corner and unrecognised started to run through the town as if he were one of the contestants. Being fresh he quickly passed the two foremost runners and triumphantly seized the prize, to the great chagrin of the next runner who thought himself beaten when already victor and resented having the victory snatched from his grasp. But he realised at once that this victor was not muddy enough and that he was wearing a cloak in which he could not possibly have finished so long a course. The judges shaking with laughter rejected the cook and gave the prize to the youth from Sarteano who came in first.

The boys' race was the best of all. There were many young lads who leapt forward naked at the signal, each trying to outstrip the others and competing with extraordinary keenness. They could not shake their feet clear of the sticky clay and now they would lose their breath and fall, now get it back and rise again. Their parents and brothers cheered them on with repeated shouts of encouragement. The course was about a *stade* to the town gate and victory wavered among many.

The Pope watched these contests from a very high window with a good deal of pleasure though while they were going on he was consulting with the cardinals on public business.

c.1483 Leonardo da Vinci Offers his Services to Ludovico, Milan, Italy Leonardo da Vinci

It is interesting how, in soliciting the patronage of Ludovico il Moro, Duke of Bari and virtual ruler of Milan, Leonardo da Vinci emphasises his skills in military and naval engineering rather than in art. Milan was at that time facing war with Venice and da Vinci's mechanical genius was channelled into the design of a range of weapons and other military devices.

Most illustrious Lord. Having now sufficiently seen and considered the proofs of all those who count themselves masters and inventors of instruments of war, and finding that the invention and working of the said instruments do not differ in any respect from those in common use, I shall endeavour without prejudice to anyone else to explain myself to your Excellency, showing your Lordship my secrets, and then offering at your pleasure to work with effect at convenient times on all those things which are in part briefly recorded below.

1. I have plans of bridges, very light and strong and suitable for carrying very easily, and with them you may pursue, and at times flee from, the enemy; and others secure and indestructible by fire and battle, easy and convenient to lift and to place in position; and plans for burning and destroying those of the enemy.

2. When a place is besieged, I know how to remove the water from the trenches, and how to construct an infinite number of bridges, covered ways and ladders and other instruments having to do with such expeditions.

3. Also if a place cannot be reduced by the method of bombardment either owing to the height of its banks or to its strength of position, I have plans for destroying every fortress or other stronghold even if it were founded on rock.

4. I have also plans of mortars most convenient and easy to carry with which to hurl small stones in the manner almost of a storm; and with the smoke of this cause great terror to the enemy and great loss and confusion.

Leonardo da Vinci, self-portrait (1452–1519)

And if it should happen that the fight was at sea I have plans for many engines most efficient for both attack and defence, and vessels which will resist the fire of the largest cannon, and powder and smoke.

5. Also I have means of arriving at a fixed spot by caves and secret and winding passages, made without any noise even though it may be necessary to pass underneath trenches or a river.

6. Also I will make covered cars, safe and unassailable, which will enter among the enemy with their artillery, and there is no company of men at arms so great

that they will not break it. And behind these the infantry will be able to follow quite unharmed and without any hindrance.

7. Also, if need shall arise, I can make cannon, mortars, and light ordnance of very useful and beautiful shapes, different from those in common use.

8. Where the operation of bombardment fails, I shall contrive catapults, mangonels, 'trabocchi', and other engines of wonderful efficacy and in general use. In short, to meet the variety of circumstances, I shall contrive various and endless means of attack and defence.

10. In time of peace I believe I can give perfect satisfaction, equal to that of any other, in architecture and the construction of buildings both private and public, and in conducting water from one place to another.

Also I can carry out sculpture in marble, bronze or clay, and also I can do in painting whatever can be done, as well as any other, be he who may.

Christopher Columbus Meets Indians, West Indies CHRISTOPHER COLUMBUS

1492

The discovery of the 'New World' in 1492 is arguably the most important event in the history of the world, and certainly of Western Europe. For the native inhabitants, however, it was an unmitigated disaster – many of them were wiped out within the first 100 years of the arrival of Europeans.

'ALL THE MEN I saw were young. I did not see one over the age of thirty. They were very well built with fine bodies and handsome faces. Their hair is coarse, almost like that of a horse's tail and short; they wear it down over their eyebrows except for a few strands at the back, which they wear long and never cut. They are the colour of the Canary Islanders (neither black nor white). Some of them paint themselves black, others white or any colour they can find. Some paint their faces, some their whole bodies, some only the eyes, some only the nose. They do not carry arms or know them. For when I showed them swords, they took them by the edge and cut themselves out of ignorance. They have no iron. Their spears are made of cane. Some instead of an iron tip have a fish's tooth and others have points of different kinds. They are fairly tall on the whole, with fine limbs and good proportions. I saw some who had wound scars on their bodies and I asked them by signs how they got these and they indicated to me that people came from other islands near by who tried to capture them and they defended themselves. I supposed and still suppose that they come from the mainland to capture them for slaves. They should be good servants and very intelligent, for I have observed that they soon repeat anything that is said to them, and I believe that they would easily be made Christians, for they appeared to me to have no religion. God willing, when I make my departure I will bring half a dozen of them back to their Majesties, so that they can learn to speak. I saw no animals of any kind on this island except parrots.'

1498

Elephants in India VASCO DA GAMA

The menagerie of exotic birds and beasts became a fashionable accessory for the great and wealthy, particularly after the start of Portuguese and Spanish expansion oversees when many hitherto unknown species found their way to Europe from Asia, Africa and the New World.

THEY MAKE a house of wood holding four men, and this house is put on the back of the elephant with the four men in it. The elephant has attached five naked swords to each of his tusks, being ten for the two tusks. This renders him so redoubtable that none awaits his attack if flight is possible. Whatever those seated on the top order to be done is done as if he were a rational creature, for if they tell him 'kill this one, or do this thing or another', he does it.

When they wish to capture a wild elephant they take a tame female, and dig a large hole on the track frequented by elephants, and cover its mouth with brushwood. They then tell the female 'Go! and if you meet with an elephant, entice him to this hole, in such a way that he falls into it, but take care that you do not fall into it yourself.' She then goes away, and does as she has been told, and when she meets one she draws him on in such a way that he must fall into the hole, and the hole is so deep that unaided he could never get out of it.

After the elephant has fallen into this hole, five or six days are allowed to pass before he is given anything to eat. When that time has elapsed, a man brings him a very small supply of food, the supply being increased from day to day until he eats by himself. This is continued for about a month, during which time those who bring him food gradually tame him, until at last they venture to descend into the hole. This is done for several days until he permits the man to put his hands upon his tusks. He then goes into the hole and puts heavy chains around the legs, and whilst in this condition they train him so well that he learns all but to speak.

1501

The Marriage of Lucrezia Borgia, Rome

JOHANN BURCHARD

The infamous Borgia family derived their prominence in Italian politics from the head of the family, Rodrigo Borgia, who was elected Pope Alexander VI in 1492. Lucrezia was his illegitimate daughter by Vanozza Catanei. This was her third marriage – the first was annulled and her brother Cesare had arranged the murder of her second husband. Burchard was the Pope's Master of Ceremonies.

NEXT DAY, after dinner, Lucrezia rode from her residence to the Church of Santa Maria del Popolo. She was dressed in a robe of brocaded gold with the veil drawn back, and was escorted by three hundred horsemen. Four bishops rode in front of her, and she was followed by her footmen and servants, but she herself proceeded alone; the company returned in the same order to her house. On the same evening from supper-time until nine o'clock, the great Capitoline bell was tolled and many bonfires were lit on the Castel Sant' Angelo and throughout the city, whilst all the buildings were brightly illuminated and the people became wildly excited, causing some anxiety.

On the following day, Monday, September 6th, two clowns paraded through all the principal streets and piazzas of the city, shouting loudly, 'Long live the most Illustrious Duchess of Ferrara, long live Pope Alexander! Viva, viva!' One of these men was on horseback and had been given by Donna Lucrezia the golden brocaded dress and veil which she had worn as new only once on the day before and which was worth three hundred ducats or so. The other man followed on foot and was similarly the recipient of a dress from the Pope's daughter.

On Sunday evening, October 30th, Don Cesare Borgia gave a supper in his apartment in the apostolic palace, with fifty decent prostitutes or courtesans in attendance, who after the meal danced with the servants and others there, first fully dressed and then naked. Following the supper too, lampstands holding lighted candles were placed on the floor and chestnuts strewn about, which the prostitutes, naked and on their hands and knees, had to pick up as they crawled in and out amongst the lampstands. The Pope, Don Cesare and Donna Lucrezia were all present to watch. Finally, prizes were offered – silken doublets, pairs of shoes, hats and other garments – for those men who were most successful with the prostitutes. This performance was carried out in the Sala Reale and those who attended said that in fact the prizes were presented to those who won the contest.

Martin Luther Enters a Monastery, Erfurt, Germany   MARTIN LUTHER

1505

Martin Luther, the Augustinian monk and theologian who dominated the Reformation, was born at Eisleben, Germany, in 1483. After a routine academic career, the experience of a violent thunderstorm inspired him to resolve his spiritual self-doubts by entering a strict monastic order. He took holy orders in 1507, much to the disappointment of his ambitious father.

ON 16TH JULY, St Alexis Day, Luther observed: 'Today is the anniversary of my entrance into the monastery at Erfurt.' Then he began to relate how he had made the vow. Two weeks earlier while travelling near Stotternheim, not far from Erfurt, he was so frightened by a flash of lightning that he exclaimed in terror: 'Help me, St Anne, I will become a monk!' He continued: 'Afterwards I regretted this vow and many counselled me against it. None the less, I remained steadfast. On the day before St Alexis I invited my best friends to a farewell and requested that they should accompany me to the cloister the following day. When

Martin Luther
(1483–1546)

IN SILENTIO
FORTITVDO

ET SPE ERIT
VESTRA

they wanted to keep me back, I said: "You will see me today for the last time." They escorted me with tears in their eyes. My father was also very angry about my vow, but I persisted in my decision. I never thought that I would leave the cloister. I had died unto the world.'

1511–12 Michelangelo Finishes Painting the Sistene Chapel, Rome GIORGIO VASARI

When, in 1508, the egocentric Pope Julius II commissioned Michelangelo to adorn the ceiling of his private chapel with paintings, the artist initially protested that he was a sculptor, not a painter. However, he then set about his work so compulsively, without consideration for himself or his health, that he painted 343 consummate spiritual figures in four years. Vasari was a pupil and friend of Michelangelo.

JULIUS, WHO justly valued the ability of Michelagnolo, commanded that he should continue the work, judging from what he saw of the first half, that our artist would be able to improve the second materially; and the master accordingly finished the whole, completing it to perfection in twenty months, without having even the help of a man to grind the colours. It is true that he sometimes complained of the manner in which the Pope hastened forward the work, seeing that he was thereby prevented from giving it the finish which he would have desired to bestow; His Holiness constantly inquiring when it would be completed. On one occasion, therefore, Michelagnolo replied, 'It will be finished when I shall have done all that I believe required to satisfy Art.' 'And we command,' rejoined the Pontiff, 'that you satisfy our wish to have it done quickly'; adding finally, that if it were not at once completed, he would have him, Michelagnolo, thrown headlong from the scaffolding.

Hearing this, our artist, who feared the fury of the Pope, and with good cause, desisted instantly, without taking time to add what was wanting, and took down the remainder of the scaffolding, to the great satisfaction of the whole city, on All Saints' Day, when Pope Julius went into that Chapel to sing mass; but Michelagnolo had much desired to retouch some portions of the work *a secco*, as had been done by the older masters who had painted the stories on the walls; he would also gladly have added a little ultramarine to some of the draperies, and gilded other parts, to the end that the whole might have a richer and more striking effect. The Pope, too, hearing that these things were still wanting, and finding that all who beheld the Chapel praised it highly, would now fain have had the additions made, but as Michelagnolo thought reconstructing the scaffold too long an affair, the pictures remained as they were, although the Pope, who often saw Michelagnolo, would sometimes say, 'Let the Chapel be enriched with bright colours and gold; it looks poor.' When Michelagnolo would reply familiarly, 'Holy Father, the men of those days did not adorn themselves with gold; those who are painted here less than any, for they were none too rich; besides which, they were holy men, and must have despised riches and ornaments.'

For this work Michelagnolo received from the Pope, in various payments, the sum of three thousand crowns, and of these he may have spent twenty-five in colours.

At the Court of Montezuma, Mexico

BERNAL DIAZ DEL CASTILLO

1519

In 1519 Hernán Cortés and a small band of Spanish conquistadores invaded Mexico. At first they were on friendly terms with the Aztec Indians who had recently conquered large parts of it and were astonished at the magnificence and sophistication of the Aztec court.

THE GREAT Montezuma was about forty years old, of good height, well proportioned, spare and slight, and not very dark, though of the usual Indian complexion. He did not wear his hair long but just over his ears, and he had a short black beard, well-shaped and thin. His face was rather long and cheerful, he had fine eyes, and in his appearance and manner could express geniality or, when necessary, a serious composure. He was very neat and clean, and took a bath every afternoon. He had many women as his mistresses, the daughters of chieftains, but two legitimate wives who were *Caciques* in their own right, and when he had intercourse with any of them it was so secret that only some of his servants knew of it. He was quite free from sodomy.

For each meal his servants prepared him more than thirty dishes cooked in their native style, which they put over small earthenware braziers to prevent them from getting cold. They cooked more than three hundred plates of the food the great Montezuma was going to eat, and more than a thousand more for the guard. I have heard that they used to cook him the flesh of young boys. But as he had such a variety of dishes, made of so many different ingredients, we could not tell whether a dish was of human flesh or anything else, since every day they cooked fowls, turkeys, pheasants, local partridges, quail, tame and wild duck, venison, wild boar, marsh birds, pigeons, hares and rabbits, also many other kinds of birds and beasts native to their country, so numerous that I cannot quickly name them all. I know for certain, however, that after our Captain spoke against the sacrifice of human beings and the eating of their flesh, Montezuma ordered that it should no longer be served to him.

1520

A Maya Account of the Spanish Conquest, Mexico ANONYMOUS MAYA CHRONICLER

The introduction of European diseases to which the American Indians had no immunity, was the most profound consequence of the conquest of the New World and responsible for the decimation of its inhabitants. Here a Maya chronicler despairs over the effects of a smallpox outbreak.

DURING THE twenty-fifth year [1520] . . . the pestilence appeared, oh my sons! First they fell ill with a cough, they suffered nosebleeds and infected urine. Truly terrible was the number of deaths in this time. Then Prince Vakaki Ahmak died. Little by little deep shadows and dark night enveloped our fathers and grandfathers, and us, too, oh my sons, when the pestilence raged. . . .

Forty days after the epidemic began, our father and grandfather died. On the day Twelve Death [April 16, 1521] died King Hunyg, your great-grandfather. Two days later, our father, the Ahpop Achí Balam, also died. . . .

Great was the stench of the dead. . . . Half the people fled to the fields. Dogs and vultures devoured the corpses. The mortality was terrible. . . . Thus it was that we became orphans, oh my sons! Thus we were left when we were young . . . We were born to die! . . .

One hundred days after the death of the kings Hunyg and Lahuh Noh, Cahi Ymox and Belehé Qat were elected kings; they were elected on the day One

Serpent [August 13, 1521]; but only one ever took up office, Belehé Qat, who survived [the smallpox]. We were children and we were alone; none of our fathers had been spared.

Fate of the German Peasants and Thomas Müntzer, the Battle of Frankenhausen, Germany ANON

1525

Thomas Müntzer was a Protestant radical from Saxony who courted controversy and became the scourge of 'respectable' reformers like Luther, who dubbed him an 'arch-devil'. Müntzer has been seen as a 16th-century proletarian: his view of the 'elect' and the 'godless' became identified with the Saxon peasants' struggle against their rulers in 1525. Indeed, he had joined the peasant camp before the calamitous Battle of Frankenhausen, after which he was arrested, tortured and executed.

THEN THEY advanced towards the peasants and began to fire. The poor people just stood there and sang, 'Now we pray the Holy Spirit', as if they were insane. They neither resisted nor fled. Many comforted themselves in Thomas's great promise that God would send help from heaven, since Thomas had said he would catch all bullets in his coat sleeves. . . .

After the battle they approached the village and occupied it. They captured some three hundred men, who were beheaded. Thomas had escaped into a house near the gate. He could have escaped in the meantime or hid himself better, had God not wanted him to be captured. Nobody paid particular attention to him; nobody even looked for him.

A nobleman from Lüneburg had moved into the same house. By accident his servant went up into the attic to see what kind of house they were living in. He found a man lying on a bed as if he were sick. He asked him who he was and if he was one of the rebels. Thomas had laid himself into bed, as if he were weak, thinking that he could hide that way and escape. He answered the servant that he was a sick man and had fever and was very weak and had never taken part in the rebellion.

The servant found a purse near the bed and took it, hoping to find some booty. He found letters, written by Count Albrecht of Mansfeld, which asked Thomas to desist from his wantonness. The servant inquired of him whence he had the letters and whether he were Thomas. Thomas was frightened and denied it vehemently, and did not want to be Thomas. Finally, when the servant began to threaten him, he confessed. Then he was arrested. . . .

He publicly confessed that he had done wrong. In the spring he admonished the princes that they should not be severe with the poor people. Then they would not encounter such danger again. He told them to read *Libros Regum*. After this talk he was beheaded. His head was put on a lance and placed in the field as a memorial.

1528

Blaise de Monluc is Wounded by an Arquebus, Italy BLAISE DE MONLUC

An incident in the campaign of the French against the Kingdom of Naples. Monluc was a professional soldier who had raised a regiment of infantry in his home region of Gascony.

ONE OF THE companies of Monsieur de Luppé, our lieutenant-colonel, and mine prepared to enter at this place, and now God had granted me the thing that I had ever desired, which was to be present at an assault, there to enter the first man or lose my life. I therefore threw myself headlong into the parlour, having on a coat of mail such as the Germans used in those days, a sword in my hand, a target upon my arm and a morion upon my head. But as those who were at my heels were pressing to get in after me, the enemy poured the great tub of stones upon their heads and trapped them in the hole, by reason whereof they could not possibly follow.

I therefore remained all alone within, fighting at a door that went out into the street. But from the roof of the parlour, which was unplanked and laid open for that purpose, they peppered me in the meantime with an infinite number of arquebus shot, one of which pierced my target and shot my arm quite through, within four fingers of my hand, and another so battered the bone at the knitting of my arm and shoulder, that I lost all manner of feeling, so that letting my target fall I was constrained to retire towards my hole, against which I was borne over by those who fought at the door of the parlour; but so fortunately nevertheless for me that my soldiers had, by that means, opportunity to draw me out by the legs, but so leisurely withal, that they very courteously made me tumble heels over head from the very top to the bottom of the graffe, wherein rolling over the ruins of the stones I again broke my already wounded arm in two places. So soon as my men had gathered me up, I told them that I thought I had left my arm behind me in the town, when one of my soldiers, lifting it up from whence it hung, as in a scarf, dangling upon my buttocks, and laying it over the other, put me into a little heart.

1531

The Purity of Zwingli's Heart, the Battle of Cappel, Switzerland OSWALD MYCONIUS

Largely under the influence of the Swiss reformer Huldreich Zwingli, Zürich was effectively a Protestant town by 1525. This created a profound religious schism in the Swiss Confederation between Zürich and the five Catholic cantons. Hostility between the two sides reached its climax in a battle near Cappel, for which the Zürich forces were unprepared and were consequently crushed. Zwingli had sported helmet and armour and was among a dozen preachers, as well as many soldiers, to be killed.

THREE TIMES Zwingli was thrown down by the onstorming masses, but each time he regained his feet. The fourth time a lancet hit him below the chin. Sinking to his knees, he exclaimed, 'What does it matter? The body they can kill, but not the soul.' Soon afterwards he departed in the Lord. After the battle the enemies had time to look for Zwingli's corpse – we had withdrawn to a secure position. Who told them so quickly about his presence or his death? The corpse was found and the sentence pronounced over it. It was cut into four pieces, thrown into the fire, and burned down to ashes. Three days later, after the departure of the enemies, Zwingli's friends arrived to find some remains of him. Miraculously his heart, altogether whole and intact, was found in the ashes. The people were amazed and sensed a miracle, but did not understand it. They ascribed this to God and rejoiced. They were assured, by supernatural means, of the purity of Zwingli's heart. Shortly thereafter a man whom I know well came to me to ask if I wished to see a part of Zwingli's heart which he had with him in a capsule. I declined, since awe struck me upon hearing such unexpected words. Thus I have not seen it with my own eyes.

The Execution of Atahuallpa, King of the Incas, Peru PEDRO PIZARRO

1533

The execution of the Inca Atahuallpa was a defining moment in Francisco Pizarro's expedition of 1532–3, which began and completed the conquest of Peru. It demonstrated Pizarro's ruthlessness as governor: Atahuallpa's alleged treason was, while imprisoned, to have sent orders for his army to attack and kill the Spaniards.

ATAHUALLPA wept, and begged that they should not kill him, for not an Indian in the land would move without his orders, and since he was a prisoner, they had nothing to fear. I saw the Marquis weep with sorrow that he could not spare his life because of the danger that he might escape.

The sentence was that for the treason he had committed he should die by burning unless he chose to become a Christian; and this was for the safety of the Christians and the good of the whole land, and to secure its conquest and pacification. For once Atahuallpa was dead, the whole of that army would immediately disperse, since they would lack the courage to attack and carry out the order he had given them.

They brought Atahuallpa out to execution, and when they carried him into the square he said that he wished to become a Christian. The Governor was immediately informed and said that he must be baptised. He was baptised by the reverend father Fray Vicente de Valverde, who comforted him. The Governor then ordered that he should not be burnt but tied to a post in the square and strangled. This was done, and the body was left there till the next morning, when the friars, the Governor and other Spaniards carried him to be most solemnly buried in church, with all possible honours. Such was the end of this man who had been so cruel. He died with great courage, showing no emotion and saying that he entrusted his children to the Governor. When they took his body to be buried there was much wailing among his women and household servants. He died on a Saturday, at the same hour that he had been defeated and taken prisoner. Some said that it was for his sins that he died on this day and at this hour. He was punished for the great wrongs and cruelties he had committed on his subjects. For all said with one voice that he was the cruellest butcher that had ever been known, and that he would raze a village to the ground for a petty crime committed by one of its inhabitants, and kill ten thousand people. He subjected the whole country to his tyranny and was universally loathed.

1534

Communism in Anabaptist Münster, Germany

MEISTER HEINRICH GRESBECK

The Imperial City of Münster was officially Lutheran before its leadership was ousted and the Anabaptists assumed control under Jan Matthys and John Beukels of Leyden. There followed one of the most notorious episodes of the Reformation, in which religious reform became associated with social revolution. In its short history, the Anabaptist kingdom of Münster, a self-styled 'New Jerusalem', was witness to the communal sharing of property and even of wives.

THE PROPHETS, preachers and the entire council deliberated and felt that everything should be held in common. It was first ordered that everyone who had copper money should bring it to the City Hall, where he would receive a different currency. This was done. After the prophets and the preachers had reached an agreement with the council in this matter, it was announced in the sermons that all things should be held in common. Thus they said in the sermon: 'Dear brothers and sisters, inasmuch as we are one people, and are brothers and sisters one to another, it is God's will that we should bring our money, silver and gold together. Each one of us should have as much as any other. Therefore everyone is to bring his money to the chancellery near the City Hall. There the council will be present and receive the money.' Likewise preacher Stutenbernt said: 'A Christian should not have any money; everything which Christian brothers and sisters possess belongs to one as well as the other. You shall not lack anything, be it food, clothes, house, or goods. What you need, you shall receive, God will not suffer you to lack anything. One thing shall be held as much in common as the other. It belongs to all of us. It is mine as well as yours, and yours as well as mine.' Thus they persuaded the people so that some of them brought their money, silver and gold, indeed everything they owned. But there was much inequality in Münster, where one supposedly had as much as any other.

Some people in the city turned in all their money, silver and gold and did not keep anything. Others turned in part and kept part. Still others did not turn in anything.

The Trial and Execution of Sir Thomas More, England ANTHONY CASTELNAU

1535

Sir Thomas More, formerly Henry VIII's chief minister, paid with his life for his princi-ples – he was the King's servant at a time when the necessary proof of loyalty was to sup-port the royal divorce, which his conscience prevented. Anthony Castelnau was the Bishop of Tarbes between 1534 and 1539.

THEY ORDERED an usher to summon 12 men according to the custom of the country, and these articles were given to them that they might judge whether More had maliciously contravened the Statute. After a quarter of an hour's absence they declared him guilty of death, and sentence was pronounced by the Chancellor 'selon la lettre de la noble loy'.

More then spoke as follows: 'Since I am condemned, and God knows how, I wish to speak freely of your Statute, for the discharge of my conscience. I know well that the reason why you have condemned me is because I have never been willing to consent to the King's second marriage, but I hope in the divine goodness and mercy, that as St Paul and St Stephen whom he persecuted, are now friends in Paradise, so we, though differing in this world, shall be united in perfect charity in the other. I pray God to protect the King and give him good counsel.'

Sir Thomas More (1478–1535)

On his way to the Tower one of his daugh-ters, named Margaret, pushed through the archers and guards, and held him in her embrace some time without being able to speak. Afterwards More, asking leave of the archers, bade her have patience, for it was God's will, and she had long known the secret of his heart. After going 10 or 12 steps she returned and embraced him again, to which he said nothing, except to bid her pray to God for his soul; and this without tears or change of colour. On the Tuesday following he was beheaded in the open space in front of the Tower. A little before his death he asked those present to pray to God for him and he would do the same for them [in the other world]. He then besought them earnestly to pray to God to give the King good counsel, protesting that he died his faithful servant, but God's first.

Maya Blood Sacrifice, Yucatan, Mexico

Diego de Landa

Diego de Landa, a Spanish Franciscan friar, accepted the missionary challenge of Catholic spiritual conquest of the New World, travelling to Yucatan in the late 1540s. There he developed an intimate understanding of Maya people and customs, not least the sacrificial rituals he intended to prevent.

Besides the feasts in solemnification of which they sacrificed [animals], they also commanded the priests or Chilans to sacrifice persons to remedy some misfortune or necessity, and everyone contributed to this, either by giving money to buy slaves [for sacrifice] or, out of devotion, by offering up their own small children, who were much feted until the feast day on which they were to be sacrificed, and carefully guarded so that they should not run away or defile themselves by some carnal sin; and while they processed from village to village with dancing, the priests fasted with the Chilans and officials.

When the day came the people gathered in the courtyard of the temple, and if the victim was to be sacrificed with arrows, they stripped him naked and anointed his body with blue, placing a cap upon his head. When they had come to the place where the devil stood, the people performed a solemn dance around the pole, all carrying arrows and bows, and, still dancing, they tied the victim to the pole, dancing all the while and all watching him. The foul priest in vestments then climbed up, and with an arrow wounded him in the secret parts, be he man or woman, and drew off the blood and anointed the face of the devil with it. He then made a certain signal to the dancers and they, as if dancing, passed swiftly one after another and began to shoot at his heart, which had been marked with a white mark. In this fashion, they turned that point in his chest into a hedgehog of arrows.

If they were to remove his heart, they took him to the courtyard with great ceremony and attended by a large company of people, and, having smeared him with blue and put on his cap, they led him to the round altar, which was the sacrificial stone. After the priests and officials had anointed that stone with the blue colour and driven out the devil by purifying the temple, the Chacs seized the poor wretch they were going to sacrifice, and with great speed placed him on his back against the stone and held him by his legs and arms so that they divided him down the middle. This done, the executioner came with a large stone knife and dealt him, with great skill and cruelty, a blow between the ribs on the left-

hand side under the nipple. He then plunged his hand in there and seized the heart and, like a raging tiger, drew it out alive and, placing it on a plate, handed it to the priest, who went very hurriedly and anointed the faces of the idols with that fresh blood.

The Expulsion of the 'Useless Mouths', Siena, Italy BLAISE DE MONLUC

1555

The siege of Siena was one of the last acts of the great Italian Wars which, after nearly seventy years, were brought to an end by the Treaty of Cateau Cambresis in 1559. It was standard procedure during a 16th-century siege to expel all civilians so as to reduce the demand on food and other resources. Often the unfortunate victims were stranded between the garrison and the besiegers and starved to death.

I CREATED six commissaries to take a list of all the useless people, and afterwards delivered the roll to a knight of Malta, accompanied with five and twenty or thirty soldiers, to put them out of the town; which in three days after I had delivered in the list, was performed. A thing that had I not very good witness of, both of the Sienese, the King's officers, and the captains who were then present in Siena, I should not however have mentioned in this place lest the world should take me for a liar; but it is most perfectly true.

The list of these useless mouths I do assure you amounted to four thousand and four hundred people or more, which of all the miseries and desolations that I have ever seen was the greatest my eyes ever yet beheld or that I believe I shall ever see again. For the master was hereby necessitated to part with his servant who had served him long, the mistress with her maid, besides an infinite number of poor people who only lived by the sweat of their brows; which weeping and desolation continued for three days together. And these poor wretches were to go through the enemy, who still beat them back again towards the city, the whole camp continuing night and day in arms to that only end. So that they drove them up to the very foot of the walls that they might the sooner consume the little bread we had left, and to see if the city out of compassion to those miserable creatures would revolt. But that prevailed nothing, though they lay eight days in this condition where they had nothing to eat but herbs and grass, and above the one half of them perished, for the enemy killed them, and very few escaped away. There were a great many maids and handsome women indeed, who found means to escape, the Spaniards by night stealing them into their quarters for their own provision. But it was unknown to the Marquis for it had otherwise been death; and some strong and vigorous men also forced their way and escaped by night. But all those did not amount to the fourth part and all the rest miserably perished.

OPPOSITE PAGE Design for a tapestry showing the defeat of the Spanish Armada 1588

1555

The Burning of Archbishop Cranmer, London

ANON

The accession to the throne of the Catholic Queen Mary in 1553 meant the complete reversal of the Protestant Reformation started by Henry VIII and continued by his son Edward. The burning of Protestant clergy at Smithfield Market was the inspiration for Foxe's Book of Martyrs *and ensured that on Mary's death the country would fight tenaciously to defend itself against any forcible imposition of the 'Old Religion'.*

THEN HE was carried away, and a great number that did run to see him go so wickedly to his death, ran after him, exhorting him, while time was, to remember himself. And one Friar John, a godly and well-learned man, all the way travelled with him to reduce him. But it would not be. What they said in particular I cannot tell, but the effect appeared in the end. For at the stake he professed that he died in all such opinions as he had taught, and oft repented him of his recantation.

Coming to the stake with a cheerful countenance and willing mind, he put off his garments with haste, and stood upright in his shirt. And a Bachelor of Divinity, named Elye, of Brasenose College, laboured to convert him to his former recantation, with the two Spanish friars. But when the friars saw his constancy, they said in Latin one to another, 'Let us go from him, we ought not to be nigh him, for the devil is with him.' But the Bachelor in Divinity was more earnest with him. Unto whom he answered, that as concerning his recantation he repented it right sore, because he knew it to be against the truth, with other words more. Whereupon the Lord Williams cried, 'Make short, make short.' Then the bishop took certain of his friends by the hand. But the bachelor of divinity refused to take him by the hand, and blamed all others that did so, and said he was sorry that ever he came in his company. And yet again he required him to agree to his former recantation. And the bishop answered (shewing his hand), 'This is the hand that wrote it, and therefore shall it suffer first punishment.'

Fire being now put to him, he stretched out his right hand and thrust it into the flame, and held it there a good space, before the fire came to any other part of his body, where his hand was seen of every man sensibly burning, crying with a loud voice, 'This hand hath offended.' As soon as the fire was got up, he was very soon dead, never stirring or crying all the while.

Bᵖ Ridley: Bᵖ Latimer. Arch·Bᵖ Cranmer

The burning of
Archbishop Cranmer

A Cannibal Feast, Brazil   JEAN DE LERY

1556

A Calvinist missionary describes the methods used by the Tupinamba tribe to cook and eat their prisoners. Jean de Lery stayed in Brazil for two years and left a vivid account of the customs and habits of the Brazilian tribes which was the basis of much later anthropological study.

THE ONE who owned the prisoner, with as many neighbours of his own choosing as he pleases, will take this poor body, cleave it and immediately cut it into pieces; no butcher in this country could more quickly dismember a sheep. But even beyond that – O more than prodigious cruelty – just as our huntsmen over here, after taking a stag, give the quarry to their hounds, so, too, these barbarians, in order to incite their children to share their vengefulness, take them one at a time and rub their bodies, arms, thighs, and legs with the blood of their enemies. Since the arrival of Christians in that region, the savages have been using the knives and other iron tools they have received from them to cut up the bodies of their prisoners or of animals, as well as other kinds of food. But before that time, as I have heard from the old men, they had no tools for the task other than sharp-edged stones shaped for the purpose.

Now after all the pieces of the body, including the guts, have been thoroughly cleaned, they are immediately put on the *boucans*. While it all cooks according to their style, the old women (who, as I have said, have an amazing appetite for human flesh) are all assembled beside it to receive the fat that drips off along the posts of the big, high wooden grilles, and exhort the men to do what it takes to provide them always with such meat. Licking their fingers, they say, '*Yguatou*'; that is, 'It is good.'

And there you have it, just as I have seen it, the way the American savages cook the flesh of their prisoners of war: that is, on the *boucan*, which is a way of roasting unknown to us.

An 'Auto-da-fé', Seville, Spain   ANON

1559

Autos, or 'acts of faith', were the public ceremonies in which the judicial sentencing of offenders against the Catholic faith was performed by the Inquisition. The convicted heretic would be burnt at the stake following the reading of Psalms. The Inquisition was a potent weapon in the battle against Protestant heresy, particularly in Italy and Spain.

ON THE square of San Francisco two large platforms were erected – one for the Inquisitors and the cathedral chapter, the supreme tribunal and the monks of San Francisco. The other platform was for the penitents, the clergy and monks of other orders. An altar was erected here for the degradation of the Licentiate Juan Gonzalez. On one side of the square another large platform was erected for the town chapter; alongside the platform of the Inquisitors a platform for the Duchess of Bejar, other marquises, and eminent gentlemen. Many noble ladies were found here. Alongside the platform for the penitents was another platform for other earls and lords and noble ladies. All around the square were numerous scaffolds upon which stood a great throng of people. It was said that some people who came to see the *auto* had arrived three days early. The crowd of people was so huge that it was impossible to find lodging in the city. . . . Between two and three hundred men, equipped with lances, well-dressed and decorated, were selected to accompany the penitents. They were a pleasure to behold. They marched orderly with drums and flags to the Castle, where they received the penitents with whom they then walked to the square. About four o'clock in the morning fifty priests arrived with the cross of St Ann and went to the Castle, where forty monks of all orders had gathered. Together they accompanied the penitents . . . eighty penitents with habit and candles, twenty-one persons condemned to fire with a statue of Francisco de Cafra (who had escaped). Then came the magistrates with their marshal, then the Cathedral Chapter with the sextons in front. Finally came the Inquisitors with their banner. . . .

Don Juan Ponce de Leon was turned over to them so that his confession could be heard and he brought back to the Catholic faith. He was a damned Lutheran who, despite two years in prison, had not given up his Lutheran errors. The rector heard his confession and led him back to the faith. Don Juan swore that he would die as a true Christian. He had been involved in great error and heresy: for example, that there was no purgatory, that the Inquisitors were antichristian, that one should not believe or obey the Pope. Also that one should not accept any papal bulls or heed the Pope's word in any matter; that it was not necessary to make confession to monks or priests, but only to God, everyone in his heart. Also the most holy sacrament should not be adored.

This Don Juan was sentenced to die at the stake. . . . But our Lord, in his immeasurable goodness, caused him to see his error, and led him back to the holy Catholic faith. He died with many tears of remorse over his sins. Indeed, still at the stake he endeavoured to persuade the others to desist from their errors and to convert themselves to the holy Catholic faith and to the Roman Church.

The Usefulness of Camels to Turks

c.1560

OGIER GHISELIN DE BUSBECQ

The Turkish letters of Ogier Ghiselin de Busbecq, imperial ambassador in Istanbul at the height of the Ottoman Empire's glory, provide an invaluable appreciation of the Turkish character.

I HAVE SIX female camels, which I have bought to carry baggage; but my real object is to take them back for my royal masters, in the hope that they may be induced by the consideration of their usefulness to breed this kind of animal.

There are two things from which, in my opinion, the Turks derive the greatest advantage and profit, rice among cereals and camels among beasts of burden; both are admirably adapted to the distant campaigns which they wage. Rice keeps well and provides a wholesome food, a little of which suffices to feed a large number. Camels can carry very heavy burdens, endure hunger and thirst, and require very little attention. One driver is enough to look after six camels; and no animal is more amenable to discipline. The camel does not require combing or scraping, but, like one's clothes, can be kept clean by brushing. They lie, or, to be more accurate, kneel on the bare ground and allow themselves to be loaded. If the burden is heavier than they can reasonably carry, they protest by grunting and refuse to get up. They are apt, however, to rupture themselves if their load is too heavy, especially if the road be muddy or slippery. It is a pleasure to see how they kneel in a circle with their heads close together, eating and drinking with the utmost goodwill out of the same manger or basin, content with the scantiest fare. If necessary, owing to lack of fodder, they chew up brambles and thorns, and the more these make their mouths bleed the more they are pleased. Some of these camels are supplied from Scythia, but the majority come from Sinai and Assyria, where they are fed in great herds, and are so plentiful and cheap that a well-bred mare is sometimes exchanged for a hundred camels.

The Great Turkish Assault, Malta

1565

FRANCISCO BALBI DI CORREGGIO

In May 1565 a Turkish army led by the Sultan Suleiman laid siege to the strategically important island of Malta, garrisoned by the Knights of St John. With help from virtually every Christian country in Europe, the attackers were finally beaten off in September. This was the high-water mark of Turkish conquest in the Mediterranean. There are only two eyewitness accounts – this is one of them.

THROUGHOUT the night preceding the assault the Turks had been assembled on the high ground near the fort, shouting at the top of their voices, as is their custom when praying. Two hours before dawn their priests absolved them of their sins, exhorting them to fight well and to die for their false faith. We knew this because we could hear first one man singing for a time, then all the army responding in unison. They kept this up until the sun rose, which was the signal for their attack. The men of St Elmo were ready to meet them.

At the appointed hour the general assault began. It was concentrated, determined, and ferocious, but was met with an equal courage and determination by the defenders. In fact, the courage and tenacity of the garrison was greater than that of the enemy.

The attack was marked by considerable use of incendiaries and fireworks on both sides. Our men suffered more from their own fire than they did from that of the Turks, due to the fresh westerly breeze which drove the smoke from their own fire, as well as from that of the Turks, into the defenders' eyes. But a far greater misfortune than this was that all the fireworks in St Elmo caught alight, depriving the defenders of these invaluable weapons, and also burning many of them to death.

At the peak of the battle, over thirty Turks, using scaling ladders, got on to the point of the Spur of the cavalier facing Marsamuscetto – the post of Colonel Mas. When the Grand Master saw from St Angelo what had happened, he had our gunners open fire on it to try and help the defence. But in the confusion and haste, so much a part of battle, the gunner laid his cannon further to the right than he should have done, with the result that the shot killed eight of the defenders. This accident could well have lost us St Elmo, if the knights and soldiers at that post had not displayed great calmness.

The Murder of David Rizzio, Scotland

1565

LORD RUTHVEN

Rizzio was secretary to Mary Queen of Scots and also, probably, her lover. His increasing power and influence antagonised the Scottish nobility who arranged his murder in the presence of the Queen.

THE SAID Lord Ruthven at his entering in, said unto the Queen's Majesty, 'Let it please your Majesty that yonder man David come forth of your privy chamber, where he hath been overlong.' The Queen answered, 'What offence hath he done?' Ruthven answered, that he made a greater and more heinous offence to her Majesty's honour, the King her husband, the Nobility and the Commonwealth. 'If it please your Majesty, he hath offended your honour, which I dare not be so bold to speak of. As to the King your husband's honour, he hath hindered him of the Crown-Matrimonial, which your Grace promised him, besides many other things which are not necessary to be expressed; and hath caused your Majesty to banish a great part of the Nobility, and to forfeit them, that he might be made a Lord'. . . .

Then the said Lord Ruthven said to the King, 'Sir, take the Queen your wife and sovereign to you', who stood all amazed and wist not what to do. Then her Majesty rose upon her feet, and stood before David, he holding her Majesty by the plates of her gown, leaning back over the window, his dagger drawn in his hand, and Arthur Erskine, and the Abbot of Holyroodhouse, and the Lord Keith, master of the household, with the French apothecary; and one of the chamber began to lay hands on the Lord Ruthven, none of the King's party being there present. Then the said Lord Ruthven pulled out his dagger, and defended himself until more came in, and said to them, 'Lay no hands on me, for I will not be handled.' At the coming in of others into the cabinet, the said Lord Ruthven put up his dagger; and with the rushing in of men, the board fell into the wall, meat and candles being thereon, and the Lady of Argyll took one of the candles in her hand. At the same instant the Lord Ruthven took the Queen in his arms and put her into the King's arms, beseeching her Majesty not to be afraid, for there was no man there that would do her body any more harm than they would do their own hearts; and assured her Majesty that all that was done was the King's own deed. And the remnant of the gentlemen being in the cabinet took David out of the window, and after they had him out of the Queen's chamber, the said Lord Ruthven followed, and bade take him away down to the King's chamber the privy way; and the said Lord returned to the cabinet, thinking that the said David had been taken down to the King's chamber; the press of the people hurled him forth to the outer-chamber, where there was a great number standing who were vehemently moved against him, so that they could not abide any longer, but slew him at the Queen's foredoor in the other chamber. . . .

And David was thrown down the stairs from the Palace where he was slain, and brought to the Porter's lodge, who taking off his clothes said, 'This was his destiny; for upon this chest was his first bed when he came to this place, and now he lieth a very niggard and misknown knave.' The King's dagger was found sticking in his side. The Queen enquired at the King where his dagger was? who answered that he wist not well. 'Well,' said the Queen, 'it will be known hereafter.'

John Hawkins' Voyage to the West Indies

1567–8

JOHN HAWKINS

English trading missions to new markets were largely inspired by economic depression at home and unsettled conditions in Europe which threatened trade. The voyage described here was backed by the City, Court and Crown – Queen Elizabeth provided two ships from her small force – and Hawkins was later appointed Treasurer of the Navy.

WE ARRIVED at Cape Verde, the eighteenth of November: where we landed 150 men, hoping to obtain some Negros, where we got but fewe, and those with great hurt and damage to our men, which chiefly proceeded of their envenomed arrowes: and although in the beginning they seemed to be but small hurts, yet there hardly escaped any that had blood drawen of them, but died in strange sort, with their mouthes shut some tenne dayes before they died, and after their wounds were whole; where I my selfe had one of the greatest woundes, yet thankes be to God, escaped. From thence we past the time upon the coast of Guinea, searching with all diligence the rivers from Rio Grande, unto Sierra Leona, till the twelfth of Januarie, in which time we had not gotten together a hundreth and fiftie Negros: yet notwithstanding the sicknesse of our men, and the late time of the yeere commanded us away: and thus having nothing where-with to seeke the coast of the West Indias, I was with the rest of our company in consultation to goe to the coast of the Mine, hoping there to have obtained some golde for our wares, and thereby to have defraied our charge. But even in that present instant, there came to us a Negro, sent from a king, oppressed by other Kings his neighbours, desiring our aide, with promise that as many Negros as by these warres might be obtained, as well of his part as of ours, should be at our pleasure: whereupon we concluded to give aide, and sent 120 of our men, which the 15 of Januarie, assaulted a towne of the Negros of our Allies adversaries, which had in it 8000 Inhabitants, being very strongly impaled and fenced after their manner, but it was so well defended, that our men prevailed not, but lost six men and fortie hurt.

1576

Martin Frobisher Encounters some Eskimos

Christopher Hall

The challenges facing captains like Martin Frobisher on voyages of exploration were considerable, not the least of which was controlling a fractious crew which had to endure immense hardship and tedium in between the rare excitement of encountering an unknown people. Frobisher was given command of the fourth squadron against the Armada in 1588.

A head and shoulder engraving of Martin Frobisher (c. 1535–94)

THE 19 DAY in the morning, being calme, and no winde, the Captaine and I tooke our boate, with eight men in her, to rowe us a shoare, to see if there were there any people, or no, and going to the toppe of the Island, we had sight of seven boates, which came rowing from the East side, toward that Island: whereupon we returned aboord againe: at length we sent our boate with five men in her, to see whither they rowed, and so with a white cloth brought one of their boates with their men along the shoare, rowing after our boate, till such time as they sawe our ship, and then they rowed a shoare: then I went on shoare my selfe, and gave every of them a threadden point, and brought one of them aboord of me, where hee did eate and drinke, and then carried him on shoare againe. Whereupon all the rest came aboord with their boates, being nineteene persons, and they spake, but we understoode them not. They bee like to Tartars, with long blacke haire, broad faces, and flatte noses, and tawnie in colour, wearing Seale skinnes, and so doe the women, not differing in the fashion, but the women are marked in the face with blewe streekes downe the cheekes, and round about the eyes. Their boates are made all of Seales skinnes, with a keele of wood within the skin: the proportion of them is like a Spanish shallop, save only they be flat in the bottome, and sharpe at both ends.

A Hutterite Community, Moravia ANON

1578

As a result of the religious tolerance of its local rulers, Moravia became a magnet for Anabaptists in the 16th century. Under the inspirational leadership of Jakob Hutter, who championed the ideal of communal living, a number of close-knit, self-sufficient and egalitarian communities sprang up, whose resilience meant that many of their characteristics have survived in the region into the present day.

STIGNITZ IS A large village belonging to the Lord of Löben, who at one time had been supervisor in Moravia. It was reported to me at last Whitsuntide he and his wife attended the Anabaptist communion or breaking of bread. He is fond of them and does not burden them. At Stignitz I found my second sister, Sara, who is married to a vineyard worker. She herself looks after little children in the Anabaptist school. Each Anabaptist community has a school in which the children are placed to learn to pray and to read when they reach the age of two years. Until that time they stay with their mothers. The children do not study more than that. Girls only learn to pray and to read a little. Boys learn to write and read. When they grow up they learn a trade or some other work.

Once a day the children go into the fields or to the nearest woods, so that they are not always close together, but get some fresh air. Certain women do nothing else but watch for the children, wash them, care for them, and keep their beds and clothes clean. Two or three, according to their age, sleep together. Mornings and evenings they say their prayers that they may be brought up in the fear of God, that they may be given good rulers, that they may be kept in God's knowledge, that their brethren and sisters be kept from all harm. After this prayer, during which they kneel, they pray the Lord's Prayer.

My sister Sara did not want to marry her husband, but could not say anything against it. This is the way it is handled: On a certain Sunday, the elders call all marriageable young men and women together, place them opposite each other and give each girl the choice of two or three fellows. She has to take one of them. She is not compelled, but she is not to do anything against the elders. I met my stepbrother Sebastian at the brewery, but like Christman he did not offer me his hand. His first words were that I was a false prophet; therefore he would not give me his hand.

1585

Search for a Priest-Hole, England

FR WILLIAM WESTON

Catholic priests were subject to the death penalty in Elizabethan England. They frequently had to use secret hiding places to avoid detection by pursuivants. Many such places were constructed by a Jesuit lay-brother, Nicholas Owen, who later died under torture in the Tower of London. Weston was a Jesuit priest who was captured in 1586. He later became the rector of the English College at Valladolid, Spain.

A HOUSE WHERE I used secretly to be given hospitality was visited once by certain Catholics, who gave a satisfactory account of themselves, both to me and to the head of the family, and said that they wished to hear Mass. After the end of Mass, when the people had left, I stayed on as usual and went upstairs to the room where I kept my books and resumed my work. Not quite two hours later the house was surrounded by a large mob of men. Whether they came on information or on chance, I do not know. But the servant rushed up to my room – I was still there – and warned me of the danger. She made me come downstairs at once and showed me a hiding-place underground; Catholic houses have several places like this, otherwise there would be no security. I got down into it, taking my breviary with me – it was all I had near me at the time, and to loiter would have been dangerous. Meantime the heretics had already made their way into the house and were examining the remoter parts. From my cave-like hide I could follow their movements by the noise and uproar they raised. Step by step they drew closer, and when they entered my room the sight of my books was an added incentive to their search. In that room also there was a secret passage-way for which they demanded the key, and as they opened the door giving on to it they were standing immediately above my head. I could hear practically every word they said. 'Here! Look!' they called out. 'A chalice! And a missal!' The things were, in fact, there. There had been no time to hide them, and, in any case, it would have been impossible. Then they demanded a hammer and other tools, to break through the wall and panelling. They were certain now that I could not be far away.

Meanwhile I was praying fervently to God that He would avert the danger. At the same time I reflected that it would be better to surrender myself into the enemy's hands than be dragged out ignominiously. I believed that some Judas had given information and betrayed me, but, to cover up the traitor, they wanted my discovery to appear accidental, and not the result of treachery.

While I was reflecting in this way, one of the men, either by mistake or on purpose or at the prompting of a good angel, shouted out: 'Why waste time getting hammers and hatchets? There's not enough space here for a man. Look at the corners. You can see where everything leads to. There can't be a hiding-place here.'

They took the fellow's word for it, and the party abandoned their plan of search and destruction.

Attack on a Spanish Galleass, off Calais

RICHARD TOMSON

The defeat of the Spanish Armada by the English fleet was arguably one of the most important events in European history. It ensured the survival of the Protestant succession and gave encouragement to other Protestant countries, particularly the Dutch who were fighting to free themselves of Spanish rule. The crucial point of the battle came off the French coast when several Spanish ships were captured and sunk, and the rest scattered by fire ships.

M Y LORD ADMIRAL, seeing he could not approach the galleass with his ship, sent off his long boat unto her with fifty or sixty men, amongst whom were many gentlemen as valiant in courage as gentle in birth, as they well showed. The like did our ship send off her pinnace, with certain musketeers, amongst whom myself went. These two boats came hard under the galleass sides, being aground; where we continued a pretty skirmish with our small shot against theirs, they being ensconced within their ship and very high over us, we in our open pinnaces and far under them, having nothing to shroud and cover us; they being 300 soldiers, besides 450 slaves, and we not, at the instant, 100 persons. Within one half hour it pleased God, by killing the captain with a musket shot, to give us victory above all hope or expectation; for the soldiers leaped overboard by heaps on the other side, and fled with the shore, swimming and wading. Some escaped with being wet; some, and that very many, were drowned. The captain of her was called Don Hugo de Moncada, son to the viceroy of Valencia. He being slain, and they seeing our English boats under her sides and more of ours coming rowing towards her some with ten and some with eight men in them, for all the smallest shipping were the nearest the shore, put up two handkerchers [handkerchiefs] upon two rapiers, signifying that they desired truce.

1588

The End of the Armada, Ireland

CAPTAIN FRANCISCO DE CUELLAR

The aftermath of the Armada is much less well-known than the battle itself. Many Spanish ships foundered in storms off the Irish coast and Queen Elizabeth ordered any survivors to be hanged. This extract is from a letter by an officer on the San Pedro *who swam ashore and subsequently returned to Spain via the underground escape route set up by Catholic Irish sympathisers.*

I PLACED myself on the top of the poop of my ship, after having commended myself to God and Our Lady, and from thence I gazed at the terrible spectacle. Many were drowning in the ships, others, casting themselves into the water, sank to the bottom without returning to the surface; others on rafts and barrels, and gentlemen on pieces of timber; others cried out aloud in the ships calling upon God; captains threw their jewelled chains and crown-pieces into the sea; the waves swept others away, washing them out of the ships. While I was watching this sorrowful scene, I did not know what to do, nor what means to adopt as I did not know how to swim and the waves and storm were very great; and, on the other hand, the land and the shore were full of enemies, who went about jumping and dancing with delight at our misfortunes; and when any one of our people reached the beach two hundred savages and other enemies fell upon him and stripped him of what he had on until he was left in his naked skin.

A typical English galleon from the time of the Armada

Such they maltreated and wounded without pity, all of which was plainly visible from the battered ships.

I went to the Auditor – God pardon him! – he was very sorrowful and depressed, and I said to him that he should make some provision for saving his life before the ship went to pieces, as she could not last for half a quarter of an hour longer; nor did she last it. Most of her complement of men and all the captains and officers were already drowned and dead when I determined to seek means of safety for my life, and placed myself upon a piece of the ship that had broken off, and the Auditor followed me, loaded with crown-pieces which he carried stitched up in his waistcoat and trousers.

The Torture of a Jesuit Priest, Tower of London, England FATHER JOHN GERARD

1597

Torture was frequently used in Elizabethan England. Here Father Gerard undergoes suspension by the hands in order to make him betray his fellow priests and Catholic associates.

WE WENT TO the torture-room in a kind of solemn procession, the attendants walking ahead with lighted candles.

The chamber was underground and dark, particularly near the entrance. It was a vast place and every device and instrument of human torture was there. They pointed out some of them to me and said that I would try them all. Then they asked me again whether I would confess.

'I cannot,' I said.

I fell on my knees for a moment's prayer. Then they took me to a big upright pillar, one of the wooden posts which held the roof of this huge underground chamber. Driven in to the top of it were iron staples for supporting heavy weights. Then they put my wrists into iron gauntlets and ordered me to climb two or three wicker steps. My arms were then lifted up and an iron bar was passed through the rings of one gauntlet, then through the staple and rings of the second gauntlet. This done, they fastened the bar with a pin to prevent it slipping, and then, removing the wicker steps one by one from under my feet, they left me hanging by my hands and arms fastened above my head. The tips of my toes, however, still touched the ground, and they had to dig away the earth from under them. They had hung me up from the highest staple in the pillar and could not raise me any higher, without driving in another staple.

Hanging like this I began to pray. The gentlemen standing around asked me whether I was willing to confess now.

'I cannot and I will not,' I answered.

But I could hardly utter the words, such a gripping pain came over me. It was worst in my chest and belly, my hands and arms. All the blood in my body seemed to rush up into my arms and hands and I thought that blood was oozing out from the ends of my fingers and the pores of my skin. But it was only a sensation caused by my flesh swelling above the irons holding them. The pain was so intense that I thought I could not possibly endure it, and added to it, I had an interior temptation. Yet I did not feel any inclination or wish to give them the information they wanted. The Lord saw my weakness with the eyes of His mercy, and did not permit me to be tempted beyond my strength.

The Tower of London

1598

Queen Elizabeth in Old Age, Greenwich, England PAUL HENTZNER

'Gloriana', as she was affectionately known, was the longest reigning English monarch for 200 years, ascending the throne in 1558 and dying some five years after this unflinching portrait of her by a German traveller.

NEXT CAME the Queen, in the 65th year of her age (as we were told), very majestic; her face oblong, fair but wrinkled; her eyes small, yet black and pleasant; her nose a little hooked, her lips narrow, and her teeth black, (a defect the English seem subject to, from their too great use of sugar); she had in her ears two pearls with very rich drops; her hair was of an auburn colour, but false; upon her head she had a small crown, reported to be made of some of the gold of the celebrated Luneburg table; her bosom was uncovered, as all the English ladies have it till they marry; and she had on a necklace of exceeding fine jewels; her hands were slender, her fingers rather long, and her stature neither tall nor low; her air was stately, her manner of speaking mild and obliging. That day she was dressed in white silk, bordered with pearls of the size of beans, and over it a mantle of black silk shot with silver threads; her train was very long, the end of it borne by a marchioness; instead of a chain, she had an oblong collar of gold and jewels.

1603

The Death of Queen Elizabeth LADY SOUTHWELL

This account of the Queen's death, by one of her ladies-in-waiting, illustrates her irascible and volatile character even in extremis. She was in fact succeeded by James VI of Scotland, the son of her old enemy, Mary Queen of Scots.

NOW FALLING into extremity, she sat two days and three nights upon her stool, ready dressed, and could never be brought by any of her council, to go to bed, or eat, or drink: only, my lord admiral one time persuaded her to drink some broth. For any of the rest, she would not answer them to any question; but said softly to my lord admiral's earnest persuasions, that, if he knew what she had seen in her bed, he would not persuade her as he did. And secretary Cecil, overhearing her, asked if her majesty had seen any spirits; to which she said she scorned to answer him to so idle a question. Then he told her how, to content the people, her majesty must go to bed: to which she smiled, wonderfully contemning him, saying that the word *must* was not to be used to princes; and thereupon said, 'Little man, little man, if your father had lived, ye durst not have said so much: but thou knowest I must die, and that maketh thee so presumptuous.' And presently, commanding him and the rest to depart from her chamber, she willed my lord admiral to stay; to whom she shook her head, and, with a pitiful voice, said, 'My lord, I am tied with a chain of iron about my neck.' He alleging her wonted courage to her, she replied, 'I am tied, and the case is altered with me.'

Now being given over by all, and at the last gasp, keeping still her sense in every thing, and giving, ever, when she spake, apt answers (though she spake very seldom, having then a sore throat) she desired to wash it, that she might answer more freely to what the council demanded; which was, to know whom she would have king: – but they, seeing her throat troubled her so much, desired her to hold up her finger, when they named whom liked her. Whereupon they named the king of France – the king of Scotland – at which she never stirred. They named my lord Beauchamp; whereto she said, 'I will have no rascal's son in my seat, but one worthy to be a king.' Hereupon, instantly she died.

The last medal struck in 1602 to celebrate Elizabeth's triumphs

The Gunpowder Plotters at Holbeach House, England FATHER JOHN GERARD

1605

The failure of the Gunpowder Plot and the pursuit and capture of the plotters ended at Holbeach in Worcestershire. The survivors were executed in the following year.

ABOUT AN hour before mid-day the High Sheriff came with the forces of the country and beset the house. Mr Thomas Winter going into the court of the house was shot in the shoulder with which he lost the use of his arm. The next shot was the elder Wright, who was stricken dead. After him the younger Wright, and fourthly Mr Rookwood, but he was only wounded in four or five places, and so taken and afterwards put to death at London. So were also Mr Thomas Winter and Mr Grant and all the rest but Mr Catesby and Mr Percy, who resolved they would not be taken, but rather suffer death at that time in the field. Wherefore Mr Catesby took from his neck a cross of gold which he always used to wear about him, and blessing himself with it and kissing it, showed it unto the people, protesting there solemnly before them all, it was only for the honour of the Cross, and the exaltation of that Faith which honoured the Cross, and for the saving of their souls in the same Faith, that had moved him to undertake the business; and

The Gunpowder
Plotters

sith he saw it was not God's will it should succeed in that manner they intended
or at that time, he was willing and ready to give his life for the same cause, only
he would not be taken by any, and against that only he would defend himself with
his sword. This done, Mr Catesby and Mr Percy turned back to back, resolving to
yield themselves to no man, but to death as to the messenger of God. None of
their adversaries did come near them; but one fellow standing behind a tree with
a musket shot them both with one bullet, and Mr Catesby was shot almost dead,
the other lived three or four days. Mr Catesby being fallen to the ground, as they
say, went upon his knees into the house, and there got a picture of our Blessed
Lady in his arms (unto whom he was accustomed to be very devout), and so
embracing and kissing the same he died.

Conditions in Peru after the Spanish Conquest

C. 1605

HUAMÁN POMA

*The narrator was himself an Hispanicised Inca, related to the Inca royal family, who
travelled throughout the Peruvian highlands observing the conditions there. His findings
were reported in a lengthy letter to King Philip III of Spain, in the hope that the terrible
oppression of the Incas could be alleviated, alas without any noticeable success.*

I NEXT VISITED the village of San Cristóbal, where I fell in with a foreman of
ten Indian labourers called Juan Quille. This man employed me at a wage of
50 pesos, part of which was paid in the form of a light chestnut horse valued at

10 pesos. He had an Indian wife and therefore his legitimate daughter was a half-caste, whom he kept in his kitchen with other girls and used for baking bread and tilling his fields. The deputy to the royal administrator came on a visit to the village and the local priest complained to this official about girls who were living with men without being married. The deputy and the priest put their heads together and sent off three of the most beautiful girls to Huancavelica, ostensibly to work for the deputy's mother but really so that they could sleep with the Spaniards.

Juan Quille and I felt ourselves impotent to prevent these particular girls from being removed from the village. We discussed with one another the tendency of the priests to take advantage of the religious instruction which they impart to the young and we agreed that it would be advisable to limit the priesthood to men of over 70 years of age, by which time their passions were likely to have cooled. It so happened that we were talking in front of Juan Quille's daughter, who promptly went off and reported what she had heard to her mother. The mother then went at midnight to call on the parish priest and passed on the gist of the conversation. On the following morning the priest sent for me and ordered me to leave the village. I was to say nothing to anyone and do nothing which would put heart into the Indians. Otherwise he would have me tied over the back of a llama and flogged. The interview ended at this point and I was escorted out of San Cristóbal.

Idolatry and Witchcraft in Mayombe, Portuguese Africa   ANDREW BATTELL

c.1610

Andrew Battell is one of four Englishmen known to have visited Angola towards the close of the 16th century. He spent years of captivity as a prisoner-of-war in Portuguese Africa. He offers a rare account of the interior of this part of Africa at this time, and insights into the religion and customs of the peoples of Angola, the Congo and Luangu.

IN THE TOWN of Mani Mayombe is a fetish called Maramba, and it standeth in a high basket made like a hive, and over it a great house. This is their house of religion, for they believe only in him, and keep his laws, and carry his reliques always with them. They are for the most part witches, and use their witchcraft for hunting and killing of elephants and fishing, and helping of sick and lame men, and to forecast journeys, whether they shall speed well or evil. By this Maramba are all thefts and murders tried, for in this country they use sometimes to bewitch one another to death. And when any dieth, their neighbours are brought before the Maramba; and if it be a great man that dieth, the whole town cometh to swear. The other is, when they come before Maramba, to kneel and clasp Maramba in their arms, and to say: *Emeno, eyge bembet Maramba*, that is, 'I come to be tried, O Maramba.' And if any of them be guilty, they fall down stark dead for ever. And if any of them that swear hath killed any man or child before, although it may be twenty years past, he presently dieth. And so it is for any other matter.

From this place, as far as it is to Cape de Lopo Gonsalves, they are all of this superstition. I was twelve months in this place, and saw many die after this sort.

These people be circumcised, as they are through all Angola, except the kingdom of Congo, for they be Christians. And those that will be sworn to Maramba come to the chief Gangas, which are their priests or men-witches, as boys of twelve years of age, and men and women. Then the Gangas put them into a dark house, and there they remain certain days with very hard diet. After this they are let abroad, and commanded not to speak for certain days, what injury soever they be offered, so that they suffer great penury before they be sworn. Lastly, they are brought before Maramba, and have two marks cut upon their shoulders before, like a half moon, and are sworn by the blood that falleth from them, that they shall be true to him. They are forbidden some one kind of flesh and some one kind of fish, with many other toys [trifles]. And if they eat any of this forbidden meat they presently sicken, and never prosper. They all carry a relique of Maramba in a little box, and hang it about their necks, under their left arms.

1613

The Galileo Debate, Tuscany, Italy

BENEDETTO CASTELLI

After the publication of The Starry Messenger *(1610), in which Galileo Galilei stated his controversial theory of the motion of the Earth, conservative scientists and philosophers had increasingly to rely on religious and biblical arguments to support their belief in a static Earth. In the following extract, Benedetto Castelli reports to Galileo a meeting with the Grand Duchess Dowager Christina of Lorraine, in which he encountered just such traditional views. Castelli had succeeded Galileo in the chair of mathematics at the University of Pisa.*

THURSDAY morning I had breakfast with our Lordships, and, when asked about school by the Grand Duke, I gave him a detailed account of everything, and he seemed to be very satisfied. He asked me whether I had a telescope, and I told him Yes and so began to relate the observation of the Medicean planets which I had made just the previous night. Then Her Most Serene Ladyship inquired about their position and began saying to herself that they had better be real and not deceptions of the instrument. So their Highnesses asked Mr Boscaglia, who answered that truly their existence could not be denied. I used the occasion to add whatever I knew and could say about your wonderful invention and your proof of the motions of these planets. At the table was also Don Antonio, who smiled at me in such a dignified manner that it was a clear sign that he was pleased with what I was saying. Finally, after many other things, all handled properly, the meal ended and I left. As soon as I had come out of the palace, the porter of Her Most Serene Ladyship caught up with me and called me back. However, before I say what followed, you must know that at the table Boscaglia had been whispering for a long time to the ear of Her Ladyship; he admitted as true all the celestial novelties you have discovered, but he said that the earth's motion was incredible and could not happen, especially since the Holy Scripture was clearly contrary to this claim.

An Aristocratic Duel, Holland

c.1615

EDWARD SACKVILLE, EARL OF DORSET

In the 17th century duelling was an established part of the code of gentlemanly honour which required every insult to be avenged. This duel was fought between the Earl of Dorset and Lord Bruce between whom there had been a long-standing feud, and was related in a letter by the Earl.

A ND THERE we wrestled for the two greatest and dearest prizes we could ever expect trial for – honour and life; in which struggling, my hand, having but an ordinary glove on it, lost one of her servants, though the meanest, which hung by a skin, and to sight yet remaineth as before, and I am put in hope one day to recover the use of it again. But at last, breathless, yet keeping our holds, there passed on both sides propositions of quitting each other's swords; but when amity was dead, confidence could not live, and who should quit first was the question which on neither part either would perform; and re-striving again afresh, with a kick and a wrench together I freed my long-captive weapon, which incontinently levying at his throat, being master still of his, I demanded if he would ask his life or yield his sword? both which, though in that imminent danger, he bravely denied to do. Myself being wounded, and feeling loss of blood, having three conduits running on me, began to make me faint, and he courageously persisting not to accord to either of my propositions, remembrance of his former bloody desire, and feeling of my present estate, I struck at his heart, but with his avoiding missed my aim, yet passed through his body and drawing back my sword, repassed it through again, through another place, when he cried, 'Oh, I am slain!' seconding his speech with all the force he had to cast me; but being too weak, after I had defended his assault, I easily became master of him, laying him on his back, when, being upon him, I redemanded if he would request his life. But it seems he prized it not at so dear a rate to be beholden for it, bravely replying he scorned it! which answer of his was so noble and worthy, as I protest I could not find in my heart to offer him any more violence, only keeping him down; till at length his surgeon, afar off, cried out he would immediately die if his wounds were not stopped; whereupon I asked if he desired his surgeon should come, which he accepted of, and so, being drawn away, I never offered to take his sword, accounting it inhumane to rob a dead man, for so I held him to be.

The Pilgrim Fathers Land in America

NATHANIEL MORTON

In August 1620 a band of 100 Puritan dissenters set sail for America in the Mayflower, intending to found a colony where they should practise their faith free of persecution. They landed in November in what is now Massachusetts. This is not a direct eyewitness account but the details were obtained by the narrator from his uncle, William Bradford, who was one of the original settlers.

NECESSITY NOW calling them to look out a place for habitation, as well as the master's and mariners' importunity urging them thereunto; while their carpenter was trimming up of their boat, sixteen of their men tendered them selves to go by land and discover those nearest places, which was accepted; and they being well armed, were sent forth on the 16th of November, 1620, and having marched about a mile by the seaside, they espied five Indians, who ran away from them, and they followed them all that day sundry miles, but could not come to speech with them; so night coming on, they betook themselves to their rendezvous, and set out their sentinels, and rested in quiet that night; and the next morning they followed the Indians' tracks, but could not find them nor their dwellings, but at length lighted on a good quantity of clear ground near to a pond of fresh water, where formerly the Indians had planted Indian corn, at which

The landing of the pilgrims

place they saw sundry of their graves; and proceeding further they found new stubble where Indian corn had been planted the same year; also they found where lately an house had been, where some planks and a great kettle was remaining, and heaps of sand newly paddled with their hands, which they digged up and found in them divers fair Indian baskets filled with corn, some whereof was in ears, fair and good, of divers colours, which seemed to them a very goodly sight, having seen none before, of which rarities they took some to carry to their friends on shipboard, like as the Israelites' spies brought from Eshcol some of the good fruits of the land; but finding little that might make for their encouragement as to situation, they returned, being gladly received by the rest of their company.

An Indian Chief has a Nosebleed, America

EDWARD WINSLOW

c.1621

The Pilgrim Fathers' best friend and ally in their new colony was the Indian Chief Massassoit. The narrator, Winslow, was a senior member of the founding fathers and later the Governor of the colony.

THE FOWL being extraordinary fat, I told Hobbamock I must take off the top thereof, saying it would make him very sick again if he did eat it. This he acquainted Massassowat therewith, who would not be persuaded to it, though I pressed it very much, showing the strength thereof, and the weakness of his stomach, which could not possibly bear it. Notwithstanding, he made a gross meal of it, and ate as much as would well have satisfied a man in health. About an hour after he began to be very sick, and straining very much, cast up the broth again; and in overstraining himself, began to bleed at the nose, and so continued the space of four hours. Then they all wished he had been ruled, concluding now he would die, which we much feared also. They asked me what I thought of him. I answered, his case was desperate, yet it might be it would save his life; for if it ceased in time, he would forthwith sleep and take rest, which was the principal thing he wanted. Not long after his blood stayed, and he slept at least six or eight hours. When he awaked, I washed his face, and bathed and suppled his beard and nose with a linen cloth. But on a sudden he chopped his nose in the water, and drew up some therein, and sent it forth again with such violence, as he began to bleed afresh. Then they thought there was no hope; but we perceived it was but the tenderness of his nostril, and therefore told them I thought it would stay presently, as indeed it did.

The messengers were now returned; but finding his stomach come to him, he would not have the chickens killed, but kept them for breed. Neither durst we give him any physic, which was then sent, because his body was so much altered since our instructions; neither saw we any need, not doubting now of his recovery, if he were careful. Many, whilst we were there, came to see him; some, by their report, from a place not less than an hundred miles. To all that came one of his chief men related the manner of his sickness, how near he was spent, how amongst others his friends the English came to see him, and how suddenly they recovered him to this strength they saw, he being now able to sit upright of himself.

1623

The Collapse of a Church at Blackfriars, England THOMAS GOAD

The residences of foreign ambassadors from Catholic countries were exempt from the penal laws against Catholics. Hence many Catholics used to attend Mass there. In this incident, the very large number of people at the Chapel of the French ambassador caused its spectacular collapse. The author of this extract was the rector of Hadleigh in Suffolk, who wrote theological tracts.

WHEN THE said Jesuit had proceeded about half an hour ... there befell that preacher and auditory the most unexpected and sudden calamity that hath been heard of to come from the hand, not of man but God, in the midst of a sacred exercise of what kind of religion soever. The floor whereon that assembly stood or sat, not sinking by degrees, but at one instant failing and falling, by the breaking asunder of a main summer or dormer of that floor, which beam, together with the joists and planking thereto adjoined, with the people thereon, rushed down with such violence that the weight and fall thereof broke in sunder another far stronger and thicker summer of the chamber situated directly underneath; and so both the ruined floors, with the people overlapped and crushed under or between them, fell (without any time of stay) upon the lower third floor, being the floor of the said Lord Ambassador's withdrawing chamber, which was supported underneath with archwork of stone (yet visible in the gatehouse there) and so became the boundary or term of that confused and doleful heap of ruins, which otherwise had sunk yet deeper by the own weight and height of the downfall, the distance from the highest floor, whence the people fell, to the lowest, where they lay, being about two and twenty feet in depth.

Such was the noise of this dreadful and unexpected downfall that the whole city of London presently rang of it, and forthwith the officers of the city (to whom the care of good order chiefly appertaineth) and in special Sergeant Finch, the Recorder, repaired thither the same evening, carefully providing for the safety of the said Ambassador's house and family, and, for preventing all disorders in such a confusion that might arise by the confluence of the multitude, shut up the gates and set guards upon the passages. With all speed possible some were employed for the relieving and saving such as yet struggled for life under this heavy load; which could not so soon be effected as they in charity desired, for that the ruins, which oppressed the sufferers, did also stop up entrance to the helpers, who thereupon were fain to make a breach in through an upper window of stone. From whence they hasted down with pickaxes and other instruments, to force asunder and take off by piecemeal the oppressing load of beams, joists and boards. At the opening thereof, what a chaos! what fearful objects! what lamentable representations! Here some bruised, some dismembered, some only parts of men; there some wounded and weltering in their own and others blood, other some putting forth their fainting hands and crying out for help. Here some gasping and panting for breath, others stifled for want of breath. To the most of them being thus covered with dust, this their death was a kind of burial....

The Battle of Brietenfeld, Germany

ROBERT MONRO

1631

In 1618 a dispute between Protestant nobles in Bohemia and the Catholic authorities of the Holy Roman Empire started the last of the great European Wars of Religion. Sweden intervened (supported by French financial subsidies) on the side of the Protestants in 1630. The victory of King Gustavus Adolphus over the Catholic Imperialist armies of Count Tilly was the crowning achievement of the first phase of Swedish intervention in the Thirty Years War. This eyewitness account is by a Scots mercenary in the Swedish Army.

OUR ARMIE of foote standing firme, not having loosed one Musket; the smoake being great, by the rising of the dust, for a long time we were not able to see about us; but being cleared up, we did see on the left hand of our reserve two great Battailes of foote, which we imagined to have beene *Saxons*, that were forced to give ground; having heard the service, though not seene it, we found they were enemies, being a great deale neerer than the *Saxons* were: His Majestie having sent Baron *Tyvell* to know the certaintie, coming before our Briggad I certified him they were enemies, and he returning towards his Majestie, was shot dead; his Majestie coming by, gave direction to Colonell *Hepburne*, to cause the Briggads on his right and left wing to wheele, and then to charge the enemy, the Orders given, his Majestie retired, promising to bring succour unto us.

Gustavus Adolphus II (1594–1632)

The enemies Battaile standing firme, looking on us at a neere distance, and seeing the other Briggads and ours wheeleing about, making front unto them, they were prepared with a firme resolution to receive us with a salve of Cannon and Muskets; but our small Ordinance being twice discharged amongst them, and before we stirred, we charged them with a salve of muskets, which was repaid, and incontinent our Briggad advancing unto them with push of pike, putting one of their battailes in disorder, fell on the execution, so that they were put to the route.

I having commanded the right wing of our musketiers, we advanced on the other body of the enemies, which defended their Cannon, and beating them from their Cannon, we were masters of their Cannon, and consequently of the field, but the smoake being great, the dust being raised, we were as in a darke cloude, not seeing the halfe of our actions, much lesse discerning, either way of our enemies, or yet the rest of our Briggads: whereupon, having a drummer by me, I caused him beate the *Scots* march, till it cleered up, which recollected our friends unto us, and dispersed our enemies being overcome; so that the Briggad coming together, such as were alive missed their dead and hurt Camerades.

Colonel Lumsdell was hurt at the first, and Lievetenant Colonell Maflen also, with divers other Ensignes were hurt and killed, and sundry Colours were missing for that night, which were found the next day; The enemy thus fled, our horsemen were pursuing hard, till it was darke, and the blew Briggad, and the commanded musketiers were sent by his Majesty to helpe us, but before their coming, the victory and the credit of the day, as being last ingaged, was ascribed to our Briggad, being the reserve, were thanked by his Majesty for their service, in publique audience, and in view of the whole Army, we were promised to be rewarded.

The Indian Inhabitants of Maryland, America

1634

FATHER ANDREW WHITE

The missionary activity of the Jesuit order, particularly in the Americas, became legendary during the 17th century. One of the first priests to found a mission in Maryland here gives a well-observed account of the native population.

THE NATIVES are very tall and well proportioned, their skin is naturally rather dark, and they make it uglier by staining it generally with red paint mixed with oil, to keep off the mosquitoes, thinking more of their own comfort than of appearances. They disfigure their countenances with other colours, too, painting them in various and truly hideous and frightful ways, either a dark blue above the nose and red below, or the reverse. And as they live almost to extreme old age without having beards, they counterfeit them with paint, drawing lines of various colours from the extremity of the lips to the ears. They generally have black hair, which they carry round in a knot to the left ear, and then fasten with a band, adding some ornament which is in estimation among them. Some of them wear on their foreheads the figure of a fish, made of copper. They adorn their necks with glass beads strung on a thread like necklaces, though these beads are getting to be less valued among them and less useful for trade.

They are clothed for the most part in deer skins, or some similar kind of covering, which hangs down behind like a cloak. They wear aprons round the middle, and leave the rest of the body naked. The soles of their feet are as hard as horn, and they tread on thorns and briers without being hurt.

Possessed by the Demons of Loudun, France

1636

JEAN-JOSEPH SURIN

Following the infamous torture, trial and burning of the Loudun priest and accused witch, Urbain Grandier, in 1636, Father Jean-Joseph Surin was sent to exorcise the demons Grandier was supposed to have summoned. In the following passage, he describes how he was himself possessed and the sensations he experienced.

I AM NEVER without a Devil at my side, exerting himself. Things have gone so far that God has permitted, for my sins, I think, something never seen, perhaps, in the Church: that during the exercise of my ministry, the Devil passes from the body of the possessed person, and coming into mine, assaults me and overturns me, shakes me, and visibly travels through me, possessing me for several hours like an energumen. I would not know how to explain to you what occurs inside of me during this time, and how this Spirit unites with mine, without depriving me either of the knowledge or the liberty of my soul, while nevertheless making himself like another me, and how it is as if I had two souls one of which is deprived of its body, of the use of its organs, and stands apart, watching the actions of the one which has entered. The two Spirits battle on the same field, which is the body, and the soul is as if it were divided; following one part of itself, it is the subject of diabolical impressions; following the other, of movements which are its own, or which God gives to it. At the same time, I feel a great peace, under the absolute will of God; and without my knowing how, there comes an extreme rage, and aversion to Him, which becomes almost violent trying to separate itself from the other feeling, which astounds those who see it; on the one hand a great joy and *douceur*, and on the other, a sadness which reveals itself by lamentations and cries similar to those of the Demons: I feel the state of damnation and am frightened by it, and I feel as if I were pierced by sharp points of despair in this foreign soul which seems to be mine, and the other soul, which is full of confidence, makes light of such feelings, and in full liberty curses the one which causes them; verily, I feel that the same cries which leave my mouth come equally from these two souls, and I am hard-pressed to discern if it is the mirth which produces them, or the extreme fury which fills me. The tremblings which overcome me when the Holy Sacrament is bestowed upon me come equally, it seems to me, from horror at its presence, which is unbearable to me, and from a sweet and gentle reverence, without my being able to attribute them more to one than to the other, and without its being in my power to restrain them. When one of these two souls moves me to want to make the sign of the cross on my mouth, the other turns my hand away with great speed, and seizes my finger with my teeth, in order to gnaw on it in a rage. I almost never find prayer easier and more tranquil than during these agitations; while my body rolls on the ground, and the Ministers of the Church speak to me as if to a Devil, and accuse me of maledictions, I could not tell you the joy that I feel, having become a Devil not out of rebellion to God, but by virtue of the distress which depicts ingenuously for me the state to which sin has reduced me; so that appropriating to myself all of the maledictions which are offered to me, my soul has cause to sink in its nothingness.

1636

Post-Mortem on an Old Man, England

WILLIAM HARVEY

Harvey is famous as the discoverer of the circulation of blood in the human body. Here he performs an autopsy on the body of Thomas Parr, allegedly 154 years old.

THE APPEARANCE of the body was well nourished, the chest was hairy, and the hair on the forearm was still black although the shins were hairless and smooth.

The genital organs were in good condition, the penis was neither retracted nor thin, nor was the scrotum, as is usual in old persons, distended by any watery hernia, while the testicles were large and sound − so good in fact as not to give the lie to the story commonly told of him that, after reaching his hundredth year, he was actually convicted of fornication and punished. Moreover his wife, a widow, whom he had married in his hundred and twentieth year, in reply to questions, could not deny that he had had intercourse with her exactly as other husbands do, and had kept up the practice to within twelve years of his death.

The chest was broad and full; his lungs were not spongy but, particularly on the right side, were attached to the ribs by fibrous bands. The lungs also were considerably distended with blood as is usual in pulmonary consumption (peripneumonia), so much so that before the blood was drawn off, a quantity seemed to become black. To this cause, too, I attributed the bluish colour of the face, and, a little before death, a difficulty in breathing and orthopnoea. As a result, the armpits and chest remained warm long after death. To sum up, there were clearly visible in his dead body this and other signs customarily found in those dying from suffocation. I concluded that he was suffocated, and that death was due to inability to breathe, and a similar report was given to his most Serene Majesty by all the physicians present. Later, when the blood had been drained off and wiped away from the lungs, they were seen to have a quite white and almost milky parenchyma.

The heart was large, thick, and fibrous with a considerable mass of fat around its wall and partition. The blood in the heart was blackish, liquid, and scarcely grumous. Only in the right ventricle were some clots seen.

When the sternum was dissected, the cartilages were not more osseous than in other men, but rather were flexible and soft.

The intestines were in excellent condition, fleshy and vigorous: the stomach was the same. The small intestine appeared muscular, but had some ring-shaped constrictions due to the fact that frequently he ate any kind of food both by day and night without any rules of diet or regular hours for meals. He was quite happy with half-rancid cheese and all kinds of milk dishes, brown bread, small beer, but most usually sour milk. By living frugally and roughly, and without cares, in humble circumstances, he in this way prolonged his life. He had taken a meal about the midnight shortly before his death.

The Siege of Gloucester, England JOHN DORNEY

1643

The English Civil War was mainly one of sieges with only a few set-piece battles. Numerous siege diaries were published, of which this is a typical example by the Town Clerk of Gloucester. The city was held by Parliamentary troops against an attack by Royalists from August to September 1643.

FRYDAY, AUGUST 25. Some few musketteers of ours this morning sallied forth of the north port, and gave the enemy an alarm, who through the suddennesse of the alarm, and hurly burly thereupon, had a barrell of powder blowne up In the afternoone their ordnance playd from Gawdie-Greene, and they likewise from thence shot many granadoes, two fell into the south-gate-streete, whereof one mortally wounded a woman, but did no other harme; some others fell upon severall houses in the citie, and shrewdly battered them, but did no other hurt; one fell downe upon the enemie's workes. They shot likewise great fire-balls, which did no harme. They also shot great stones out of their morter-pieces, which did little hurt, and killed none. In the evening and night following, they shot from their battery, at Lanthony, above twenty fiery melting hot iron bullets, some eighteen pound, others twenty-two pound waight; in the night wee perceived them flying in the ayre like a starre shooting, most of them fell into houses and stables where hay was, but by God's great providence did no hurt at all. One came through three houses, and fell into a chamber of Mr. Comelin's the apothecary, and being perceived, many payles of water were cast upon it to quench the same, but that little avayling, it was cast into a cowle of water, where after a good space it cooled. This night (it being suspected that false rumours of our being taken might be spread abroad to hinder our reliefe) it was ordered that some lights should be set up on the colledge-tower, to give notice abroad of our holding out, the performance whereof was committed to the care of Captain Pury junior, who performed it accordingly. The enemy vexed thereat levelled some shot at the tower, one whereof came close by the said Captain Pury, as he was looking towards Lanthony, whence their fiery bullets came, who for all that continued the burning of his linkes till the moone was fully risen.

1649

The Execution of King Charles I, London

ROBERT COTCHETT

At the end of the Civil War in 1646, Charles surrendered to Parliamentary forces and was imprisoned. For the next two years he engaged in secret and tortuous negotiations with the Scots who ultimately declared for him – this was the start of the second Civil War, which was swiftly suppressed by Cromwell's New Model Army. In the aftermath the King was tried and condemned to death by Parliament and executed in Whitehall on 30 January. Robert Cotchett was the son of a provincial gentleman who lived in Derby.

'THE SCAFFOLD erected before Whitehall, the King about 2 of the clocke came out of the banqueting house at a passage made through a window upon the scaffold, where the block and axe lay, at which he smilingly looking found fault with the block for being made too lowe. The scaffold was covered with black cloth. His Majestie turned about and spake something to the Bishop of London who replied to him and administered the Lord's supper. I think none heard what was said, but only those few on the scaffold with him, being about 14. Haveing spoke a quarter of an hour he putt off his hat and one of the executioners putt on his head a white capp and gathered upp his hair under it. Then he putt off his doublet and lay flatt downe on his belly with his neck on the block with

The execution of King Charles at Whitehall

his arms spread out giving the signe by spreading his hands wider. The executioner, haveing on his knees asked him pardon, cutt off his head at one blow and his mate took it upp and held it up to the spectators which was very many. The executioners were disguised being masqued with great beards and I believe not known to many. The King seemed to dye resolutely. I heard he left a speech in writing to be published. It may be it will come forth the morrow. I shall send it as soon as I can gett it.

All the army was uppon guard at their severall posts at Whitehall, Charing Cross, Westminster, St James parke and fields, Covent Garden etc.

Two Ambassadors at the importunity of the Prince are come from ye States of Holland to intercede but too late. They delivered the message yesterday in French and Dutch to the House, which the House not skilled at required the message in plain English, which is thought but a dilatory complaint on both sides. The Lord Loughborough is escaped from Windsor. There was much scrabbling for the King's blood.

The Great Mogul Prohibits Alcohol, India

NICCOLAO MANUCCI

1659

The author of this account was an Italian mercenary soldier who served at the court of Aurangzeb, the last of the great Mogul emperors of India who reigned from 1659 to 1707. Being a strict Muslim, he was strongly against the use of alcohol and prohibited it when he ascended the throne.

IT WAS SO common to drink spirits when Aurangzeb ascended the throne, that one day he said in a passion that in all Hindustan no more than two men could be found who did not drink, namely, himself and Abd-ul-wahhab, the chief *kazi* [magistrate]. But with respect to Abd-ul-wahhab he was in error, for I myself sent him every day a bottle of spirits, which he drank in secret, so that the king could not find it out. Aurangzeb wished to repress this disorder, and therefore ordered that all Christians, excepting physicians and surgeons, should leave the city and remove to near the park of artillery, which was beyond the suburbs at one league's distance from the city. There they had leave to prepare and drink spirits on condition they did not sell them.

After the issue of this order he directed the *kotwal* (chief of police) to search out Mahometans and Hindus who sold spirits, every one of whom was to lose one hand and one foot. Without fail the *kotwal* went out to search for the vendors, although himself one of the consumers. One day I saw him carry out such a sentence on six Mahometans and six Hindus; after the punishment he ordered them to be trailed to a dung-heap, leaving them there to die discreetly.

A Boyhood Experiment of Sir Isaac Newton, Grantham, England   Dr Stukeley

It is perhaps fitting, given early evidence of his approach to problems in childhood experiments, such as the one described here, that the mature philosophy of Sir Isaac Newton was digested for younger readers in the 18th century.

E VERY ONE that knew Sir Isaac, or have heard of him, recount the pregnancy of his parts when a boy, his strange inventions, and extraordinary inclination for mechanics. That instead of playing among the other boys, when from school, he always busied himself in making knick-knacks and models of wood in many kinds. For which purpose he had got little saws, hatchets, hammers, and all sorts of tools, which he would use with great dexterity. In particular they speak of his making a wooden clock. About this time, a new windmill was set up near Grantham, in the way to Gunnerby, which is now demolished, this country chiefly using water mills. Our lad's imitating spirit was soon excited and by frequently prying into the fabric of it, as they were making it, he became master enough to make a very perfect model thereof, and it was said to be as clean and curious a piece of workmanship, as the original. This sometimes he would set upon the house-top, where he lodged, and clothing it with sail-cloth, the wind would readily turn it; but what was most extraordinary in its composition was, that he put a mouse into it, which he called the miller, and that the mouse made the mill turn round when he pleased; and he would joke too upon the miller eating the corn that was put in. Some say that he tied a string to the mouse's tail, which was put into a wheel, like that of turn-spit dogs, so that pulling the string, made the mouse go forward by way of resistance, and this turned the mill. Others suppose there was some corn placed above the wheel, this the mouse endeavouring to get to, made it turn.

Robert Boyle's Classic Experiments with the Air-pump, Oxford, England   William Wotton

Since the time of Aristotle it had traditionally been believed that vacuums were physically impossible. Von Guericke's development of a prototype air-pump in Germany, however, paved the way for their detailed study. The Hon. Robert Boyle improved the design of the air-pump and introduced objects into a partial vacuum, conducting a series of classic experiments, such as the extinction of a flame, described in the following extract from William Wotton's Life of Boyle.

M R BOILE try'd afterwards several Experiments upon Fire & Flame in an exhausted Receiver, that he might find what Influence the Air had upon their Duration. First he put a Tallow-Candle of eight to the pound into a

Receiver & hung so that the Flame might burn about the middle of the Vessel. The Flame went out upon pumping in half a minute. Afterwards before he pumpt he freed the Receiver of Smoke by blowing with Bellow's, & thereby clearing the Receiver & the Flame went out with pumping in two Minutes. At first the Flame contracted itself in all its Dimensions. Then it appeared exceeding blew, except at Top, & still went from the Tallow, till it got all up to the Top before it went out. It lasted much longer when the Receiver was full of Air, & as it expired it went from the Tallow, tho slower than it did before. When it went out of it self, & the Receiver was unexhausted the Wick would remain kindled, & would emit a Smoke which ascended to the Top in a slender Cylinder. Whereas when it was extinguished by exsuction, it sometimes emitted no Smoke, & at other Times very little, which instead of ascending upwards, unless perhaps a very little way, usually fell down. If Wax Candles were used & the Flame was large, tho the lower Stopcock & Valve were left open, yet for want of Air sufficient to cherish the Flame, it could go out before every thing could be got ready for pumping. If a small Taper of white wax were put in, tho that emits much less Smoke than Yellow, yet the Flame would not last upon pumping above a minute; whereas if the Receiver was kept full of Air, & carefully cemented, the same Taper would keep its Flame above five Minutes.

The Smoke of London   JOHN EVELYN

1661

Modern-day London-dwellers would probably sympathise with John Evelyn's tirade against pollution, which in the later 17th century was due in large part to the coal trade there. John Evelyn was a member of the Royal Society and a man of broad cultural interests, including science.

OF ALL THE common and familiar materials which emit it, the immoderate use of, and indulgence to *Sea-coale* alone in the City of *London*, exposes it to one of the fowlest Inconveniences and reproaches, than possibly beffall so noble, and otherwise incomparable City: And that, not from the *Culinary* fires, which for being weak, and less often fed below, is with such ease dispelled and scattered above, as it is hardly at all discernible, but from some few particular Tunnells and Issues, belonging only to *Brewers, Diers, Lime-burners, Salt,* and *Sope-Boylers,* and some other private Trades, *One* of whose *Spiracles* alone, does manifestly infect the *Aer,* more than all the Chimnies of *London* put together besides. And that this is not the least *Hyperbolic,* let the best of Judges decide it, which I take to be our senses: Whilst these are belching it forth their sooty jaws, the City of *London* resembles the face rather of *Mount Ætna,* the *Court of Vulcan, Stromboli,* or the Suburbs of *Hell,* than an Assembly of Rational Creatures, and the imperial seat of our incomparable *Monarch.* For when in all other places the *Aer* is most Serene and Pure, it is here Ecclipsed with such a Cloud of Sulphure, as the Sun itself, which gives day to all the World besides, is hardly able to penetrate and impart it here; and the weary *Traveller*, at many Miles distance, sooner smells, than sees the City to which he repairs. This is that pernicious Smoake which sullyes all her Glory, superinducing a sooty Crust or Fur upon all that it lights, spoyling the moveables, tarnishing the Plate, Gildings and Furniture, and corroding the very Iron-bars and hardest Stones with those piercing and acrimonious Spirits which accompany its Sulphure; and executing more in one year, than exposed to the pure *Aer* of the Country it could effect in some hundreds.

1665

The Great Plague, London   SAMUEL PEPYS

In the summer of 1665 the Bubonic Plague (the Black Death) struck London in its last serious outbreak, causing an estimated 68,000 deaths in the capital alone. The diarist Samuel Pepys was present. His celebrated Diary is of extraordinary interest for the vivid picture it gives of contemporary life.

PUT ON MY coloured silk suit very fine, and my new periwigg, bought a good while since but durst not wear because the plague was in Westminster when I bought it; and it is a wonder what will be the fashion after the plague is done as to periwiggs, for nobody will dare to buy any haire for fear of the infection, that it had been cut off of the heads of people dead of the plague. To church, where a sorry dull parson. I up to the Vestry at the desire of the Justices of the Peace, in order to the doing something for the keeping of the plague from growing; but Lord! to consider the madness of the people of the town, who will (because they are forbid) come in crowds along with the dead corps to see them buried; but we

Fleeing from the Great Plague

agreed on some orders for the prevention thereof. Among other stories one was very passionate methought, of a complaint brought against a man in the towne for taking a child from London from an infected house. Alderman Hooker told us it was the child of a very able citizen in Gracious Street, a saddler, who had buried all the rest of his children of the plague, and himself and wife now being shut up and in despair of escaping did desire only to save the life of this little child; and so prevailed to have it received stark-naked into the arms of a friend, who brought it (having put it into new fresh clothes) to Greenwich; where upon hearing the story, we did agree it should be permitted to be received and kept in the towne.

After dinner to Greenwich where I found my Lord Bruncker. We to walk in the Park, and there eat some fruit out of the King's garden, and thence walked home, my Lord Bruncker giving me a very neat cane to walk with; but it troubled me to pass by Coome farme where about twenty-one people have died of the plague, and three or four days since I saw a dead corps in a coffin lie in the Close unburied; and a watch is constantly kept there night and day to keep the people in, the plague making us cruel as doggs one to another.

The Great Fire of London JOHN EVELYN

1666

From 2–6 September the Great Fire of London raged, burning down a large part of the capital including Old St Pauls Cathedral. Evelyn was partly responsible, with Sir Christopher Wren, for the designs for the new city which replaced the warren of medieval buildings

THE FIRE having continu'd all this night (if I may call that night which was light as day for ten miles round about, after a dreadfull manner) when conspiring with a fierce Eastern wind in a very drie season; I went on foote to the same place, and saw the whole South part of the Citty burning from Cheapeside to the Thames, and all along Cornehill (for it likewise kindl'd back against the wind as well as forward), Tower Streete, Fen-church Streete, Gracious Streete, and so along to Bainard's Castle, and was now taking hold of St Paule's Church, to which the scaffolds contributed exceedingly. The conflagration was so universal, and the people so astonish'd, that from the beginning, I know not by what despondency or fate, they hardly stirr'd to quench it, so that there was nothing heard or seene but crying out and lamentation, running about like distracted creatures, without at all attempting to save even their goods; such a strange consternation there was upon them, so as it burned both in breadth and length, the Churches, Public Halls, Exchange, Hospitals, Monuments, and ornaments, leaping after a prodigious manner from house to house and streete to streete, at greate distances one from the other; for the heate with a long set of faire and warme weather had even ignited the aire and prepar'd the materials to conceive the fire, which devour'd after an incredible manner houses, furniture, and every thing. Here we saw the Thames cover'd with goods floating, all the barges and boates

The Great Fire as seen from Southwark

laden with what some had time and courage to save, as, on the other, the carts, &c. carrying out to the fields, which for many miles were strew'd with moveables of all sorts, and tents erecting to shelter both people and what goods they could get away. Oh the miserable and calamitous spectacle! Such as happly the world had not seene the like since the foundation of it, nor be outdon till the universal conflagration of it. All the skie was of a fiery aspect, like the top of a burning oven, and the light seene above 40 miles round about for many nights. God grant mine eyes may never behold the like, who now saw above 10,000 houses all in one flame; the noise and cracking and thunder of the impetuous flames, the shrieking of women and children, the hurry of people, the fall of Towers, Houses and Churches, was like an hideous storme, and the aire all about so hot and inflam'd that at the last one was not able to approch it, so that they were forc'd to stand still and let the flames burn on, which they did for neere two miles in length and one in bredth.

Newton's Experiments on Light, Cambridge, England SIR ISAAC NEWTON

1666

Sir Isaac Newton's first great field of research and publication was optics, not mathematics, mechanics or gravitation where his work is perhaps better known. The following passage describes his discovery of the colours which always arise when white light is refracted by lenses or prisms, a high point of his inventiveness during the plague years of 1665–6.

I PROCURED me a Triangular glass-Prisme, to try therewith the celebrated *Phaenomena* of *Colours*. And in order thereto having darkened my chamber, and made a small hole in my window-shuts, to let in a convenient quantity of the Suns light, I placed my Prisme at his entrance, that it might be thereby refracted to the opposite wall. It was at first a very pleasing divertisement, to view the vivid and intense colours produced thereby; but after a while applying my self to consider them more circumspectly, I became surprised to see them in an *oblong* form; which, according to the received laws of Refraction, I expected should have been *circular*.

And I saw that the light, tending to [one] end of the Image, did suffer a Refraction considerably greater than the light tending to the other. And so the true cause of the length of that Image was detected to be no other, then that *Light* consists of *Rays differently refrangible*, which, without any respect to a difference in their incidence, were, according to their degrees of refrangibility, transmitted towards divers parts of the wall.

Then I placed another Prisme ... so that the light ... might pass through that also, and be again refracted before it arrived at the wall. This done, I took the first Prisme in my hand and turned it to and fro slowly about its *Axis*, so much as to make the several parts of the Image ... successively pass through ... that I might observe to what places on the wall the second Prisme would refract them.

When any one sort of Rays hath been well parted from those of other kinds, it hath afterwards obstinately retained its colour, notwithstanding my utmost endeavours to change it.

I have refracted it with Prismes, and reflected with it Bodies which in Daylight were of other colours; I have intercepted it with the coloured film of Air interceding two compressed plates of glass; transmitted it through coloured Mediums, and through mediums irradiated with other sorts of Rays, and diversely terminated it; and yet could never produce any new colour out of it.

But the most surprising, and wonderful composition was that of *Whiteness*. There is no one sort of Rays which alone can exhibit this. 'Tis ever compounded, and to its composition are requisite all the aforesaid primary Colours, mixed in a due proportion. I have often with Admiration beheld, that all the Colours of the Prisme being made to converge, and thereby to be again mixed, reproduced light, intirely and perfectly white.

Hence therefore it comes to pass, that *Whiteness* is the usual colour of *Light*; for, Light is a confused aggregate of Rays indued with all sorts of Colours, as they are promiscuously darted from the various parts of luminous bodies.

1670

The Buccaneers Sack Panama, Central America

A. O. EXQUEMELIN

For nearly thirty years, from 1660, English and French interlopers, usually referred to as buccaneers, waged war against the Spanish authorities in the Caribbean. In their most famous exploit, under their leader Henry Morgan, they captured and looted the wealthy city of Panama in August 1670.

WHILE SOME of his men went marauding by sea, others scoured the countryside. A party of 200 men marched out each day, and as soon as one expedition came back, another was ready to go out. From these sorties they brought back considerable booty, and many prisoners, whom day by day they made to suffer the greatest cruelties and tortures, to make them disclose where their money had been hidden.

One of their captives was a poor cripple whom they found in a gentleman's house outside the city. This wretched man had come across a good shirt in the house, and a pair of silk breeches, which he had put on. A silver key was tied to the points of these breeches. The buccaneers asked him about the coffer which this key had been designed to fit. He had no coffer, he told them, but had simply found the key in the house.

When it became plain this was all he was going to tell them, they strappado'd him until both his arms were entirely dislocated, then knotted a cord so tight round the forehead that his eyes bulged out, big as eggs. Since he still would not admit where the coffer was, they hung him up by his male parts, while one struck him, another sliced off his nose, yet another an ear, and another scorched him with fire – tortures as barbarous as man can devise. At last, when the wretch could no longer speak and they could think of no new torments, they let a Negro stab him to death with a lance.

They committed many more such cruelties. They showed little mercy, even to the monks, and would have shown none but for the hope of extracting money from them. Nor did they spare the women, except for those who yielded themselves completely. The rovers had a way of dealing with those women who held out. They would let them leave the church, which was being used as their prison, as if giving them a chance to go and wash themselves – but once a woman was in their hands they would work their will upon her, or beat her, starve her, or simply torment her. Morgan, being the general, should have set a better example, but he was no better than the rest. Whenever a beautiful prisoner was brought in, he at once sought to dishonour her.

Christmas Day at Sea HENRY TEONGE

1678

The narrator was an impoverished parson with a large family who became a naval chaplain in order to repair his fortunes. Like many 17th-century clerics, he had more of an eye for food and good living than for the spiritual.

GOOD Christmas Day. We go to prayers at 10; and the wind rose of such a sudden that I was forced (by the Captain's command) to conclude abruptly at the end of the Litany; and we had no sermon. And soon after, by the carelessness of some, our barge at stern was almost sunk, but recovered. We had not so great a dinner as was intended, for, the whole fleet being in this harbour, beef could not be got. Yet we had to dinner an excellent rice pudding in a great charger, a special piece of Martinmas English beef, and a neat's tongue, and good cabbage, a charger full of excellent fresh fish fried, a dozen of woodcocks in a pie, which cost 15d., a couple of good hens roasted, three sorts of cheese, and, last of all, a great charger full of blue figs, almonds, and raisins; wine and punch galore, and a dozen of English pippins.

The wind was so high all this night that we ever expected when it would have broke our cable or anchor. But the greatest loss we yet sustained was this: about 11 or 12 a-clock our honest Lieutenant, Mr Will. New, died, and left a mournful ship's-company behind him. Yesterday our Captain bought three Spanish hogs: the roughness of the weather made them so sea-sick that no man could forbear laughing to see them go reeling and spewing about the decks.

The Great Frost Fair, London JOHN EVELYN

1684

The unusually harsh winter of 1683–4, which affected all Europe, froze the River Thames to a depth that allowed a fair, booths and entertainment to be held on the ice.

THE FROST continuing more and more severe, the Thames before London was still planted with boothes in formal streetes, all sorts of trades and shops furnish'd and full of commodities, even to a printing presse, where the people and ladyes tooke a fancy to have their names printed, and the day and yeare set down when printed on the Thames; this humour tooke so universally, that 'twas estimated the printer gain'd £5. a day, for printing a line onely, at sixpence a name, besides what he got by ballads, &c. Coaches plied from Westminster to the Temple, and from several other staires to and fro, as in the streetes, sleds, sliding with skeetes, a bull-baiting, horse and coach races, puppet plays and interludes, cookes, tipling, and other lewd places, so that it seem'd to be a bacchanalian triumph, or carnival on the water, whilst it was a severe judgment on the land, the trees not onely splitting as if by lightning-struck, but men and cattle perishing in divers places, and the very seas so lock'd up with ice, that no vessells could stir out or come in. The fowles, fish, and birds, and all our exotiq plants and greenes

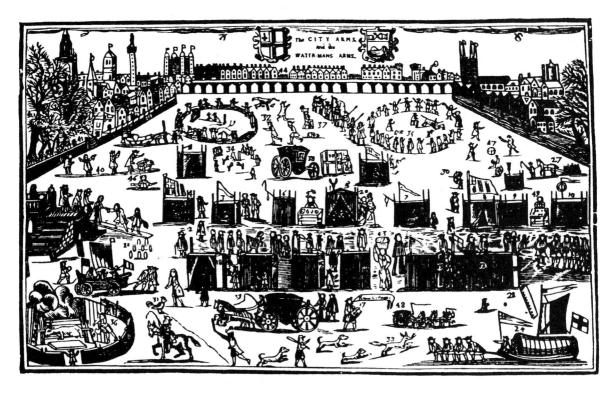

The Great Frost Fair
on the Thames

universally perishing. Many parkes of deer were destroied, and all sorts of fuell so deare that there were greate contributions to preserve the poore alive. Nor was this severe weather much lesse intense in most parts of Europe, even as far as Spaine and the most Southern tracts. London, by reason of the excessive cold-nesse of the aire hindering the ascent of the smoke, was so fill'd with the fuliginous steame of the sea-coale, that hardly could one see crosse the streetes, and this filling the lungs with its grosse particles, exceedingly obstructed the breast, so as one could scarcely breathe. Here was no water to be had from the pipes and engines, nor could the brewers and divers other tradesmen worke, and every moment was full of disastrous accidents.

An Experiment into the Eduction of Light, England   John Evelyn

1685

John Evelyn was close friends with Samuel Pepys, at whose house the experiment described here took place.

Dining at Mr Pepys's, Dr Slayer shewed us an experiment of a wonderful nature, pouring first a very cold liquor into a glass, and super-fusing on it another, to appearance cold and clear liquor also; it first produced a white cloud, then boiling, divers corruscations and actual flames of fire mingled with the liquor, which being a little shaken together, fixed divers sunns and starrs of real fire, perfectly globular, on the sides of the glasse, and which there stuck like so many constellations, burning most vehemently, and resembling starrs and heavenly bodies, and that for a long space. It seemed to exhibit a theorie of the eduction of light out of chaos, and the fixing or gathering of the universal light into luminous bodys. This matter or phosphorus was made out of human blood and urine, elucidating the vital flame or heate in animal bodys. A very noble experiment.

The Marriage of the Duc de Chartres, Versailles, France DUC DE SAINT-SIMON

1692

Louis XIV, much against the wishes of the groom's mother, arranged for the marriage of his illegitimate daughter Francoise Marie de Blois to the Duc de Chartres. In this typically entertaining and waspish account, the court gossip Saint-Simon witnesses the anger of the hapless Duke's mother.

IN THE LONG gallery, Madame was marching up and down with Châteautiers, her favourite. She strode about handkerchief in hand, weeping unrestrainedly, speaking rather loud, gesticulating, and looking for all the world like Ceres after the rape of Proserpine. Everyone made way for her respectfully, and only passed her when they wished to reach the Appartement. Monseigneur and Monsieur went back to their lansquenet. The former appeared quite as usual, but no one has ever looked more ashamed of himself than Monsieur, nor more embarrassed, and he remained in this condition for several weeks. M. de Chartres, looked utterly miserable, and his intended was in a state of great distress and unhappiness. She was very young and the marriage a marvellous one for her, yet she could see and feel the effects of it and dreaded the consequences. Indeed, the dismay was pretty general, except amongst a few. As for the Lorraines, they triumphantly rejoiced in their success, and, having no shame, they had good reason.

Next day, the entire Court called upon Monsieur, Madame, and M. le Duc de Chartres, but nothing was said. People merely made their bows and everything passed off in perfect silence. Afterwards, everyone waited as usual in the long gallery for the Council to rise and the King to pass on his way to mass. Madame was there too, and when her son came up to her to kiss her hand, she dealt him such a resounding box on the ear that it could be heard some distance away. Receiving this, as he did, in the presence of the whole Court, the poor prince was covered with embarrassment and the vast crowd, myself included, were prodigiously amazed. On that same day the details of the bride's enormous dowry were announced, and on the following, the King visited Monsieur and Madame. It was all very unhappy. After that, no one thought of anything but the wedding.

1704

A Surgical Bleeding, Versailles, France

DUC DE SAINT-SIMON

Bleeding, either by lancet or by the use of leeches, was a commonplace of medical treatment for most of the 17th and 18th centuries. It was believed to rid the body of the 'ill humours' which were thought to cause disease.

ABOUT THIS time I met with an unfortunate accident and allowed myself to be bled because the blood was rushing to my head. The operation seemed to me vastly well done. During the night, however, I felt a pain in my arm which Ledran, the well-known surgeon, who had performed the blood-letting, assured me was due to a tight bandage. To make a long story short, in two days' time the arm had swollen bigger than my thigh and I was in great pain and feverish. They kept me for two days longer with applications over the wound to draw out the poison, following the advice of the most renowned Paris surgeons. M. de Lauzun, rightly thinking that I was very ill indeed, insisted upon my seeing Maréchal, the King's surgeon, and himself went to Versailles to ask the King's permission, for without it Maréchal could not come to Paris and rarely slept away from the King. He was allowed to come and to spend the night and even to remain with me, and as soon as he arrived, he opened the arm from end to end. It was high time, for the abscess had spread to the body and was manifesting itself by fits of shivering. Maréchal stayed for two days, then came to see me every day, and afterwards, every two days. The skill and speed with which he performed the operation and dressings, and the pains he took to make me comfortable, pass all description. He made this accident an excuse to speak to the King on my behalf, who overwhelmed me with kindness after my recovery. A short time before this happened, Chamillart had managed to mend matters somewhat between us and what Maréchal said finally healed the breach.

On the day that I was bled I had strained my arm slightly, to which I attributed my accident, and during the course of the operation I asked Ledran to bleed me again, so that I might not lose the use of it. Maréchal and Fagon thought that a tendon might have been damaged, but they put weights upon my arm so that it remained its natural length and I felt no ill-effects.

c. 1706

Experimenting with a Live Mare, England

STEPHEN HALES

The turn of the century witnessed an emergence of reports on experiments, such as the botanist and chemist Stephen Hales' description here, both for the special purpose of scientists and the general interest of philosophers.

I N DECEMBER I caused a mare to be tied down alive on her back; she was fourteen hands high, and about fourteen years of age, had a *Fistula* on her Withers, was neither very lean, nor yet lusty: Having laid open the left crural Artery about three inches from her belly, I inserted into it a brass Pipe, whose bore was one sixth of an inch in diameter; and to that, by means of another brass Pipe which was fitly adapted to it, I fixed a glass Tube, of nearly the same diameter, which was nine feet in Length: Then untying the Ligature on the Artery, the blood rose in the Tube eight feet three inches perpendicular above the level of the left Ventricle of the heart: But it did not attain to its full height at once; it rushed up about half way in an instant, and afterwards gradually at each Pulse twelve, eight, six, four, two, and sometimes one inch: When it was at its full height, it would rise and fall at and after each Pulse two, three, or four inches; and sometimes it would fall twelve or fourteen inches, and have there for the same Vibrations up and down at and after each Pulse, as it had, when it was at its full height; to which it would rise again, after forty or fifty Pulses.

Rescue of Alexander Selkirk, Juan Fernandez Island WOODES ROGERS

1709

Captain Woodes Rogers' journal of his privateering expedition to the South Sea in the time of Queen Anne includes the following description of his bizarre encounter with Alexander Selkirk – a Scotsman marooned on Juan Fernandez Island for more than four years, whose tale of solitary survival inspired Daniel Defoe's Robinson Crusoe *(1719).*

I MMEDIATELY our pinnace return'd from the shore, and brought abundance of craw-fish with a man cloth'd in goat-skins, who look'd wilder than the first owner's of them. He had been on the island four years and four months, being left there by Captain Stradling in the ship 'Cinque-Ports'. His name was Alexander Selkirk, a Scotchman, who had been master of the 'Cinque-Ports', a ship that came here last with Capt. Dampier, who told me this was the best man in her; so I immediately agreed with him to be mate on board our ship.

The reason of his being left here was a difference betwixt him and his captain. When left, he had with him his clothes and bedding, with a firelock, some powder, bullets, and tobacco, a hatchet, a knife, a kettle, a Bible, some practical pieces, and his mathematical instruments and books.

He diverted and provided for himself as well as he could; but for the first eight months had much ado to bear up against melancholy, and the terror of being alone in such a desolate place. He built two huts with piemento trees, cover'd them with long grass, and lin'd them with the skins of goats which he killed with his gun as he wanted, so long as his powder lasted, which was but a pound, and that being near spent, he got fire by rubbing two sticks of piemento wood together on his knees. In the lesser hut, at some distance from the other, he dressed his victuals, and in the larger he slept, and employed himself in reading, singing Psalms, and praying, so that he said he was a better Christian while in this solitude, than ever he was before, or than he was afraid he should ever be again. At first he never eat anything till hunger constrain'd him, partly for grief, and partly for want of bread and salt; nor did he go to bed till he could watch no longer.

1709

Royal Irish Regiment at the Battle of Malplaquet, Flanders Robert Parker

Malplaquet was the bloodiest of Marlborough's victories over the French during the War of the Spanish Succession. Total casualties in one day of fighting exceeded 36,000 out of the 190,000 men engaged. This extract, by a lieutenant in the Royal Irish Regiment, demonstrates the relative efficiency of British musketry.

THE PART which our Regiment acted in this battle was something remarkable. We happened to be the last of the regiments that had been left at Tournai to level our approaches, and therefore could not come up till the lines were all formed and closed, so that there was no place for us to fall into. We were ordered therefore to draw up by ourselves, on the right of the whole army, opposite to a skirt of the wood of Sart [*or Taisnières*]; and when the army advanced to attack the enemy, we also advanced into that part of the wood, which was in our front. We continued marching slowly on, till we came to an open in the wood. It was a small plain, on the opposite side of which we perceived a battalion of the enemy drawn up, a skirt of the wood being in the rear of them. Upon this Colonel Kane, who was then at the head of the Regiment, having drawn us up, and formed our platoons, advanced gently toward them, with the six platoons of our first fire made ready. When we had advanced within a hundred paces of them, they gave us a fire of one of their ranks: whereupon we halted, and returned them the fire of our six platoons at once; and immediately made ready the six platoons of our second fire, and advanced upon them again. They then gave us the fire of another rank, and we returned them a second fire, which made them shrink; however, they gave us the fire of a third rank after a scattering manner, and then retired into the wood in great disorder: on which we sent our third fire after them, and saw them no more. We advanced cautiously up to the ground which they had quitted, and found several of them killed and wounded; among the latter was one Lieutenant O'Sullivan, who told us the battalion we had engaged was the Royal Regiment of Ireland. Here, therefore, there was a fair trial of skill between the two Royal Regiments of Ireland, one in the British, the other in the French service; for we met each other upon equal terms, and there was none else to interpose. We had but four men killed, and six wounded: and found near forty of them on the spot killed and wounded.

Death of the Sun King, Versailles, France

DUC DE SAINT-SIMON

1715

Louis XIV – the Sun King – was France's longest reigning monarch, ascending the throne at the age of five in 1643. Saint-Simon, diarist and courtier, records the King's last moments.

THE DAY AND night of August 31st were very dreadful. There were only short moments of consciousness at rare intervals. The gangrene spread over the knee and the whole of the thigh. They gave him medicine of the late Abbé d'Aignan, which had been suggested by the Duchesse du Maine, and was an excellent remedy for smallpox, but by this time the doctors were consenting to any suggestion because they no longer had any hope. At eleven o'clock, the King was seen to be so ill that they said the prayers for the dying. The service brought him back to consciousness, and he recited the prayers in so strong a voice that it could be heard clearly above the many priests and all the other persons who had entered the room. At the end of the prayers, he recognised Cardinal de Rohan and said to him, 'These are then the last favours of the Church.' The Cardinal was the last person to whom he ever spoke. Several times he was heard to repeat the words, 'Nunc et in hora mortis', also, 'Oh! God help me. Haste Thou to succour me.' Those were his last words. All the rest of that night he lay unconscious. His long-protracted agony ended at a quarter past eight in the morning of Sunday 1st September 1715, just three days before his seventy-seventh birthday, in the seventy-second year of his reign.

A Total Eclipse of the Sun, London

1715

DR EDMUND HALLEY

Edmund Halley recorded his impressions of a total eclipse of the sun in 1715 in the Philosophical Transactions of the Royal Society. His description reveals the aesthetic concerns of the 18th century in its alliance of science and spirituality. The particular popularity of astronomy among laymen is perhaps demonstrated by Halley's request that people all over England should record their own observations of the eclipse.

ON TUESDAY the sixth of *March, st. vet.* in the current Year 1716, (the Afternoon having been very serene and calm, and somewhat warmer than ordinary) about the Time it began to grow dark, (much about seven of the Clock) not only in *London*, but in all Parts of *England*, where the Beginning of this wonderful Sight was seen; out of what seem'd a dusky Cloud, in the N.E. Parts of the Heavens, and scarce ten Degrees high, the Edges whereof were tinged with a reddish Yellow, like as if the Moon had been hid behind it, there arose very long luminous Rays or Streaks perpendicular to the Horizon, some of which seem'd nearly to ascend to the Zenith. Presently after, that reddish Cloud was swiftly propagated along the Northern Horizon into the N.W. and still farther Westerly; and immediately sent forth its Rays from all Parts, now here, now there, they observing no Rule or Order in their rising. Many of these Rays seeming to concur near the *Zenith*, formed there a *Corona*, or Image which drew the Attention of all Spectators. Some liken'd it to that Representation of *Glory* wherewith our Painters in Churches surround the Holy *Name of God*. Others to those radiating *Stars*, wherewith the Breasts of the *Knights* of the Order of the *Garter* are adorn'd. Many compar'd it to the *Concave* of the great *Cupola* of St Paul's Church, distinguish'd with Streaks alternately light and obscure, and having in the middle a Space less bright than the rest, resembling the Lantern. Whilst others, to express as well the Motion as Figure thereof, would have it to be like the Flame in an Oven, reverberated and rouling against the arched Roof thereof: Some thought it liker to that tremulous Light which is cast against a Ceiling by the Beams of the Sun, reflected from the Surface of Water in a bason that's a little shaken; whose reciprocal Motion it very much imitated. But all agree, that this *Spectrum* lasted only a few Minutes, and exhibited itself variously tinged with Colours, Yellow, Red, and a dusky Green: Nor did it keep in the same Place; for when first it began, it appear'd a little to the Northwards of the *Zenith*, but by Degrees declining towards the South, the long *Striae* of Light, which arise from all parts of the Northern Semicircle of the Horizon, seem'd to meet together, not much above the Head of *Castor*, or the Northern Twin, and there soon disappear'd.

The Practice of Inoculation, Turkey

LADY MARY WORTLEY-MONTAGU

1717

Lady Mary was the wife of the British Ambassador to Constantinople where she discovered the local custom of inoculation against smallpox. She introduced it to England in 1721 by inoculating her own daughter, happily with beneficial results.

THE SMALL-POX, so general and so fatal amongst us, is entirely harmless by the invention of *ingrafting*, which is the term they give it. There is a set of old women who make it their business to perform the operation every autumn, in the month of September, when the great heat is abated. People send to one another to know if any one has a mind to have the small-pox. They make parties for this purpose, and when they are met (commonly fifteen or sixteen together), the old woman comes with a nut-shell full of the matter of the best sort of small-pox, and asks you what vein you please to have opened. She immediately rips open that you offer to her with a large needle (which gives you no more pain than a common scratch), and puts into the vein as much matter as can lie upon the head of her needle, and after that binds up the little wound with a hollow bit of shell, and in this manner opens four or five veins. . . . The children or young patients play together all the rest of the day, and are in perfect health till the eighth. Then the fever begins to seize them, and they keep their beds two days, very seldom three. They have very rarely above twenty or thirty on their faces, which never mark, and in eight days' time they are as well as they were before their illness. Where they are wounded there remain running sores during the distemper, which, I don't doubt, is a great relief to it. Every year thousands undergo the operation; and the French ambassador says pleasantly that they take the small-pox here by way of diversion, as they take the waters in other countries.

Lady Mary
Wortley-Montagu
(1689 1762)

Turkish Baths, Adrianople, Turkey

LADY MARY WORTLEY-MONTAGU

Having eloped with Edward Wortley in 1712, Lady Mary Wortley-Montagu journeyed with him to Constantinople in 1716 where she wrote her Embassy Letters, *from which this passage is an extract. She spent many of her later years abroad, mainly in Italy, in solitude and increasingly alienated from England.*

I WENT TO the bagnio about ten o'clock. It was already full of women. It is built of stone in the shape of a dome with no windows but in the roof, which gives light enough.

I was in my travelling habit, which is a riding dress, and certainly appeared very extraordinary to them, yet there was no one of 'em that showed the least surprise or impertinent curiosity, but received me with all the obliging civility possible. I know no European court where the ladies would have behaved themselves in so polite a manner to a stranger. I believe in the whole there were two hundred women and yet none of those disdainful smiles or satiric whispers that never fail in our assemblies when anybody appears that is not dressed exactly in fashion. They repeated over and over to me, 'Uzelle, pek uzelle', which is nothing but, 'Charming, very charming'. The first sofas were covered with cushions and rich carpets, on which sat the ladies, and on the second their slaves behind 'em, but without any distinction of rank by their dress, all being in the state of nature, that is, in plain English, stark naked, without any beauty or defect concealed, yet there was not the least wanton smile or immodest gesture amongst 'em. They walked and moved with the same majestic grace which Milton describes of our General Mother. There were many amongst them as exactly proportioned as ever any goddess was drawn by the pencil of Guido or Titian, and most of their skins shiningly white, only adorned by their beautiful hair divided into many tresses hanging on their shoulders, braided either with pearl or riband, perfectly representing the figures of the Graces.

'Tis no less than death for a man to be found in one of these places.

Lightning Strikes in Northamptonshire, England J. WASSE

The following extract gives a detailed account of the terrible wounds inflicted on a man by a bolt of lightning. It is evident that the writer, rather than eulogizing on the miraculousness of the natural world, takes a coldly empirical, 'realist' approach. Electrical storms were one of the prime means of studying the force of electricity.

ON SATURDAY July 3 at *Mixbury*, a storm of thunder and lightning began about half past 1 in the afternoon, and lasted with intermissions for an hour.

About 2 W. Hall, aged about sixty, was found dead in a hard gravelly field, together with five sheep which lay round him at about 30 yards Distance; but that only which lay nearest him had a visible Wound, through the head. The Shepherd lay partly upon his Side; the upper part of his Head was terribly fractur'd, and his right knee was out of joint; He had a wound in the sole of his foot, towards the heel; his right Ear was cut off and beaten into his Skull, and blood flowed out of that Part upon the ground. All his Cloaths and Shirt were torn into small Pieces and hung about him; but from the Girdle downwards were carried away entirely, and scattered up and down the Field. Particularly, the Soles of a new strong Pair of Shoes were rent off. His Hat was driven to Pieces: I have a Hand-breadth of it full of irregular slits, and in some few Places cut as with a very sharp Pen-knife, and a little singed in the upper Part. His Beard and the Hair of his Head were for the most part close burnt off. The Iron Buckle of his belt was thrown 40 yards off, and a knife in the right Side Pocket of his Breeches. Near each Foot appear two round Holes five inches in diameter, but after that grew narrower; in both of them the matter divided into two parts, and formed horizontal cavities about three inches diameter. In one we found a hard glazed stone, about ten inches long, six wide, and four thick, cracked in two: others it could not pierce, but was turned here and there out of his course, yet left not the least blackness or other discolouring any where. I have seen an iron ball shot out of a mortar almost perpendicular which upon a like gravelly soil made not a greater impression. To make a gross estimate of the force, I took a cohorn charged with three quarters of a pound of very good powder wadded with thick paper, and fired it against a stone of the same dimensions, but not so hard, which it shattered to pieces at half an inch distance. But in the other blow we have above treble the effect, without any discoverable particles at all; and yet it seems to fly like small shot, pieces only here and there, and leaves a good many places quite untouch'd, as is evident from the hat which I have by me.

Farinelli: the Great Castrato, Rome

Charles Burney

The castrati *were the superstars of Italian opera in the 17th and 18th centuries. Farinelli, the stage name of Carlo Broschi, was perhaps the most famous* castrato *of all – he sang to great acclaim in several European cities, then served the Spanish court in Madrid between 1737 and 1759. Charles Burney here relates a famous episode from Farinelli's early years in Rome, which he probably checked at first-hand when, in 1770, he visited the singer in Bologna.*

During the run of an opera, there was a struggle every night between him and a famous player on the trumpet, in a song accompanied by that instrument: this, at first, seemed amicable and merely sportive, till the audience began to interest themselves in the contest, and to take different sides: after severally swelling out a note, in which each manifested the power of his lungs, and tried to rival the other in brilliancy and force, they both had a swell and a shake together, by thirds, which was continued so long, while the audience eagerly awaited the event, that both seemed to be exhausted; and in fact, the trumpeter, wholly spent gave it up, thinking, however, his antagonist as much tired as himself, and that it would be a drawn battle; when Farinelli with a smile on his countenance, shewing he had been only sporting with him all this time, broke out all at once in the same breath, with fresh vigour, and not only swelled and shook the note, but ran the most rapid and difficult divisions, and was at last silenced only by the acclamations of the audience.

1735 Fleet Marriages, London

ANON (GRUB STREET JOURNAL)

The area around the Fleet prison was notorious as a place where irregular or suspect marriages could be celebrated – often by de-frocked clergy with no questions asked, a state of affairs only remedied by Lord Hardwicke's Marriage Act of 1753 which required weddings to be celebrated only in churches with a proper record kept.

SOME TIME after, I went in a coach to Ludgate Hill in the daytime, to see the manner of their picking up people to be married. As soon as our coach stopped near Fleet Bridge, up comes one of the myrmidons. 'Madam,' says he, 'you want a parson?' 'Who are you?' says I. 'I am the clerk and register of the Fleet.' 'Shew me the chapel.' At which comes a second, desiring me to go along with him. Says he: 'That fellow will carry you to a pedling alehouse.' Says a third: 'Go with me, he will carry you to a brandy-shop.' In the interim comes the doctor. 'Madam,' says he, 'I'll do your job for you presently!' 'Well, gentlemen,' says I, 'since you can't agree, and I can't be married quietly, I'll put it off till another time;' and so drove away. The truthfulness of this description is attested by Pennant: 'In walking along the street, in my youth, on the side next the prison, I have often been tempted by the question: "*Sir, will you be pleased to walk in and be married?*" Along this most lawless space was hung up the frequent sign of a male and female hand enjoined, with *Marriages performed within*, written beneath. A dirty fellow invited you in. The parson was seen walking before his shop; a squalid profligate figure, clad in a tattered plaid nightgown, with a fiery face, and ready to couple you for a dram of gin or a roll of tobacco.

Capture of the Manila Treasure Ship, Pacific

1743

RICHARD WALTER

In 1740 the British government fitted out a squadron for a voyage round the world. The commander was George Anson, and the intention was both to explore and chart unknown areas and to attack Spanish commerce and trade in their colonies. The climax of the voyage was the capture of one of the richest prizes ever seized by a privateer. The action is narrated by the captain on board the flag-ship Centurion.

AND NOW the engagement began in earnest, and for the first half-hour Mr. Anson over-reached the galeon and lay on her bow, where, by the great wideness of his ports, he could traverse almost all his guns upon the enemy, whilst the galeon could only bring a part of hers to bear. Immediately on the commencement of the action, the mats with which the galeon had stuffed her netting took fire and burnt violently, blazing up half as high as the mizen-top. This accident, supposed to be caused by the *Centurion's* wads, threw the enemy into the utmost terror, and also alarmed the commodore, for he feared lest the galeon should be burnt, and lest he himself too might suffer by her driving on board him. However, the Spaniards at last freed themselves from the fire, by cutting away the netting and tumbling the whole mass, which was in flames, into the sea. All this interval the *Centurion* kept her first advantageous position, firing her cannon with great regularity and briskness, whilst at the same time the galeon's decks lay open to her top-men, who having at their first volley driven the Spaniards from their tops, made prodigious havock with their small arms, killing or wounding

The fight between the treasure ship and Anson's fleet

every officer but one that appeared on the quarter-deck, and wounding in particular the general of the galeon himself. Thus the action proceeded for at least half an hour; but then the *Centurion* lost the superiority arising from her original situation, and was close alongside the galeon, and the enemy continued to fire briskly for near an hour longer; yet even in this posture the commodore's grape-shot swept their decks so effectually, and the number of their slain and wounded became so considerable, that they began to fall into great disorder, especially as the general, who was the life of the action, was no longer capable of exerting himself. Their confusion was visible from on board the commodore, for the ships were so near that some of the Spanish officers were seen running about with much assiduity, to prevent the desertion of their men from their quarters. But all their endeavours were in vain, for after having, as a last effort, fired five or six guns with more judgment than usual, they yielded up the contest, and, the galeon's colours being singed off the ensign staff in the beginning of the engagement, she struck the standard at her main top-gallant mast-head; the person who was employed to perform this office having been in imminent peril of being killed, had not the commodore, who perceived what he was about, given express orders to his people to desist from firing.

Thus was the *Centurion* possessed of this rich prize, amounting in value to near a million and a half of dollars. She was called the *Nostra Signora de Cabadonga*, and was commanded by General Don Jeronimo de Mentero, a Portuguese, who was the most approved officer for skill and courage of any employed in that service. The galeon was much larger than the *Centurion*, and had five hundred and fifty men, and thirty-six guns mounted for action, besides twenty-eight pedreroes in her gunwale, quarters, and tops, each of which carried a four-pound ball. She was very well furnished with small arms, and was particularly provided against boarding, both by her close quarters, and by a strong network of two-inch rope which was laced over her waist, and was defended by half-pikes. She had sixty-seven killed in the action, and eighty-four wounded, whilst the *Centurion* had only two killed, and a lieutenant and sixteen wounded, all of whom but one recovered: of so little consequence are the most destructive arms in untutored and unpractised hands.

The End of the Battle of Culloden, Scotland

1746

CHEVALIER JOHNSTONE

The Jacobite Rebellion of 1745, led by Prince Charles Edward Stuart (Bonnie Prince Charlie) came very close to toppling the Hanoverian regime. The rebels were finally defeated at Culloden in April 1746.

BEING NO longer able to keep myself on my legs, and the enemy always advancing very slowly but redoubling their fire, my mind was agitated and undecided whether I should throw away my life or surrender a prisoner, which was a thousand times worse than death on the field of battle. All at once I perceived a horse without a rider about thirty paces before me. The idea of being yet able to escape, gave me fresh strength and served as a spur to me. I ran and laid hold of the bridle which was fast in the hand of a man lying on the ground, whom I supposed dead. What was my surprise, when the cowardly poltroon, who was suffering from nothing but fear, dared to remain in the most horrible fire to dispute the horse with me at twenty paces from the enemy? All my menaces could not induce him to quit the bridle. Whilst we were disputing, a discharge from a cannon loaded with grape-shot fell at our feet and covered us with mud, without, however, producing any effect upon this singular individual, who obstinately persisted in retaining the horse. Fortunately for me, Finlay Cameron, an officer in Lochiel's regiment, a youth of twenty years of age, six feet high, and very strong and vigorous, happened to pass near us. I called on him to assist me. 'Ah! Finlay,' said I, 'this fellow will not give me up the horse.' Finlay flew to me like lightning, immediately presented his pistol to the head of this man and threatened to blow out his brains if he hesitated a moment to let go the bridle. The fellow, who had the appearance of a servant, at length yielded and took to his heels.

The Charms of Handel, London   CHARLES BURNEY

c.1750

The German born composer George Frideric Handel had received a life pension from Queen Anne, which was increased when George I ascended the throne. However, it was only in the last eleven years of his life that he achieved great repute, though his enjoyment of such success was blighted by the onset of blindness in 1753. Dr Burney describes Handel's 'rich' life away from music.

THE FIGURE of Handel was large and he was somewhat corpulent and unwieldy in his motions; but his countenance, which I remember as perfectly as that of any man I saw but yesterday, was full of fire and dignity, and such as impressed ideas of superiority and genius. He was impetuous, rough and peremptory in his manners and conversation, but totally devoid of ill-nature or malevolence; indeed, there was an original humour and pleasantry in his most lively sallies of anger or impatience, which, with his broken English, were extremely risible. His natural propensity to wit and humour and happy manner of relating common occurrences in an uncommon way enabled him to throw persons and things into very ridiculous attitudes. Had he been as great a master of the English language as Swift, his *bons mots* would have been as frequent and somewhat of the same kind.

Handel, with many virtues, was addicted to no vice that was injurious to society. Nature, indeed, required a great supply of sustenance to support so huge a mass, and he was rather epicurean in the choice of it; but this seems to have been the only appetite he allowed himself to gratify.

The late Mr Brown, leader of His Majesty's band, used to tell me several stories of Handel's love of good cheer, liquid and solid, as well as of his impatience. Of the former he gave an instance which was accidentally discovered at his own house in Brook Street, where Brown, in the oratorio season, among other principal performers, was at dinner. During the repast Handel often cried out – 'Oh – I have de taught'; when the company, unwilling that, out of civility to them, the public should be robbed of anything so valuable as his musical ideas, begged he would retire and write them down; with which request, however, he so frequently complied that at last one of the most suspicious had the ill-bred curiosity to peep through the keyhole into the adjoining room; where he perceived that *dese taughts* were only bestowed on a fresh hamper of Burgundy, which, as was afterward discovered, he had received as a present from his friend, the late Lord Radnor, while his company was regaled with more generous and spirited port.

c.1755

First Experience of a Slave-Ship

Olaudah Equiano

Olaudah Equiano was an African from the river Niger who was captured at the age of ten and transported as a slave to the West Indies. He wrote his autobiography from which this extract is taken.

I WAS SOON put down under the decks, and there I received such a salutation in my nostrils as I had never experienced in my life: so that with the loathsomeness of the stench and crying together, I became so sick and low that I was not able to eat, nor had I the least desire to taste anything. I now wished for the last friend, death, to relieve me; but soon, to my grief, two of the white men offered me eatables, and on my refusing to eat, one of them held me fast by the hands and laid me across I think the windlass, and tied my feet while the other flogged me severely. I had never experienced anything of this kind before, and although, not being used to the water, I naturally feared that element the first time I saw it, yet nevertheless could I have got over the nettings I would have jumped over the side, but I could not; and besides, the crew used to watch us very closely who were not chained down to the decks, lest we should leap into the water: and I have seen some of these poor African prisoners most severely cut from attempting to do so, and hourly whipped for not eating. This indeed was often the case with myself. In a little time after, amongst the poor chained men I found some of my own nation, which in a small degree gave ease to my mind. I inquired of these what was to be done with us; they gave me to understand we were to be carried to these white people's country to work for them. I then was a little revived, and thought if it were no worse than working, my situation was not so desperate: but still I feared I should be put to death, the white people looked and acted, as I thought, in so savage a manner; for I had never seen among my people such instances of brutal cruelty, and this not only shewn towards us blacks but also to some of the whites themselves. One white man in particular I saw, when we were permitted to be on deck, flogged so unmercifully with a large rope near the foremast that he died in consequence of it; and they tossed him over the side as they would have done a brute.

The Lisbon Earthquake, Portugal   MR BRADDOCK

1755

The Lisbon earthquake lasted approximately ten minutes. In its wake it left a dark cloud of stifling dust which descended upon the ruins. Fires spread throughout the city, and the river Tagus broke its banks in three huge tidal waves. Repercussions of the disturbance were felt as far away as France, the African coast and even the West Indies. Here is an extract from Mr Braddock's vivid eyewitness account.

'IT WAS ON the morning of this fatal day, between the hours of nine and ten, that I sat down in my apartment, just finishing a letter, when the papers and table I was writing on began to tremble with a gentle motion, which rather surprised me, as I could not perceive a breath of wind stirring. Whilst I was reflecting with myself what this could be owing to, but without having the least apprehension of the real cause, the whole house began to shake from the very foundation, which I at first imputed to the rattling of several coaches in the main street, which usually passed that way at this time from Belem to the palace; but on hearkening more attentively, I was soon undeceived, as I found it was owing to a strange, frightful kind of noise underground, resembling the hollow, distant rumbling of thunder. All this passed in less than a minute, and I must confess I now began to be alarmed, as it naturally occurred to me that this noise might possibly be the fore-runner of an earthquake, as one I remembered, which had happened about six or seven years ago in the island of Madeira, commenced in the same manner, though it did little or no damage.

Upon this I threw down my pen, and started up on my feet, remaining a moment in suspense whether I should stay in the apartment or run into the street, as the danger in both places seemed equal, and still flattering myself that this tremor might produce no other effects than such inconsiderable ones as had been felt at Madeira; but in a moment I was roused from my dream, being instantly stunned with a most horrid crash, as if every edifice in the city had tumbled down at once. The house I was in shook with such violence that the upper stories immediately fell, and though my apartment (which was the first floor) did not then share the same fate, yet everything was thrown out of its place in such a manner that it was with no small difficulty I kept my feet, and expected nothing less than to be soon crushed to death, as the walls continued rocking to and fro in the frightfulest manner, opening in several places, large stones falling down on every side from the cracks, and the ends of most of the rafters starting out from the roof. To add to this terrifying scene, the sky in a moment became so gloomy,

The devastation caused by the Lisbon Earthquake

that I could now distinguish no particular object; it was an Egyptian darkness indeed, such as might be felt; owing, no doubt, to the prodigious clouds of dust and lime raised from so violent a concussion, and, as some reported, to sulphurous exhalations, but this I cannot affirm; however, it is certain I found myself almost choked for near ten minutes.

As soon as the gloom began to disperse, and the violence of the shock seemed pretty much abated, the first object I perceived in the room was a woman sitting on the floor with an infant in her arms, all covered with dust, pale, and trembling. I remember the poor creature asked me, in the utmost agony, if I did not think that the world was at an end.

1758

Drunken Frivolity, Sussex, England

Thomas Turner

Thomas Turner was a highly moralistic man who regarded the age in which he lived as a degenerate one. The cause, he had little doubt, was the excessive consumption of liquor. The following passage amuses, therefore, as it describes Turner himself indulging in rather wanton jollity, then suffering a pang of guilt the next day. Thomas Turner was a shopkeeper in East Hoathly, a small village in East Sussex.

THIS MORN about 6 o'clock, just as my wife was gladly got to bed and had laid herself down to rest, we was awakened by Mrs Porter, who pretended she wanted some cream of tartar. But as soon as my wife got out of bed, she vowed she should come down, which she complied with and found she, Mr Porter, Mr Fuller and his wife with a lighted candle, part of a bottle of wine and a glass. Then the next thing in course must be to have me downstairs, which I being apprised of, fastened my door. But, however upstairs they came and threatened as also attempted to break open my door, which I found they would do; so I therefore ordered the boys to open it. But as soon as ever it was open, they poured into my room, and as modesty forbid me to get out of my bed in the presence of women, so I refrained. But their immodesty permitted them to draw me out of bed (as the common phrase is) tipsy turvy. But, however, at the intercession of Mr Porter they permitted me to put on my breeches (though it was no more than to cast a veil over what undoubtedly they had before that time discovered); as also, instead of my clothes, they gave me time to put on my wife's petticoat. In this manner they made me dance with them without shoes or stockings until they had emptied their bottle of wine and also a bottle of my beer. They then contented themselves with sitting down to breakfast on a dish of coffee etc. They then obliged my wife to accompany them to Joseph Durrant's, where they again breakfasted on tea etc. They then all adjourned to Mr Fuller's, where they again breakfasted on tea, and there they also stayed and dined; and about 3.30 they all found their ways to their respective homes, beginning by that time to be a little serious, and in my opinion ashamed of their stupid enterprise, or drunken perambulation. Now let anyone but call in reason to his assistance and seriously reflect on what I have before recited, and they must I think join with me in thinking that the precepts delivered from the pulpit on Sundays by Mr Porter, though delivered with the greatest ardour, must lose a great deal of their efficacy by such examples.

Coalminers Brush with Death, Cumberland, England JOHN WESLEY

1759

John Wesley was the founder of Methodism, which appealed in particular to the lower and middle classes. Indeed Wesley, who travelled widely during his life, was remarkably skilled at preaching to the poor, such as the 'new nation' in mining and manufacturing areas.

I INQUIRED into a signal instance of providence. When a coal-pit runs far under the ground, it is customary here to build a partition-wall, nearly from the shaft to within three or four yards of the end, in order to make the air circulate, which then moves down one side of the wall, turns at the end, and then moves briskly up on the other side. In a pit two miles from the town,

(Whitehaven) which ran full four hundred yards under the ground, and had been long neglected, several parts of this wall were fallen down. Four men were sent down to repair it. They were about three hundred yards from the shaft, when the foul air took fire. In a moment it tore down the wall from end to end, and burning on till it came to the shaft it then burst, and went off like a large cannon. The men instantly fell on their faces, or they would have been burnt to death in a few moments. One of them, who once knew the love of God, (Andrew English) began crying aloud for mercy: but in a very short time his breath was stopped. The other three crept on their hands and knees, till two got to the shaft and were drawn up; but one of them died in a few minutes: John M'Comlie was drawn up next, burnt from head to foot, but rejoicing and praising God. They then went down for Andrew, whom they found senseless, the very circumstance which saved his life: for, losing his senses, he lay flat on the ground, and the greatest part of the fire went over him; whereas had he gone forward on his hands and knees, he would undoubtedly have been burnt to death. But life or death was welcome; for God had restored the light of his countenance.

1763

A Rake in London   JAMES BOSWELL

Boswell, the biographer of Dr Samuel Johnson, was also a reluctant lawyer and an enthusiastic man-about-town, with a keen appetite for amorous affairs. Here he relates, with some relish, his final seduction of an actress, Mrs Louisa Lewis. Unfortunately he contracted from his brief liaison one of many venereal infections which were eventually to cause his death from kidney failure.

I CAME SOFTLY into the room, and in a sweet delirium slipped into bed and was immediately clasped in her snowy arms and pressed to her milk-white bosom. Good heavens, what a loose did we give to amorous dalliance! The friendly curtain of darkness concealed our blushes. In a moment I felt myself animated with the strongest powers of love, and, from my dearest creature's kindness, had a most luscious feast. Proud of my godlike vigour, I soon resumed the noble game. I was in full glow of health. Sobriety had preserved me from effeminacy and weakness, and my bounding blood beat quick and high alarms. A more voluptuous night I never enjoyed. Five times was I fairly lost in supreme rapture. Louisa was madly fond of me; she declared I was a prodigy, and asked me if this was not extraordinary for human nature. I said twice as much might be, but this was not, although in my own mind I was somewhat proud of my performance. She said it was what there was no just reason to be proud of. But I told her I could not help it. She said it was what we had in common with the beasts. I said no. For we had it highly improved by the pleasures of sentiment. I asked her what she thought enough. She gently chid me for asking such questions, but said two times. I mentioned the Sunday's assignation, when I was in such bad spirits, told her in what agony of mind I was, and asked her if she would not have despised me for my imbecility. She declared she would not, as it was what people had not in their own power.

She often insisted that we should compose ourselves to sleep before I would consent to it. At last I sunk to rest in her arms and she in mine. I found the negus, which had a fine flavour, very refreshing to me. Louisa had an exquisite mixture of delicacy and wantonness that made me enjoy her with more relish. Indeed I could not help roving in fancy to the embraces of some other ladies which my lively imagination strongly pictured. I don't know if that was altogether fair. However, Louisa had all the advantage. She said she was quite fatigued and could neither stir leg nor arm. She begged I would not despise her, and hoped my love would not be altogether transient. I have painted this night as well as I could. The description is faint; but I surely may be styled a Man of Pleasure.

Attack on Fort Michillimackinac, Great Lakes, Canada ALEXANDER HENRY

1763

In the spring of 1763 an Ottawa chief, Pontiac, organised an alliance of tribes in the Great Lakes to drive out the white immigrants then beginning to settle the area in significant numbers. The attack opened on Fort Michillimackinac under cover of a game of lacrosse. This vivid account is by a trader present in the fort and captured by the Indians.

Mr TRACY had not gone more than twenty paces from the door, when I heard an Indian war-cry, and a noise of general confusion.

Going instantly to my window, I saw a crowd of Indians within the fort, furiously cutting down and scalping every Englishman they found. In particular, I witnessed the fate of Lieutenant Jemette. I had, in the room in which I was, a fowling-piece, loaded with swan-shot. This I immediately seized, and held it for a few moments, waiting to hear the drum beat to arms. In this dreadful interval I saw several of my countrymen fall, and more than one struggling between the knees of an Indian, who, holding him in this manner, scalped him while yet living.

At length, disappointed in the hope of seeing resistance made to the enemy, and sensible, of course, that no effort of my own unassisted arm could avail against four hundred Indians, I thought only of seeking shelter.

Amid the slaughter which was raging, I observed many of the Canadian inhabitants of the fort calmly looking on, neither opposing the Indians nor suffering injury. From this circumstance I conceived a hope of finding security in their houses.

A Paris woman of M. Langlade's household beckoned me to follow her. She brought me to a door, which she opened, desiring me to enter, and telling me that it led to a garret, where I must go and conceal myself. I joyfully obeyed her directions; and she, having followed me up to the garret door, locked it after me, and with great presence of mind took away the key.

This shelter obtained, if shelter I could hope to find it, I was naturally anxious to know what might still be passing without. Through an aperture which afforded me a view of the area of the fort, I beheld, in shapes the foulest and most terrible, the ferocious triumphs of barbarian conquerors. The dead were scalped and mangled; the dying were writhing and shrieking under the unsatiated knife and tomahawk, amidst the shouts of rage and victory. I was shaken not only with horror at the sight, but with terror for myself. The sufferings which I witnessed, I seemed to be on the point of experiencing. No long time elapsed before, everyone being destroyed who could be found, there was a general cry of 'All is finished!' And, at the same instant, I heard some of the Indians enter the house in which I was.

1765

James Watt's Improved Steam Engine, England

JOHN ROBISON

The mathematician John Robison met James Watt, the engineer, at Glasgow University. He encouraged Watt to improve on existing versions of the steam engine, work which bore fruit with his invention of a separate condenser to conserve steam power.

James Watt studies the improvement of the steam engine

I WAS VERY anxious, however, to learn what Mr Watt had contrived, but was obliged to go to the country in the evening. A gentleman who was going to the same house said he would give me a place in his carriage, and desired me to wait for him on the walk by the river-side. I went thither, and found Mr Alexander Brown, a very intimate acquaintance of Mr Watt's, walking with another gentleman, (Mr Craig, architect). Mr Brown immediately accosted me with, 'Well, have you seen Jamie Watt?' – 'Yes.' – 'He'll be in high spirits now with his engine, isn't he?' 'Yes,' said I, 'very fine spirits.' 'Gad,' says Mr Brown, 'the condenser's the thing: keep it but cold enough, and you may have perfect vacuum, whatever be the heat of the cylinder.' The instant he said this, the whole flashed on my mind at once. I did all I could to encourage the conversation, but was much embarrassed. I durst not appear ignorant of the apparatus, lest Mr Brown should find he had communicated more than he ought to have done. I could only learn that there was a vessel called a condenser, which communicated with the cylinder, and that this condenser was immersed in cold water, and had a pump to clear it of the water which was formed in it. I also learned that the great difficulty was to make the piston tight; and that leather and felt had been tried, and were found quite unable to stand the heat. I saw that the whole would be perfectly dry, and that Mr Watt had used steam instead of air to press up his piston, which I thought, by Mr Brown's description was inverted. We parted, and I went home, a very silent companion to the gentleman who had given me a seat. Next day, impatient to see the effects of the separate condensation, I sent to Paisley and got some tin things made there, in completion of the notion I had formed. I tried it as an air-pump, by making my steam-vessel communicate with a tea-kettle, a condenser, and a glass receiver. In less than two minutes I rarefied the air in a pretty large receiver more than twenty times. I could go no farther in this process, because my pump for taking out the air from my condenser was too large, and not tight enough; but I saw that when applied to the mere process of taking out the air generated from the water, the vacuum might be made almost complete. I saw, too, (inconsequence of a conversation the preceding day with Mr Watt about the eduction-pipe in Beighton's engine), that a long suck-pipe, or syphon, would take off all the water. In short, I had no doubt that Mr Watt had really made a perfect steam-engine.

Prodigious Ability of Mozart, England

DAINES BARRINGTON

1765

The violinist and composer Leopold Mozart took his young son, Wolfgang Amadeus, on a European tour in 1763, exhibiting his remarkably prodigious musical talent in Germany, Belgium, Paris, London and Holland. It was during his stay in London (1764–5) that the philosopher Daines Barrington rigorously tested the boy Mozart, presenting his report to the Royal Society in 1769–70.

HAVING BEEN informed that he was often visited with musical ideas, to which, even in the midst of the night, he would give utterance on his harpsichord; I told his father that I should be glad to hear some of his extemporary compositions.

The father shook his head at this, saying, that it depended entirely upon his being as it were musically inspired, but that I might ask him whether he was in humour for such a composition.

Happening to know that little Mozart was much taken notice of by Manzoli, the famous singer, who came over to England in 1764, I said to the boy, that I should be glad to hear an extemporary *Love Song*, such as his friend Manzoli might choose in an opera.

The boy on this (who continued to sit at his harpsichord) looked back with much archness, and immediately began five or six lines of a jargon recitative proper to introduce a love song.

He then played a symphony which might correspond with an air composed to the single word, *Affetto*.

·It had a first and second part, which, together with the symphonies, was of the length that opera songs generally last: if this extemporary composition was not amazingly capital, yet it was really above mediocrity, and shewed most extraordinary readiness of invention.

Finding he was in humour, and as it were inspired, I then desired him to compose a *Song of Rage*, such as might be proper for the opera stage.

The boy again looked back with much archness, and began five or six lines of a jargon recitative proper to precede a *Song of Anger*.

This lasted also about the same time with the *Song of Love*; and in the middle of it, he had worked himself up to such a pitch, that he beat his harpsichord like a person possessed, rising sometimes in his chair.

Witness as I was myself of most of these extraordinary facts, I must own that I could not help suspecting his father imposed with regard to the real age of the boy, through he had not only a most childish appearance, but likewise had all the actions of that stage of life.

For example, whilst he was playing to me, a favourite cat came in, upon which he immediately left his harpsichord, nor could we bring him back for a considerable time.

He would also sometimes run about the room with a stick between his legs by way of a horse. . . .

1766

Ball Room Rules, Bath, England

REVD JOHN PENROSE

Bath had been a fashionable spa town since the beginning of the 18th century, and owed much to Beau Nash's organisation and disciplining of it. A place where the cost of living was high and the luxury trade prosperous, the following passage by a Cornish parson reveals one manifestation of Bath's fashion and elegance.

NO CHAIR or Bench can be called on Ball Nights for any person, who does not rank as a Peer or Peeress of Great Britain or Ireland.

No Lady can be permitted to dance Minuets, without a Lappet head, and full-dress long Hoop, such as are permitted to dance Minuets at Court.

No Lady can be permitted to dance Country Dances with an Hoop of any kind; and those that chuse to pull their Hoops off, will always find a servant maid ready to assist them, and a proper Place to retire to for that purpose.

The Master of the Ceremonies is under a Necessity of causing all Ladies infringing on this Rule, to sit down.

No Lady, be her Rank or Quality ever so high, has a Right to take place in Country Dances after they have been begun.

Every Gentleman chusing to dance Minuets, must present himself in a full Dress, or a French Frock Suit compleat, and a Bag wig.

Officers Regimentals are an Exception to this Rule, being every where proper; but every other kind of Lapel is improper for a minuet, at Bath.

It is recommended to the Gentlemen frequenting the Rooms to remember that leather Breeches are by no means suitable to the Decorum of the Place.

Before the French Dances begin, such Ladies as chuse to dance minuets, are desired to acquaint the Master of the Ceremonies with their Names and Intention.

Gentlemen are requested not to stand between the Ladies sitting down and the Country Dancers, the Benches being brought forward solely for the use of the Ladies, and sufficient Space left for the Gentlemen to pass thro' behind.

The Music is always to be dismissed as soon as the Clock strikes Eleven.

No Ladies with Hats can be admitted into the Rooms at Bath, be their Rank or Quality ever so high, during the Season.

No large Screens can be brought to any Card-Party in the Rooms on any account, as they not only divide the company into secluded Setts, which is against the fundamental Institution of these Places, but occasion such a Draught of Air, as is not only disagreeable to the rest of the Company, but often detrimental. There are small Screens provided for such Individuals as complain of Cold.

A Tahitian Funeral Ceremony Sir Joseph Banks

1769

Though something of a prima donna, Joseph Banks was a pioneer of naturalist voyagers in his capacity to absorb himself in the cultures he encountered. For example, he rapidly mastered the language of the Otahitans and, as he describes here, even performed a character in a native funeral ceremony, alongside the Heiva no Metua *(chief mourner of the dead).*

THIS EVENING, according to my yesterday's engagement, I went to the place where the *Metua* lay; there I found Tubourai, Tamio, Hoona, the *Metua's* daughter, and a young Indian prepared to receive me. Tubourai was the *Heiva*, the three others and myself were to be *Nineveh*. Tubourai put on his most fantastical though not unbecoming dress. I was next prepared by stripping off my European clothes and putting on a small strip of cloth round my waist, the only garment I was allowed to have. They then began to smut me and themselves with charcoal and water, the Indian boy was completely black, the women and myself as low as our shoulders; we then set out. Tubourai began by praying twice, once near the corpse, and again near his own house. We then proceeded towards the fort; it was necessary, it seems, that the procession should visit that place, but they dare not do it without our sanction, indeed it was not until they had received many assurances of our consent that they ventured to perform any part of their ceremonies.

To the fort then we went, to the surprise of our friends and affright of the

Indians who were there, for they everywhere fly before the *Heiva*, like sheep before a wolf; we soon left it and proceeded along shore towards a place where above a hundred Indians were collected together. We, the *Ninevehs*, had orders from the *Heiva* to disperse them; we ran towards them, but before we came within a hundred yards of them they dispersed every way, running to the first shelter and hiding themselves under grass or whatever else would conceal them. We now crossed the river into the woods and passed several houses, all deserted; not another Indian did we see during the half-hour that we spent in walking about. We (the *Ninevehs*) then came to the *Heiva* and said *imatata* (there are no people), after which we repaired home; the *Heiva* undressed, and we went into the river and scrubbed one another until it was dark, before the blacking came off.

1769

A Duel Between Two Cadets, Comoro Islands

WILLIAM HICKEY

Duelling, in spite of many attempts to outlaw it, was almost universal in Europe up to the 1830s. The outcome, however, was not always as harmless as in this case!

THE CEREMONY of loading the pistols by the seconds being finished, they next spoke of distance, the doctor proposing six paces! upon which both violently protested against being so near, one of them saying he understood thirty yards was the usual space. The seconds told them the pistols would not carry much further. After much argument and discussion, it was resolved that twelve paces should be the distance. This the parties concerned pronounced absolute butchery. They, nevertheless, were obliged to yield, and finding that to be the case, insisted that the fourth mate, who had much longer legs than the deputy surgeon, should measure the space; and he accordingly did so. The antagonists were then desired to take their stations, there being no time to spare. The object the principals appeared to have in view was to squabble and dispute until it really became too late to fight; but the seconds, seeing that, insisted upon their presenting and discharging their pistols at each other upon the word being given. Unwillingly they took their respective stations, when one of them turned to his second, saying his antagonist owed him forty dollars, and it was very hard that he should be obliged to risk his money as well as his life. This created another pause, but was settled by the seconds engaging, in the event of the debtor being slain, that he would pay to the survivor the amount due, gravely adding, he conceived he was not in much danger of being called upon, as in all probability two such desperate champions would both end their lives upon the spot. The poor devils, not being able to devise any further mode of delay, and the signal being given to fire, they did so in the same moment, when to our surprise and alarm down dropped one of them, apparently dead.

This led us to apprehend that the seconds had not kept the private agreement, or at least that one of them had loaded with ball. We all ran up to the prostrate youth, and had the satisfaction to find him unhurt, having fallen through sheer terror. A glass of brandy from the pocket flask of one of the company soon restored him, when he positively declared he heard the ball whizz by close to his ear, which he thought it had hit. The combatants were then congratulated upon the gallantry they had both shown and were assured that they had done all that was required of men of honour and gentlemen, upon which they shook hands, mutually rejoiced at having got so well out of a dangerous scrape.

Cannibalism and Human Trophies, New Zealand SIR JOSEPH BANKS

1770

It is evident from Captain Cook's own journal of his first voyage round the world of the importance of Banks to his expedition to the Southern Hemisphere. It was he who investigated the native customs and language of New Zealand – his skills as interpreter for the party were often essential to their receiving food. Despite evidence of native barbarity, such as in the following passage, voyages of exploration ultimately transformed the European view of primitive society.

THAT THEY eat the bodies of such of their enemies as are killed in war, is a fact which they universally acknowledged from our first landing at every place we came to. It was confirmed by an old man, whom we supposed to be the chief of an Indian town very near us, bringing at our desire six or seven heads of men, preserved with the flesh on. These it seems the people keep, after having eaten the brains, as trophies of their victories, in the same manner as the Indians of North America do scalps; they had their ornaments in their ears as when alive, and some seemed to have false eyes. The old man was very jealous of showing them; one I bought, but much against the inclination of its owner, for though he liked the price I offered, he hesitated much to send it up; yet, having taken the price, I insisted either on having that returned or the head given, but could not prevail until I enforced my threats by showing him a musket, on which he chose to part with the head rather than the price he had, which was a pair of old drawers of my white linen. The head appeared to have belonged to a person of about fourteen or fifteen years of age, and evidently showed, by the contusions on one side, that it had received many violent blows which had chipped off a part of the skull near the eye. From this, and many other circumstances, I am inclined to believe that these Indians give no quarter, or even take prisoners to eat upon a future occasion, as is said to have been practised by the Floridan Indians; for had they done so, this young creature, who could not make much resistance, would have been a very proper subject.

1770

Dealing with a Smuggler, England

William Hickey

Smuggling of tea, spirits, playing cards and other heavily taxed items, was as much of a problem in the 18th century as drug smuggling is today, and as profitable. Many sea captains brought back cargoes of tea from China and, as in this account, transferred them to smugglers while at sea, thus avoiding the Revenue Men.

THE TEA being all removed to the cutter pen, ink, and paper was produced; the smuggler, sitting down at a table in the round house, calculated the amount due for his purchase; which Captain Waddell admitting correct, he took from his pocket-book a cheque, which filled up for twelve hundred and twenty-four pounds he signed and delivered it to the captain. I observed it was drawn upon Walpole and Company, Bankers in Lombard Street, and was astonished to see Captain Waddell with the utmost composure deposit it in his escritoire. The smuggler then being asked whether he chose a glass of wine or would stay dinner, he answered he could not afford to lose a minute; so must be off; but would take a *drap* of brandy. The liquor being brought, he chucked off a bumper, the servant directly filling a second. 'That's right, my good fellow,' said he, 'always wet both eyes.' He swallowed the second and returned to his cutter. The moment he departed, I asked Captain Waddell whether he felt secure in a draft for so large a sum by such a man as that; to which he answered, 'Perfectly, and wish it was for ten times as much; it would be duly paid. These people always deal with the strictest honour. If they did not, their business would cease.' For what he purchased from the officers he paid in guineas, to the amount of upward of eight hundred.

1773

A Feast with Musquito Indians, South America

Olaudah Equiano

Travelling on behalf of his employer, the freed slave, Olaudah Equiano, arrived at the Mosquito Coast (present-day Belize) and gives an entertaining account of the eating habits of the local population.

OPPOSITE PAGE The Frost Fair on the Thames by A. Hondius 1684

OPPOSITE PAGE 115 The death of Captain Cook in 1779 by J. Cleveley

WE HAD timely notice given to us of the entertainment. A white family within five miles of us told us how the drink was made, and I and two others went before the time to the village where the mirth was appointed to be held, and there we saw the whole art of making the drink and also the kind of animals that were to be eaten there. I cannot say the sight of either the drink or the meat were enticing to me. They had some thousands of pineapples roasting, which they squeezed, dirt and all, into a canoe they had there for the purpose.

The casade drink was in beef barrels and other vessels and looked exactly like hog-wash. Men, women and children were thus employed in roasting the pine-apples and squeezing them with their hands. For food they had many land torpins or tortoises, some dried turtle, and three large alligators alive, and tied fast to the trees. I asked the people what they were going to do with these alligators, and I was told they were to be eaten. I was much surprised at this, and went home not a little disgusted at the preparations. The alligators were killed and some of them roasted. Their manner of roasting is by digging a hole in the earth and filling it with wood, which they burn to coal, and then they lay sticks across on which they set the meat. I had a raw piece of the alligator in my hand. It was very rich. I thought it looked like fresh salmon, and it had a most fragrant smell, but I could not eat any of it.

Dr Johnson in the Highlands, Scotland

1773

JAMES BOSWELL

Dr Samuel Johnson, poet, polemicist, writer and savant, was accompanied by his friend and biographer, James Boswell, on a trip to the Highlands of Scotland. A culture more different from 18th-century England could hardly be imagined.

WE HAD A considerable circle about us, men, women, and children, all M'Craas, Lord Seaforth's people. Not one of them could speak English. I observed to Dr Johnson, it was much the same as being with a tribe of Indians. JOHNSON. 'Yes, Sir, but not so terrifying.' I gave all who chose it snuff and tobacco. I also gave each person a piece of wheat bread, which they had never tasted before. I then gave a penny apiece to each child. I told Dr Johnson of this: upon which he called to Joseph and our guides, for change for a shilling, and declared that he would distribute among the children. Upon this being announced in Erse, there was a great stir; not only did some children come running down from neighbouring huts, but I observed one black-haired man, who had been with us all along, had gone off, and returned, bringing a very young child. My fellow-traveller then ordered the children to be drawn up in a row, and he dealt about his copper, and made them and their parents all happy.

There was great diversity in the faces of the circle around us; some were as black and wild in their appearance

Dr Samuel Johnson (1709–84)

as any American savages whatever. One woman was as comely almost as the figure of Sappho, as we see it painted. We asked the old woman, the mistress of the house where we had the milk (which, by the by, Dr Johnson told me, for I did not observe it myself, was built not of turf, but of stone), what we would pay. She said what we pleased. One of our guides asked her, in Erse, if a shilling was enough. She said, 'Yes.' But some of the men bade her ask more. This vexed me; because it showed desire to impose upon strangers, as they knew that even a shilling was high payment. The woman, however, honestly persisted in her first price; so I gave her half a crown. Thus we had one good scene of life uncommon to us. The people were very much pleased, gave us many blessings, and said they had not had such a day since the old Laird of Macleod's time.

Treatment of Slaves, Surinam JOHN STEDMAN

1773

A slave rebellion in Surinam (Dutch Guiana) brought the author of this extract to the colony as a mercenary soldier in Dutch service.

INSTEAD OF gaiety and dissipation, disease and mortality now began to rage among us, and the devastation increased from day to day among the private men in a most alarming proportion. The remains of the deceased officer were interred with military honours in the centre of the fortress Zelandia, where all criminals are imprisoned and all field officers buried. At this place I was not a little shocked to see the captive rebel negroes and others clanking their chains, and roasting plantains and yams upon the sepulchres of the dead; they presented to my imagination, the image of a number of diabolical fiends in the shape of African slaves, tormenting the souls of their European persecutors. From these gloomy mansions of despair, on this day, seven captive negroes were selected, who being led by a few soldiers to the place of execution, which is in the savannah where the sailors and soldiers are interred, six were hanged and one broken alive upon the rack with an iron bar; besides which a white man was scourged before the court house by the public executioner, who is in this country always a black. The circumstance which led me to take particular notice of this affair, was the shameful injustice of showing a partiality to the European, who ought to have been better informed, by letting him escape with only a slight corporal punishment, while the poor uneducated African for the same crime – stealing money out of the Town Hall – lost his life under the most excruciating torments, which he supported without heaving a sigh or making a complaint. One of his companions, with the rope about his neck and just on the point of being turned off, uttered a laugh of contempt at the magistrates who attended the execution. I ought not in this place to omit that the negro who flogged the white man inflicted the punishment with the greatest marks of commiseration. These transactions almost induced me to decide between the Europeans and Africans in this colony, that the first were the greater barbarians of the two.

Publication of Edward Gibbon's *Decline and Fall*, London   EDWARD GIBBON

Published in the same year as the American Declaration of Independence, the first volume of Gibbon's account of the Roman Empire, Decline and Fall, *struck at the whole question of the viability of empire. The following passage reveals that Gibbon did not anticipate the huge success of his work, nor the heated debate it would foster, particularly through its sceptical attitude to Christianity.*

THE VOLUME of my *History*, which had been somewhat delayed by the novelty and tumult of a first session, was now ready for the press. After the perilous adventure had been declined by my timid friend Mr Elmsley, I agreed, upon very easy terms, with Mr Thomas Cadell, a respectable bookseller, and Mr William Strahan, an eminent printer; and they undertook the care and risk of the publication, which derived more credit from the name of the shop than from that of the author. The last revisal of the proofs was submitted to my vigilance; and many blemishes of style, which had been invisible in the manuscript, were discovered and corrected in the printed sheet. So moderate were our hopes, that the original impression had been stinted to five hundred, till the number was doubled by the prophetic taste of Mr Strahan. During this awful interval I was neither elated by the ambition of fame, nor depressed by the apprehension of contempt. My diligence and accuracy were attested by my own conscience. History is the most popular species of writing, since it can adapt itself to the highest or the lowest capacity. I had chosen an illustrious subject. Rome is familiar to the schoolboy and the statesman; and my narrative was deduced from the last period of classical reading. I had likewise flattered myself, that an age of light and liberty would receive, without scandal, an inquiry into the human *causes* of the progress and establishment of Christianity.

A Skirmish in the American Revolution

JOSEPH MARTIN

Martin joined the American Revolutionary Army at the start of the war in 1776 and served throughout until peace in 1783. This account of one of his early battles gives a foretaste of his main preoccupation – food and how to get enough of it!

OUR REGIMENT was now ordered into the field, and we arrived on the ground just as the retreating enemy were entering a thick wood, a circumstance as disagreeable to them as it was agreeable to us at that period of the war. We soon came to action with them. The troops engaged, being reinforced by our regiment, kept them still retreating until they found shelter under the cannon of some of their shipping lying in the North River.

We remained on the battleground till nearly sunset, expecting the enemy to attack us again, but they showed no such inclination that day. The men were very much fatigued and faint, having had nothing to eat for forty-eight hours; at least, the greater part were in this condition, and I among the rest. While standing on the field after the action had ceased, one of the men near the lieutenant colonel complained of being hungry. The colonel, putting his hand into his coat pocket, took out a piece of an ear of Indian corn burnt as black as a coal. 'Here,' said he to the man complaining, 'eat this and learn to be a soldier.'

1777

A Tahitian Massage, Tahiti   CAPTAIN JAMES COOK

Captain Cook embarked on his first voyage round the world in HMS Endeavour in 1768. Cook, like many other explorers before him, discovered native methods of healing and realised that they were not without their uses.

I NOW RETURNED on board my ship, attended by Otoo's mother, his three sisters, and eight more women. At first I thought that this numerous train of females came into my boat with no other view than to get a passage to Matavai. But when we arrived at the ship they told me they intended passing the night on board for the express purpose of undertaking the cure of the disorder I had complained of, which was a pain of the rheumatic kind. I accepted the friendly offer, had a bed spread for them upon the cabin floor, and submitted myself to their directions. They began to squeeze me with both hands from head to foot, but more particularly on the parts where the pain was lodged, till they made my bones crack, and my flesh became a perfect mummy. In short, after undergoing this discipline about a quarter of an hour, I was glad to get away from them. However, the operation gave me immediate relief, which encouraged me to submit to another rubbing down before I went to bed, and it was so effectual that I found myself pretty easy all the night after. My female physicians repeated their prescription the next morning before they went ashore, and again in the evening when they returned on board; after which I found the pains entirely removed, and the cure being perfected, they took their leave of me the following morning. This they call romee; an operation which, in my opinion, far exceeds the flesh-brush or anything of the kind that we make use of externally. It is universally practised amongst these islanders, being sometimes performed by the men, but more generally by the women.

The Death of Captain Cook, Hawaii

CAPTAIN JAMES KING

Cook's three voyages of discovery to the South Seas made him the most famous explorer and navigator of his day. His death at the hands of Hawaiians however, was largely his own fault due to his tactless handling of a series of thefts by curious natives eager to sample the strangers' goods.

THE BOATS, which had been stationed across the bay, having fired at some canoes that were attempting to get out, unfortunately had killed a chief of the first rank. The news of his death arrived at the village where Captain Cook was, just as he had left the king and was walking slowly toward the shore. The ferment it occasioned was very conspicuous; the women and children were immediately sent off, and the men put on their war mats, and armed themselves with spears and stones. One of the natives, having in his hands a stone and a long iron spike (which they called a pahooa), came up to the Captain, flourishing his weapon by way of defiance, and threatening to throw the stone. The Captain desired him to desist, but the man persisting in his insolence, he was at length provoked to fire a load of small shot. The man having his mat on, which the shot was not able to penetrate, this had no other effect than to irritate and encourage them. Several stones were thrown at the marines, and one of the earees attempted to stab Mr Phillips with his pahooa, but failed in the attempt, and received from him a blow with the but-end of his musket. Captain Cook now fired his second barrel loaded with ball, and killed one of the foremost of the natives. A general attack with stones immediately followed, which was answered by a discharge of musketry from the marines and the people in the boats. The islanders, contrary to the expectations of every one, stood the fire with great firmness; and before the marines had time to reload, they broke in upon them with dreadful shouts and yells. What followed was a scene of the utmost horror and confusion.

Four of the marines were cut off amongst the rocks in their retreat, and fell a sacrifice to the fury of the enemy; three more were dangerously wounded, and the lieutenant, who had received a stab between the shoulders with a pahooa, having fortunately reserved his fire, shot the man who had wounded him just as he was going to repeat his blow. Our unfortunate commander, the last time he was seen distinctly, was standing at the water's edge, and calling out to the boats to cease firing and to pull in. Whilst he faced the natives none of them had offered him any violence, but having turned about to give his orders to the boats, he was stabbed in the back and fell with his face into the water. On seeing him fall, the islanders set up a great shout, and his body was immediately dragged on shore and surrounded by the enemy, who, snatching the dagger out of each other's hands, shewed a savage eagerness to have a share in his destruction.

1780

The Gordon Riots, London   GEORGE CRABBE

In July 1780, the London mob, incited by the half-mad Lord George Gordon, rioted against Catholics. Several hundred people were killed, untold damage caused, and the army called in to restore order.

BY EIGHT o'clock, Akerman's house was in flames. I went close to it, and never saw any thing so dreadful. The prison was, as I said, a remarkably strong building; but, determined to force it, they broke the gates with crows and other instruments, and climbed up the outside of the cell part, which joins the two great wings of the building, where the felons were confined; and I stood where I plainly saw their operations. They broke the roof, tore away the rafters, and having got ladders they descended. Not Orpheus himself had more courage or better luck; flames all around them, and a body of soldiers expected, they defied and laughed at all opposition.

The prisoners escaped. I stood and saw about twelve women and eight men ascend from their confinement to the open air, and they were conducted through the street in their chains. Three of these were to be hanged on Friday. You have no conception of the phrensy of the multitude. This being done, and Akerman's

The Gordon Riots at Newgate, 1780

house now a mere shall of brickwork, they kept a store of flame there for other purposes. It became red-hot, and the doors and windows appeared like the entrance to so many volcanoes. With some difficulty they then fired the debtor's prison – broke the doors – and they, too, all made their escape.

But I must not omit what struck me most. About ten or twelve of the mob getting to the top of the debtors' prison, whilst it was burning, to halloo, they appeared rolled in black smoke mixed with sudden bursts of fire – like Milton's infernals, who were as familiar with flame as with each other. On comparing notes with my neighbours, I find I saw but a small part of the mischief. They say Lord Mansfield's house is now in flames.

Surrender at Yorktown, Virginia, America

JOHANN CONRAD DOHLA

1781

The surrender of British forces at Yorktown on 18 October 1781 was the culminating event of the American Revolutionary War. It convinced the British government that they could not hope to win the war, which was concluded in 1784 by the Treaty of Paris. This account is by a German mercenary soldier who was a member of the garrison.

ALL TROOPS during the last fourteen days have received much sugar and chocolate, or cocoa, as the English call it, with the daily ration. These were taken from a Dutch merchant ship that the English captured and divided among the regiments. We drank chocolate three, four or even more times a day. Also, we ate it with sugar on bread, but still could not use it all. It served us well during the present sleepless work and fatigue, which we had day and night with the greatest danger to our lives.

19 October   The unfortunate day for England when the otherwise so famous and brave General Lord Cornwallis, with all his troops and the ships in the harbour, had to surrender to the united French and American troops under the command of General Washington, and the Marquis de Lafayette,

On this day, in the morning, I went for the last time on the engineer watch. At twelve o'clock noon all watches and posts were cancelled. Only a regimental watch of one sergeant with twelve men remained on duty a few hours more.

Now the capitulation was final.

The French and Americans immediately occupied our works and the line and all magazines and storehouses.

Nothing of our equipment and uniform items was taken or even touched; instead we were treated according to law and fairness and the customs of war.

We were, on one side, happy that finally this siege was ended, and that it was done with a reasonable accord, because we always believed we would be taken by storm. If it had continued only a few more days, it would really have resulted in a major attack, because the French Grenadiers already had such orders.

A Captive of the Shawnee, Ohio, America

1782

JOHN GLOVER

Glover was captured at the age of eight by Miami Indians and lived with them until the age of twenty when he returned to his former life. Because of his first-hand knowledge of the Indians he was often employed as a scout. In an expedition against villages on the Sandusky River he was captured by Shawnees and threatened with burning to death, the usual fate of white prisoners at the time.

BEING brought to the post, I had my arms tied behind me anew, and the thong or cord with which they were bound was fastened to the post. A fresh rope was put about my neck and also tied to the post about four feet above my head. During the time they were tying me, the piles were kindled and began to flame. Death by burning, which now appeared to be my certain fate, I had resolved to sustain with patience. The grace of God had made it less alarming to me; for on my way this day, I had been greatly exercised in regard to my latter end.

I was tied to the post as I have already said, and the flame was now kindled. The day was clear, and not a cloud to be seen: if there were clouds low in the horizon, the sides of the house prevented me from seeing them, but I heard no thunder, nor observed any sign of approaching rain. Just as the fire of one pile began to blaze, the wind rose. From the time when they began to kindle the fire and to tie me to the post, until the wind began to blow, about fifteen minutes had elapsed. The wind blew a hurricane, and the rain followed in less than three minutes. The rain fell violently, and the fire, though it began to blaze considerably, was instantly extinguished. The rain lasted about a quarter of an hour.

When the storm was over, the savages stood amazed, and were a long time silent. At last one said, 'We will let him alone till morning, and take a whole day's frolic in burning him.' The sun at this time was about three hours high. The rope about my neck was now untied, and, making me sit down, they began to dance around me. They continued dancing in this manner until eleven o'clock at night, in the meantime beating, kicking, and wounding me with their tomahawks and clubs.

Lunardi's Balloon Voyage, London

1784

VINCENT LUNARDI

Lunardi had originally planned to undertake the first aerial voyage in England with an assistant. However, at the last minute it became evident that the balloon could only take up one man, incurring incredulity and scorn of the observing masses, who considered Lunardi a lunatic, according to puns in the contemporary press.

Lunardi's Balloon

I NOW DETERMINED on my immediate ascension, being assured by the dread of any accident which might consign me and my Balloon to the fury of the populace, whose impatience had wrought them up to a degree of ferment. An affecting, because unpremeditated testimony of approbation and interest in my fate, was here given. The Prince of Wales, and the whole surrounding assembly, almost at one instant, took off their hats, hailed my resolution, and expressed the kindest and most cordial wishes for my safety and success. At five minutes after two, the last gun was fired, the cords divided, and the Balloon rose, the company returning my signals of adieu with the most unfeigned acclamations and applauses. The effect was that of a miracle on the multitudes which surrounded the place; and they passed from incredulity and menace, into the most extravagant expressions of approbation and joy.

At the height of twenty yards, the Balloon was a little depressed by the wind, which had a fine effect; it held me over the ground for a few seconds, and seemed to pause majestically before its departure.

On discharging a part of the ballast, it ascended to the height of two hundred yards. As a multitude lay before me of a hundred and fifty thousand people, who had not seen my ascent from the ground, I had recourse to every stratagem to let them know I was in the gallery, and they literally rent the air with their acclamations and applause.

Flight from Mad King George III, Kew Gardens, London FANNY BURNEY

1789

Fanny Burney was born into the elite social and intellectual circles of acquaintance in London. In 1786 she was offered the much sought-after court post of Second Keeper of the Robes to the Queen, which she reluctantly accepted to please her father. The following extract from her diary provides a comical incident of court life during the King's supposed madness.

THIS MORNING, when I received my intelligence of the King from Dr John Willis, I begged to know where I might walk in safety? 'In Kew Gardens,' he said, 'as the King would be in Richmond.'

'Should any unfortunate circumstance,' I cried, 'at any time, occasion my being seen by his Majesty, do not mention my name, but let me run off without call or notice.'

This he promised. Everybody, indeed, is ordered to keep out of sight.

Taking, therefore, the time I had most at command, I strolled into the gardens. I had proceeded, in my quick way, nearly half the round, when I suddenly perceived, through some trees, two or three figures. Relying on the instructions of Dr John, I concluded them to be workmen and gardeners; yet tried to look sharp, and in so doing, as they were less shaded, I thought I saw the person of his Majesty!

Alarmed past all possible expression, I waited not to know more, but turning back, ran off with all my might. But what was my terror to hear myself pursued! – to hear the voice of the King himself loudly and hoarsely calling after me: 'Miss Burney! Miss Burney!'

Soon after, I heard other voices, shriller, though less nervous, call out: 'Stop! stop! stop!'

As they approached, some little presence of mind happily came to my command: it occurred to me that, to appease the wrath of my flight, I must now show some confidence: I therefore faced them as undauntedly as I was able, only charging the nearest of the attendants to stand by my side.

When they were within a few yards of me, the King called out: 'Why did you run away?'

Shocked at a question impossible to answer, yet a little assured by the mild tone of his voice, I instantly forced myself forward, to meet him, though the internal sensation, which satisfied me this was a step the most proper to appease his suspicions and displeasure, was so violently combated by the tremor of my nerves, that I fairly think I may reckon it the greatest effort of personal courage I have ever made.

The effort answered: I looked up, and met all his wonted benignity of countenance, though something still of wildness in his eyes. Think, however, of my surprise, to feel him put both his hands round my two shoulders, and then kiss my cheek!

Mutiny on HMS *Bounty*, South Pacific

WILLIAM BLIGH

1789

Lt William Bligh was given command of HMS Bounty in 1787 with Admiralty orders to procure bread-fruit trees from the South Sea Islands as a source of food for the West India Islands. In the event, unexpectedly, the voyage became one of the most notorious in history: corrupted by a five-month stop-off in Tahiti, in which time the crew was largely idle and indulged by native women, the dashing and popular Fletcher Christian led a mutiny, casting Bligh and eighteen others adrift in the ship's launch.

TUESDAY, 28th. – Just before sun-rising, while I was yet asleep, Mr Christian, with the master-at-arms, gunner's mate, and Thomas Burkitt, seaman, came into my cabin, and, seizing me, tied my hands with a cord behind my back, threatening me with instant death if I spoke or made the least noise. I, however, called as loud as I could in hopes of assistance; but they had already secured the officers who were not of their party, by placing sentinels at their doors. There were three men at my cabin door, besides the four within; Christian had only a cutlass in his hand, the others had muskets and bayonets. I was hauled out of bed and forced on deck in my shirt, suffering great pain from the tightness with which they had tied

Lt. Bligh and officers cast adrift from the *Bounty*

my hands. I demanded the reason of such violence, but received no other answer than abuse for not holding my tongue. The master, the gunner, the surgeon, Mr Elphinstone, master's mate, and Nelson, were kept confined below, and the fore-hatchway was guarded by sentinels. The boatswain and carpenter, and also the clerk, Mr Samuel, were allowed to come upon deck, where they saw me standing abaft the mizen-mast, with my hands tied behind my back, under a guard, with Christian at their head. The boatswain was ordered to hoist the launch out, with a threat, if he did not do it instantly, *to take care of himself.*

When the boat was out, Mr Hayward and Mr Hallet, two of the midshipmen, and Mr Samuel, were ordered into it. I demanded what their intention was in giving this order, and endeavoured to persuade the people near me not to persist in such acts of violence; but it was to no effect. 'Hold your tongue, sir, or you are dead this instant,' was constantly repeated to me.

I continued my endeavours to turn the tide of affairs, when Christian changed the cutlass which he had in his hand for a bayonet that was brought to him, and holding me with a strong gripe by the cord that tied my hands, he with many oaths threatened to kill me immediately, if I would not be quiet; the villains round me had their pieces cocked and bayonets fixed. Particular people were called on to go into the boat, and were hurried over the side, whence I concluded that with these people I was to be set adrift. I therefore made another effort to bring about a change, but with no other effect than to be threatened with having my brains blown out.

The mutineers having forced those of the seamen whom they meant to get rid of into the boat, Christian directed a dram to be served to each of his own crew. I then unhappily saw that nothing could be done to effect the recovery of the ship; there was no one to assist me, and every endeavour on my part was answered with threats of death.

A Description of Australian Aboriginals, New South Wales   GEORGE BARRINGTON

c. 1791

Apart from occasional contacts with Malay pearl fishermen and shipwrecked Dutch sea-men, the aborigines were entirely isolated from outside influences for some 40,000 years until the landing of the English convict fleet at Botany Bay in 1788.

I HAD MANY opportunities of getting acquainted with several of the natives; and as I seldom saw them without giving them some trifle or other, soon became a great favourite with them, and mostly had one or other of them with me in my rambles. The men in general are from five feet six to five feet nine inches high; are rather slender, but strait, and well made. The women are not quite so tall, rather lustier, but are mostly well made. Their colour is of a brownish black, of a coffee cast, but many of the women are almost as light as a mulatto: now and then you may meet with some of both sexes with pretty tolerable features; but broad noses, wide mouths, and thick lips, are most generally met with; their countenances are not the most prepossessing, and what renders them still less so, is, they are abominably filthy. They know no such ceremony as washing themselves, and their skin is mostly smeared with the fat of such animals as they kill, and afterwards covered with every sort of dirt; sand from the beach, and ashes from their fires, all adhere to their filthy skin, which never comes off, except when accident, or the want of food obliges them to go into the water. Some of the men wear a piece of wood, or bone thrust through the septum of the nose, which, by raising the opposite sides of the nose, dilates the nostril, and spreads the lower part very much. Many of them want the two front teeth on the right side of the upper jaw and I have seen several of the women who have lost the two first joints of the little finger of their left hand, a circumstance which I have never been able to discover the meaning of. This want of the little finger I observed in elderly women; in girls of eight or nine years old; in young women who have had children; and in those who have had none. I have also observed that the finger has been perfect in individuals of all ages and descriptions. They have, in general, good teeth; their hair is short, strong, and curly; and they having no method of combing or cleaning it, it is always filthy and matted; the men's beards are short and curly like the hair of their heads. They all go entirely naked, men, women, and children, and seem to have no fixed place of residence, but lay down wherever night overtakes them.

The September Massacres, Paris

1792

RESTIF DE LA BRETONNE

In April 1792 the French Revolutionary government found itself at war with Austria and Prussia. After a number of military setbacks the Paris Commune took control under Danton and the French nation was called to arms. In an outburst of savagery, elements of the Paris mob massacred 1,300 prisoners between 2–6 September.

PASSING THE Conciergerie, I see a killer who, someone tells me, is a sailor from Marseilles. His wrist is swollen with fatigue. I go on my way. The front of the Châtelet is ornamented with piled-up dead. I turn to run.

But instead I followed the people. I arrived [at the Force] in the rue St-Antoine, at the end of the rue des Ballets, just at the moment when one poor wretch, having seen them kill his predecessor, instead of stopping when he came through the gate took to his heels and ran for it. A man who was not one of the killers, but just one of those unthinking machines of whom there are so many, stopped him with his pike. The miserable fugitive was overtaken by his pursuers and murdered. The pikeman said to us dispassionately: 'Well, how was I to know they wanted to kill him . . . ?'

There had been a pause in the murders. Something was going on inside . . . I deluded myself that all was over. At last, I saw a woman appear, as white as a sheet, supported by a turnkey. They said to her harshly: 'Cry: "Vive la nation!"' 'No! No!' said she. They made her climb on a heap of corpses. One of the killers grabbed the turnkey and pushed him away. 'Ah!' exclaimed the ill-fated woman, 'do not harm him!' They repeated that she must shout 'Vive la nation!' She refused, disdainfully. Then one killer seized her, tore away her dress, and ripped open her stomach. She fell, and was finished off by the others. Never has my imagination envisaged such horror. I wanted to flee; my legs gave way under me. I fainted.

When I returned to my senses, I saw the bloody head. Someone told me they were going to wash it, curl it, stick it on the end of a pike, and carry it past the windows of the Temple. What pointless cruelty! . . .

This ill-fated woman was Madame de Lamballe.

Dalton Discovers his Colour Blindness, Manchester, England JOHN DALTON

1792

John Dalton, a Quaker from Manchester and revolutionary scientist, put forward his celebrated atomic theory of matter in a book published in 1808. In so doing, he created the framework for the development of modern chemistry. Some sixteen years earlier, however, while pursuing a side-interest in botany, he had made a significant contribution to medicine: the discovery, through self-observation, of colour-blindness (or 'Daltonism' as it became known).

I WAS ALWAYS of opinion, though I might not often mention it, that several colours were injudiciously named. The term *pink*, in reference to the flower of that name, seemed proper enough; but when the term *red* was substituted for pink, I thought it highly improper; it should have been *blue*, in my apprehension, as pink and blue appear to me very nearly allied; whilst pink and red have scarcely any relation.

In the course of my application to the sciences, that of optics necessarily claimed attention; and I became pretty well acquainted with the theory of light and colours before I was apprised of any peculiarity in my vision. I had not, however, attended much to the practical discrimination of colours, owing, in some degree, to what I conceived to be a perplexity in their nomenclature. Since the year 1790, the occasional study of botany obliged me to attend more to colours than before. With respect to colours that were *White, yellow,* or *green,* I readily assented to the appropriate term. *Blue, purple, pink,* and *crimson* appeared rather less distinguishable; being, according to my idea, all referable to *blue.* I have often seriously asked a person whether a flower was blue or pink, but was generally considered to be in jest. Notwithstanding this, I was never convinced of a peculiarity in my vision, till I accidentally observed the colour of the flower of the *Geranium zonale* by candle-light, in the Autumn of 1792. The flower was pink, but it appeared to me almost an exact sky-blue by day; in candle-light, however, it was astonishingly changed, not having then any blue in it, but being what I called red, a colour which forms a striking contrast to blue. Not then doubting but that the change of colour would be equal to all, I requested some of my friends to observe the phaenomenon; when I was surprised to find they all agreed, that the colour was not materially different from what it was by day-light, except my brother who saw it in the same light as myself. This observation clearly proved, that my vision was not like that of other persons; – and, at the same time, that the difference between day-light and candle-light, on some colours, was indefinitely more perceptible to me than to others.

Jenner's Vaccination Experiments, Gloucestershire, England   EDWARD JENNER

c.1796

The country doctor and medical pioneer, Edward Jenner, here describes his discovery of the process of vaccination. This achievement was the end result of more than twenty years of research into 'cowpox', a mild disease quite common among milkmaids. The ethical propriety of Jenner's critical experiment – in which a healthy boy was infected with 'cowpox', then with smallpox – is open to criticism!

DURING THE investigation of the casual Cow Pox, I was struck with the idea that it might be practicable to propagate the disease by inoculation, after the manner of the Small Pox, first from the Cow, and finally from one human being to another. I anxiously waited some time for an opportunity of putting this theory to the test. At length the period arrived. The first experiment was made upon a lad of the name of Phipps, in whose arm a little Vaccine Virus was inserted, taken from the hand of a young woman who had been accidentally infected by a cow. Notwithstanding the resemblance which the pustule, thus excited on the boy's arm, bore to variolous inoculation, yet as the indisposition attending it was barely perceptible, I could scarcely persuade myself the patient was secure from the Small Pox. However, on his being inoculated some months afterwards, it proved that he was secure. This Case inspired me with confidence; and as soon as I could again furnish myself with Virus from the Cow, I made an arrangement for a series of inoculations. A number of children were inoculated in succession, one from the other; and after several months had elapsed, they were exposed to the infection of the Small Pox; some by Inoculation, others by various effluvia. and some in both ways; but they all resisted it. The distrust and scepticism which naturally arose in the minds of medical men, on my first announcing so unexpected a discovery, has now nearly disappeared. Many hundreds of them, from actual

The effects of the inoculation as depicted by the anti-vaccinationists

experience, have given their attestations that the inoculated Cow Pox proves a perfect security against the Small Pox; and I shall probably be within compass if I say, thousands are ready to follow their example; for the scope that this inoculation has now taken is immense. An hundred thousand persons, upon the smallest computation, have been inoculated in these realms.

1797

A Naval Surgeon at the Battle of Camperdown, off the Dutch coast   ROBERT YOUNG

One of the two great naval victories of 1797, the Battle of Camperdown destroyed the Dutch fleet which was in alliance with revolutionary France. Robert Young was the surgeon on board HMS Ardent.

NINETY WOUNDED were brought down during the action. The whole cockpit deck, cabins, wing berths and part of the cable tier, together with my platform and preparations for dressing were covered with them. So that for a time they were laid on each other at the foot of the ladder where they were brought down, and I was obliged to go on deck to the Commanding Officer to state the situation and apply for men to go down the main hatchway and move the foremost of the wounded further forward into the tiers and wings, and thus make room in the cockpit. Numbers, about 16, mortally wounded, died after they were brought down, amongst whom was the brave and worthy Captain Burgess, whose corpse could with difficulty be conveyed to the starboard wing berth. Joseph Bonheur had his right thigh taken off by a cannon shot close to the pelvis, so that it was impossible to apply a tourniquet; his right arm was also shot to pieces. The stump of the thigh, which was very fleshy, presented a large and dreadful surface of mangled flesh. In this state he lived near two hours, perfectly sensible and incessantly calling out in a strong voice to me to assist him. The bleeding from the femoral artery, although so high up, must have been inconsiderable, and I observed it did not bleed as he lay. All the service I could render this unfortunate man was to put dressings over the part and give him drink.

First Impressions of a Press Tender, London

JACK NASTYFACE (PSEUDONYM)

c.1798

During the long wars with France from 1793 to 1815, England could only man her navy by use of the Press Gang. One of its victims describes his first impressions of the 'Press tender' where newly-pressed men were detained.

ON BEING sent on board the receiving ship, it was the first time I began to repent of the rash step I had taken, but it was of no avail, submission to the events of fate was my only alternative, murmuring or remonstrating I soon found would be folly. After having been examined by the doctor and reported seaworthy, I was ordered down to the hold where I remained all night with my companions in wretchedness, and the rats running over us in numbers.

When released, we were ordered into the admiral's (press) tender which was to convey us to the Nore. There we were called over by name, nearly two hundred, including a number of Lord Mayors' Men, a term given to those who enter to relieve themselves from public disgrace, and who are sent on board by any of the city magistrates for a street frolic or a night charge. These poor fellows have a sad time of it, as they are the derision of the old and more experienced and hardened sailors, who generally cut the tails from their coats and otherwise abuse and ridicule them.

Upon getting on board this vessel we were ordered down in the hold and the gratings put over us; as well as a guard of marines placed round the hatchway with their muskets loaded and fixed bayonets as though we had been culprits of the first degree or capital convicts. In this place we spent the day and following night huddled together, for there was not room to sit or stand separate. Indeed, we were in a pitiable plight, for numbers of them were seasick, some retching, others were smoking, whilst many were so overcome by the stench that they fainted for want of air. As soon as the officer on deck understood that the men below were overcome with foul air, he ordered the hatches to be taken off, when daylight broke in upon us; and a wretched appearance we cut, for scarcely any of us were free from filth and vermin.

1800

Lake District Scene, England

Dorothy Wordsworth

Dorothy Wordsworth went to live with her brother, the poet William, in 1795 and became a life-long companion of his, even after he married. Her descriptions of the seasonal changes of appearance of the Lake District are said to have influenced the poetry of William and their friend Samuel Taylor Coleridge. The following extract is taken from her Grasmere Journal.

I SATE A LONG time upon a stone at the margin of the lake, and after a flood of tears my heart was easier. The lake looked to me, I knew not why, dull and melancholy, and the weltering on the shores seemed a heavy sound. I walked as long as I could amongst the stones of the shore. The wood rich in flowers; a beautiful yellow, palish yellow, flower, that looked thick, round, and double, and smelt very sweet – I supposed it was a ranunculus. Crowfoot, the grassy-leaved rabbit-toothed white flower, strawberries, geranium, scentless violets, anemones two kinds, orchises, primroses. The heckberry very beautiful, the crab coming out as a low shrub. Met a blind man, driving a very large beautiful Bull, and a cow – he walked with two sticks. Came home by Clappersgate. The valley very green; many sweet views up to Rydale head, when I could juggle away the fine houses; but they disturbed me, even more than when I have been happier; one beautiful view of the Bridge, without Sir Michael's. Sate down very often, though it was cold. I resolved to write a journal of the time till W and J return, and I set about keeping my resolve, because I will not quarrel with myself, and because I shall give Wm pleasure by it when he comes home again.

1800

Petticoat Lane, the Jewish East End, London

Israel Zangwill

In the following passage, the Jewish writer Israel Zangwill fondly recalls an era of the 'London Ghetto' when the Jewish community had yet to be Anglicised – a community characterised, in his words, by an 'old gaiety and brotherhood'.

THEIR SOCIAL life focussed on Petticoat Lane, a long, narrow thoroughfare which as late as Strype's day was lined with beautiful trees; vastly more pleasant they must have been than the faded barrows and beggars of after days. The Lane was always the great market-place, and every insalubrious street and alley abutting on it was covered with the overflowings of its commerce and its mud. Wentworth Street and Goulston Street were the chief branches, and in festival times the latter was a pandemonium of caged poultry, clucking and quacking, and cackling and screaming. Fowls and geese and ducks were bought alive, and taken to have their throats cut for a fee by the official slaughterer. At Purim a gaiety, as of the Roman carnival, enlivened the swampy Wentworth Street, and brought a smile into the unwashed face of the pavement. The confectioners shops, crammed with 'stuffed monkeys' and 'bolas', were besieged by hilarious crowds of handsome girls and their young men, fat women and their children, all washing down the luscious spicy compounds with cups of chocolate; temporarily erected swinging cradles bore a vociferous many-coloured burden to the skies; cardboard noses, grotesque in their departure from truth, abounded. The Purim *Spiel*, or Purim play, never took root in England, nor was Haman ever burnt in the streets, but *Shalachmonos*, or gifts of the season, passed between friend and friend, and masquerading parties burst into neighbours' houses. But the Lane was lively enough on the ordinary Friday and Sunday. The famous Sunday Fair was an event of metropolitan importance, and thither came buyers of every sect. The Friday Fair was more local, and confined mainly to edibles. The ante-festival fairs combined something of the other two, for Jews desired to sport new hats and clothes for the holidays as well as to eat extra luxuries, and took the opportunity of a well-marked epoch to invest in new everythings from oil-cloth to cups and saucers. Especially was this so at Passover, when for a week the poorest Jew must use a supplementary set of crockery and kitchen utensils. A babel of sound, audible for several streets around, denoted market day in Petticoat Lane, and the pavements were blocked by serried crowds going both ways at once

The Battle of Trafalgar, Coast of Spain

1805

CAPTAIN PIERRE SERVAUX

Nelson's victory over the combined French and Spanish fleet on 21 October set the seal on British seapower for a hundred years. This account, from the losing side, is by the Master-at-Arms on board the French ship Fougueux.

I THOUGHT THE *Fougueux* was shattered to pieces – pulverized. The storm of projectiles that hurled themselves against and through the hull on the port side made the ship heel to starboard. Most of the sails and the rigging were cut to pieces, while the upper deck was swept clear of the greater number of the seamen working there, and of the soldier sharpshooters. Our gun-decks below had, however, suffered less severely. There, not more than thirty men were put *hors de combat*. This preliminary greeting, rough and brutal as it was, did not dishearten our men. A well-maintained fire showed the Englishmen that we too had guns and could use them.

The English ship having come up to us, made to break the line between us and the *Santa Ana*. The Spanish ship, in fact, during our action with the English leader, had not fired a single shot. She had stolidly kept on and continued her course without shortening sail, thus giving an easy passage through to the enemy. After that, however, by the smart handling of our captain, we managed to come within our proper distance of her; indeed, almost with our bow-sprit over his poop. By this manoeuvre we had the enemy's ship on the port quarter in such a way that whilst we could only receive a few shots from their stern guns, they were exposed to our whole broadside, raking the enemy, end-on, along all his decks. We soon saw the English vessel's mizen-mast go by the board, and then her rudder and steering gear were damaged, making the ship unmanageable. Her sails flapped loose in the wind, and her sheets and running rigging were cut to pieces by our hail of shot. For some time she ceased firing.

We now redoubled our efforts and we next saw her main-topmast come down. At that moment the English ship hoisted two signal flags at the foremast. It made us think that she was calling for help. And we were not wrong. After a little time two fresh English men-of-war came up and began to attack us; the one on the starboard quarter, the other at the stern. Under their fire, we held out for more than an hour, but they almost overpowered us with their terrible storm of round shot and a fusillade of bullets which carried death among our men.

Nelson's address at Trafalgar, in his own handwriting

Our mizen-mast was now shot by the board, while our spars were shot from the masts and were lying in wreckage along the sides of the ship. Then, too, fire broke out in the stern walk and the poop. We tried our best, in spite of the hail of shot, to put the fire out, and with hatches to cut adrift the mass of wrecked top-hamper from the fallen masts and yards and cordage. It lay along the ship's sides by the gun-tiers and was endangering the ship and exposing her to the most imminent risk of destruction by fire. At this moment the captain ordered me to climb outboard and see if the wreckage of the mainsail was not in danger of being set on fire from the main-deck guns. I obeyed; but as I clambered from the gang-way into the chains one of the enemy fired her whole starboard broadside. The din and concussion were fearful; so tremendous that I almost fell headlong into the sea. Blood gushed from my nose and ears, but it did not prevent my carrying out my duty. Then our mainmast fell. Happily it was shot through some ten or twelve feet above the deck and fell over to port. At once we cut away the shrouds to starboard; but it was with great difficulty that in the end we were able to clear ourselves.

Seized by the Press Gang, London

ROBERT HAY

1811

During Britain's long war with Revolutionary and Napoleonic France, seizure by the Press Gang was an ever-present threat to seamen on shore, as, for that matter, to anyone who looked like a sailor. Hay had deserted his previous ship – if the numbered socks had been found, therefore, being naval issue, he might well have faced the death penalty.

I N THE MIDST of this agreeable reverie I was when crossing Towerhill accosted by a person in seamen's dress who tapped me on the shoulder enquiring in a familiar and technical strain 'what ship?' I assumed an air of gravity and surprise and told him I presumed he was under some mistake as I was not connected with shipping. The fellow, however, was too well acquainted with his business to be thus easily put off. He gave a whistle and in a moment I was in the hands of six or eight ruffians who I immediately dreaded and soon found to be a press gang. They dragged me hurriedly along through several streets amid bitter execrations bestowed on them, expressions of sympathy directed towards me and landed me in one of their houses of rendezvous. I was immediately carried into the presence of the Lieutenant of the gang, who questioned me as to my profession, wither I had ever been to sea, and what business had taken me to Towerhill. I made some evasive answers to these interrogations and did not acknowledge having been at sea: but my hands being examined and found hard with work, and perhaps a little discoloured with tar, overset all my hesitating affirmations and I was remanded for further examination.

Some of the gang then offered me Spirits and attempted to comfort me under my misfortune, but like the friends of Job, miserable comforters were they all. The very scoundrel who first laid hold of me put on a sympathising look and observed what a pity it was to be pressed when almost within sight of the mast of the Scotch Smacks. Such sympathy from such a source was well calculated to exasperate my feelings, but to think of revenge was folly and I had patiently to listen to their mock pity.

I trembled exceedingly in the fear that they would inspect my small bundle, for in it there were a pair of numbered stockings, which would not only have made them suppose I had been at sea, but would have given them good reason to think I had been in a war ship. I contrived, however, to slip them out unobserved and concealed them behind one of the benches and thus had my fears a little moderated.

1812

The Retreat of the Grande Armée, Russia

SERGEANT BOURGOGNE

In June 1812 Napoleon invaded Russia with an army of 600,000. The Russians retreated before him wasting the country as they went. By October he was forced to retreat, his army suffering terribly from the effects of cold and starvation. Only 100,000 survived to cross the River Niemen. This account is by a sergeant in the Imperial Guard Light Infantry.

As I WALKED on, thinking of my potatoes, I lost my way. I was made aware of this by hearing cries and curses from five men, who were fighting like dogs; the leg of a horse on the ground was the cause of the disturbance. One of them, on seeing me, told me that he and his companion, both artillery soldiers, had killed a horse behind the wood, and that, on returning with their portion, they had been attacked by three men of another regiment. If I would help them they would give me a share. I feared the same sort of fate for my potatoes, so I replied that I could not wait, but that if they could hold on for a little I would send some people to help them. A little further on I met two men in our regiment to whom I told the story. The next day I heard that when they got to the place they only saw a man lying dead, covered with blood, killed by a great pine cudgel at his side. Probably the three aggressors had taken advantage of the absence of one of their enemies to fall on the other.

When at length I got back to my regiment, several of the men asked me if I had found anything. I answered 'No,' and, taking my place near the fire, I hollowed out a bed in the snow, stretched my bearskin coat to lie on, a cape lined with ermine for my head. Before going to sleep, I had my potato to eat. Hiding it by my cape, I was as quiet as possible, terrified lest anyone should observe that I was eating. I had a little snow for drink, and then went to sleep, holding my bag containing the rest of my provisions fast in my arms. Several times in the night, as I woke, I put in my hand, carefully counting my potatoes; so I passed the night without sharing with my starving companions the bit of luck I had had. I shall never forgive myself for this selfishness. I was awake and sitting on my knapsack before the reveille sounded in the morning. I saw that a terrible day was in store for us, on account of the high wind. I made a hole in my bearskin coat, and put my head through it. The bear's head fell over my chest, and the rest over my back, but it was so long that it dragged on the ground. Before dawn we set out. We left behind us an enormous number of dead and dying. Further on it was worse still, as we had to stride over the dead bodies left on the road by the regiments going before us. It was worst of all for the rear-guard, as these were witnesses of all the horrors left by the whole army. The last corps were those commanded by Marshal Ney and Davoust, and the army of Italy under Prince Eugène. Daylight appeared when we had been marching for about an hour, and, as we had come up with the corps in front of us, we halted. Our *cantinière*, Mother Dubois, took advantage of the halt to feed her baby, when suddenly we heard a cry of anguish. The infant was dead, and as stiff as a piece of wood. Those nearest to her tried to comfort her by saying that it was the best thing both for the baby and herself, and, in spite of her cries and tears, they took the infant from her breast. They gave it to a sapper, who, with the child's father, went a short distance from the road. The sapper dug a hole in the snow, the father on his knees holding the child in his arms. When the grave was made, he kissed the baby, and placed it in its tomb. It was covered with snow, and all was at an end.

Beethoven: 'the Poor Deaf Maestro', Vienna, Austria   LOUIS SPOHR

1814

Louis Spohr, the German violinist, composer and conductor, who is reputed to have been one of the first to use a baton to conduct, here describes Ludwig van Beethoven struggling against his deafness to control an orchestra. By 1819, Beethoven would be completely deaf, and yet would go on to compose some of his greatest works. Ironically, it was the complexity of his compositions that necessitated conducting.

ALTHOUGH I had heard much of his conducting, yet it surprised me greatly. Beethoven was wont to give the signs of expression to his orchestra by all manner of extraordinary motions of his body. Whenever a *sforzando* occurred, he flung his arms wide, previously crossed upon his breast. At a *piano*, he bent down, and all the lower in proportion to the softness of tone he wished to achieve. Then when a crescendo came, he would raise himself again by degrees, and upon the commencement of the *forte*, would spring bolt upright. To increase the *forte* yet more, he would sometimes shout at the orchestra, without being aware of it. . . .

It was easy to see that the poor deaf maestro could no longer hear the *pianos* of his own music. This was particularly remarkable in a passage in the second part of the first 'Allegro' of the symphony (No. 7). At that part there are two holds in quick succession, the second of which is *pianissimo*. This Beethoven had probably overlooked, for he again began to give the time before the orchestra had executed this second hold. Without knowing it, therefore, he was already from ten to twelve bars in advance of the orchestra when it began the *pianissimo*. Beethoven, to signify this in his own way, had crept completely under the desk. Upon the ensuing crescendo, he again made his appearance, raising himself continually and then springing up high at the moment when, according to his calculation, the *forte* should have begun. As this did not take place, he looked around him in dismay, stared with astonishment at the orchestra, which was still playing *pianissimo*, and only recovered himself when at length the long-expected *forte* began, and was finally audible to himself.

1815

An Infantry Square at Waterloo, Belgium

Captain Gronow

'Forming square' was established drill for infantry facing cavalry attack and provided all-round defence. The attack of French cavalry on the British squares at about 2pm was the turning point of the battle.

During the battle our squares presented a shocking sight. Inside we were nearly suffocated by the smoke and smell from burnt cartridges. It was impossible to move a yard without treading upon a wounded comrade, or upon the bodies of the dead; and the loud groans of the wounded and dying were most appalling.

At four-o'clock our square was a perfect hospital, being full of dead, dying, and mutilated soldiers. The charges of cavalry were in appearance very formidable, but in reality a great relief, as the artillery could no longer fire on us: the very earth shook under the enormous mass of men and horses. I never shall forget the strange noise our bullets made against the breastplates of Kellermann's and Milhaud's Cuirassiers, six or seven thousand in number, who attacked us with great fury. I can only compare it, with a somewhat homely simile, to the noise of a violent hail-storm beating upon panes of glass.

The artillery did great execution, but our musketry did not at first seem to kill many men; though it brought down a large number of horses, and created indescribable confusion. The horses of the first rank of Cuirassiers, in spite of all the efforts of their riders, came to a standstill, shaking and covered with foam, at about twenty yards' distance from our squares, and generally resisted all attempts to force them to charge the line of serried steel. On one occasion, two gallant French officers forced their way into a gap momentarily created by the discharge of artillery: one was killed by [Colonel] Staples, the other by [Captain Robert] Adair. Nothing could be more gallant than the behaviour of those veterans, many of whom had distinguished themselves on half the battlefields of Europe.

Laennec and the Birth of the Stethoscope, Brittany, France

1816

RENÉ-THÉOPHILE-HYACINTHE LAENNEC

Laennec's invention of the stethoscope was a critical development in the history of clinical medicine, as it enabled doctors to listen to changes within the body: for example, to hear fluid within the lungs. He christened this technique for exploring the cardiaco-pulmonary system 'mediate auscultation'. It is a painful irony that this great Breton physician died at the age of forty-five from the disease, tuberculosis, which his invention did so much to help diagnose.

I WAS CONSULTED in 1816 by a young lady who presented the general symptoms of a heart-disease and with whom the application of the hand and percussion gave poor results owing to stoutness. The age and sex of the patient forbidding the type of examination of which I have just spoken (direct auscultation), I remembered a well-known phenomenon of acoustics: if the ear is applied to one end of a beam, a pin prick is most distinctly heard at the other end. I thought that maybe I could make use this fact in this particular case. I took some sheets of paper and, rolling them very tightly, I applied one end to the precordial region and placing my ear at the other end, I was as surprised as I was gratified to hear the beating of the heart much more clearly and distinctly than if I had applied my ear directly to the chest. It occurred to me that this means could become a useful method, applicable not only to the study of heart-beats but also to that of all movements that might produce sound in the thoracic cavity. It might, for example, help in the investigation of breathing, voice production, wheezing, and even pleural or pericardial effusions . . .

A Visit to a Fortune-Teller, Paris

c.1819

CAPTAIN GRONOW

Mademoiselle le Normand was a celebrated fortune-teller in Revolutionary and Napoleonic France. At the time of this incident, the practice of the occult was forbidden by law and had to be carried out in secret. She gave her name to a pack of fortune-telling cards which is still produced.

I WAS first admitted into a good-sized drawing-room, plainly but comfortably furnished, with books and newspapers lying about, as one sees them at a dentist's. Two or three ladies were already there, who, from their quiet dress and the haste with which they drew down their veils or got up and looked out of the window, evidently belonged to the upper ten thousand. Each person was summoned by an attendant to the sibyl's boudoir, and remained a considerable time, disappearing by some other exit without returning to the waiting-room. At last I was summoned by the elderly servant to the mysterious chamber, which opened by secret panels in the walls, to prevent any unpleasant surprises by the police. I confess that it was not without a slight feeling of trepidation that I entered the small square room, lighted from above, where sat Mademoiselle le Normand in all her glory.

It was impossible for imagination to conceive a more hideous being. She looked like a monstrous toad, bloated and venomous. She had one wall-eye, but the other was a piercer. She wore a fur cap upon her head, from beneath which she glared out upon her horrified visitors. The walls of the room were covered with huge bats, nailed by their wings to the ceiling, stuffed owls, cabalistic signs, skeletons – in short, everything that was likely to impress a weak or superstitious mind. This malignant-looking Hecate had spread out before her several packs of cards with all kinds of strange figures and ciphers depicted on them. Her first question, uttered in a deep voice, was whether you would have the *grand* or *petit jeu*, which was merely a matter of form. She then inquired your age, and what was the colour and the animal you preferred. Then came, in an authoritative voice, the word '*Coupez*', repeated at intervals, till the requisite number of cards from the various packs were selected and placed in rows side by side. No further questions were asked and no attempt was made to discover who or what you were, or to watch upon your countenance the effect of the revelations. She neither prophesied smooth things to you nor tried to excite your fears, but seemed really to believe in her own powers. She informed me that I was *un militaire*, that I should be twice married and have several children, and foretold many other events which have also come to pass, though I did not at the time believe one word of the sibyl's prediction.

1822

Berlioz Discovers his Musical Vocation, Paris

HECTOR BERLIOZ

Berlioz originally trained as a doctor – but as this amusing extract from his memoirs shows, he realised early on that his true talents lay elsewhere.

WHEN ROBERT and I got to Paris in 1822, I loyally kept my promise to my father by studying nothing but medicine. My first trial came when my cousin, telling me that he had bought a *subject*, took me to the hospital dissecting room.

But the foul air, the grinning heads, the scattered limbs, the bloody cloaca in which we waded, the swarms of ravenous rats and sparrows fighting for the debris of poor humanity, overwhelmed me with such a paroxysm of wild terror that, at one bound, I was through the nearest window, and tearing home as if Death and the Devil were at my heels.

The following night and day were indescribable. Hell seemed let loose upon me, and I felt that no power on earth should drag me back to that Gehenna, The wildest schemes for evading my horrible fate – each madder than the last – chased each other through my burning brain; but finally, worn out and despairing, I yielded to Robert's persuasion, and went back to the charnel house,

Strange to say, this time I felt nothing but cold, impersonal disgust, worthy of an old sawbones in his fiftieth battle. I actually got to the point of ferreting in some poor dead creature's chest for scraps of lung to feed the sparrow-ghouls of this unsavoury den, and when Robert said, laughing:

'Hallo! you are getting quite civilised. Giving the birds their meat in due season!'

I retorted: 'And filling all things living with plenteousness,' as I threw a blade-bone to a wretched famished rat that sat up watching me with anxious eyes.

Life, however, had some compensations.

Some secret affinity drew me to my anatomy demonstrator, Professor Amussat, probably because he, like myself, was a man of one idea, and was as passionately devoted to his science – medicine – as I to my beloved art, music. His marvellous discoveries have brought him world-wide fame, but, insatiable searcher after truth as he is, he takes no rest. He is a genius, and I am honoured in being allowed to call him friend,

I also enjoyed the chemistry lectures of Gay-Lussac, of Thénard (physics) and, above all, the literature course of Andrieux, whose quiet humour was my delight.

Drifting on in this sort of dumb quiescence, I should probably have gone to swell the disastrous list of commonplace doctors, had I not, one night, gone to the Opera. It was Salieri's *Danaïdes*.

The magnificent setting, the blended harmonies of orchestra and chorus, the sympathetic and beautiful voice of Madame Branchu, the rugged force of Dérivis, Hypermnestra's air – which so vividly recalled Gluck's style, made familiar to me by the scraps of *Orpheus* I had found in my father's library – all this, intensified by the sad and voluptuous dance-music of Spontini, sent me up to fever-pitch of excitement and enthusiasm.

I was like a young man, who, never having seen any boat but the cockle-shells on the mountain tarns of his homeland, is suddenly put on board a great three-decker in the open ocean. I could not sleep, of course, and consequently my next day's anatomy lesson suffered, and to Robert's frenzied expostulations I responded with airs from the *Danaïdes*, humming lustily as I dissected.

Hector Berlioz
(1803–69)

c.1826

A Hindu Widow Commits Suttee, India

CAPTAIN BURNES

The ritual suicide by burning of Hindu widows at their husbands' funeral pyres was common in India until suppressed by the British. It was viewed as being a path to virtue in the next life.

ALL FURTHER interference being useless, the ceremony proceeded. Accompanied by the officiating Brahmin, the widow walked seven times round the pyre, repeating the usual mantras, or prayers, strewing rice and coories on the ground, and sprinkling water from her hand over the bystanders, who believe this to be efficacious in preventing disease and in expiating committed sins. She then removed her jewels, and presented them to her relations, saying a few words to each, with a calm soft smile of encouragement and hope. The Brahmins then presented her with a lighted torch, bearing which,

'Fresh as a flower just blown,
And warm with life, her youthful pulses playing,'

she stepped through the fatal door, and sat within the pile. The body of her husband, wrapped in rich kinkaub, was then carried seven times round the pile, and finally laid across her knees. Thorns and grass were piled over the door; and again it was insisted, that free space should be left, as it was hoped the poor victim might yet relent, and rush from her fiery prison to the protection so freely offered. The command was readily obeyed, the strength of a child would have sufficed to burst the frail barrier which confined her, and a breathless pause succeeded; but the woman's constancy was faithful to the last; not a sigh broke the death-like silence of the crowd, until a slight smoke, curling from the summit of the pyre, and then a tongue of flame darting with bright and lightning-like rapidity into the clear blue sky, told us that the sacrifice was completed. Fearlessly had this courageous woman fired the pile, and not a groan had betrayed to us the moment when her spirit fled. At sight of the flame, a fiendish shout of exultation rent the air; the tom-toms sounded, the people clapped their hands with delight, as the evidence of their murderous work burst on their view; whilst the English spectators of this sad scene withdrew, bearing deep compassion in their hearts, to philosophise as best they might, on a custom so fraught with horror, so incompatible with reason, and so revolting to human sympathy.

1826

The Embarrassments of Travel, Hampshire, England WILLIAM COBBETT

The radical politician, soldier, journalist and farmer William Cobbett undertook a number of fact-finding tours of Southern England between 1822 and 1826, later published as Rural Rides. *Then, as now, travelling was not without its occasional difficulties and embarrassments.*

YESTERDAY, FROM Lyndhurst to this place, was a ride, including our round-abouts, of more than *forty miles*; but the roads the best in the world, one half of the way green turf; and the day as fine an one as ever came out of the heavens. We took in a breakfast, calculated for a long day's work, and for no more eating till night. We had slept in a room, the access to which was only through another sleeping room, which was also occupied; and, as I had got up about *two o'clock* at Andover, we went to bed, at Lyndhurst, about *half past seven* o'clock. I was, of course, awake by three or four; I had eaten little over night; so that here lay I, not liking (even after daylight began to glimmer) to go through a chamber, where, by possibility, there might be 'a *lady*' actually *in bed*; here lay I, my bones aching with lying in bed, my stomach growling for victuals, imprisoned by my *modesty*. But, at last, I grew impatient; for, modesty here or modesty there, I was not to be penned up and starved: so, after having shaved and dressed and got ready to go down, I thrust GEORGE out a little before me into the other room; and, through we pushed, previously resolving, of course, not to look towards *the bed* that was there. But, as the devil would have it, just as I was about the middle of the room, I, like *Lot's wife* turned my head! All that I shall say is, first, that the consequences that befel her did not befal me, and, second, that I advise those, who are likely to be hungry in the morning, not to sleep in *inner rooms*; or, if they do, to take some bread and cheese in their pockets.

Social Conditions Among Redundant Cloth Workers, Wiltshire England WILLIAM COBBETT

1826

This incident personifies the character of the writer – impulsive, compassionate, angry, and eager to speak out against appalling social conditions created by the depression that followed the end of the Napoleonic Wars.

I SET OUT from Heytesbury this morning about six o'clock. Last night, before I went to bed, I found that there were some men and boys in the house, who had come all the way from BRADFORD, about twelve miles, in order to get *nuts*. These people were men and boys that had been employed in the *cloth factories* at Bradford and about Bradford. I had some talk with some of these nutters, and I am quite convinced, not that the cloth making is at *an end*; but that it *never will be again what it has been*. Before last Christmas these manufacturers had full work, at one shilling and three-pence a yard at broadcloth weaving. They have now a quarter work, at one shilling a yard! One and three-pence a yard for this weaving has been given at all times within the memory of man! Nothing can show more clearly than this, and in a stronger light, the great change which has taken place in the *remuneration for labour*. There was a turn out last winter, when the price was reduced to a shilling a yard; but it was put an end to in the usual way; the constable's staff, the bayonet, the gaol. These poor nutters were extremely ragged. I saved my supper, and I fasted instead of breakfasting. That was three shillings, which I had saved, and I added five to them, with a resolution to save them afterwards, in order to give these chaps a breakfast for once in their lives. There were eight of them, six men and two boys; and I gave them two quartern loaves, two pounds of cheese, and eight pints of strong beer.

1827

Life On Board a Slave-Ship, West Africa

THEODORE CANOT

A rare account of the slave-trade by a slaver. Canot was born in Florence in 1807 and went to sea at an early age. He was involved in slaving for some years but derived little profit from it and retired penniless to America.

ON THE APPOINTED day, the *barracoon* or slave-pen is made joyous by the abundant 'feed' which signalises the negro's last hours in his native country. The feast over, they are taken alongside the vessel in canoes; and as they touch the deck, they are entirely stripped, so that women as well as men go out of Africa as they came into it – *naked*. This precaution, it will be understood, is indispensable; for perfect nudity, during the whole voyage, is the only means of securing cleanliness and health. In this state, they are immediately ordered below, the men to the hold and the women to the cabin, while boys and girls are, day and night, kept on deck, where their sole protection from the elements is a sail in fair weather, and a tarpaulin in foul.

At meal time they are distributed in messes of ten. Thirty years ago, when the Spanish slave-trade was lawful, the captains were somewhat more ceremoniously religious than at present, and it was then a universal habit to make the gangs say grace before meat, and give thanks afterwards. In our days, however, they dispense with this ritual, and content themselves with a '*Viva la Habana,*' or 'hurrah for Havana,' accompanied by a clapping of hands.

This over, a bucket of salt water is served to each mess by way of 'finger glasses' for the ablution of hands, after which a *kidd*, either of rice, farina, yams, or beans, according to the tribal habit of the negroes, is placed before the squad. In order to prevent greediness or inequality in the appropriation of nourishment, the process is performed by signals from a monitor, whose motions indicate when the darkies shall dip and when they shall swallow.

It is the duty of a guard to report immediately whenever a slave refuses to eat, in order that his abstinence may be traced to stubbornness or disease. Negroes have sometimes been found in slavers who attempted voluntary starvation; so that, when the watch reports the patient to be 'shamming', his appetite is stimulated by the medical antidote of a 'cat.' If the slave, however, is truly ill, he is forthwith ticketed for the sick-list by a bead or button around his neck, and despatched to an infirmary in the forecastle.

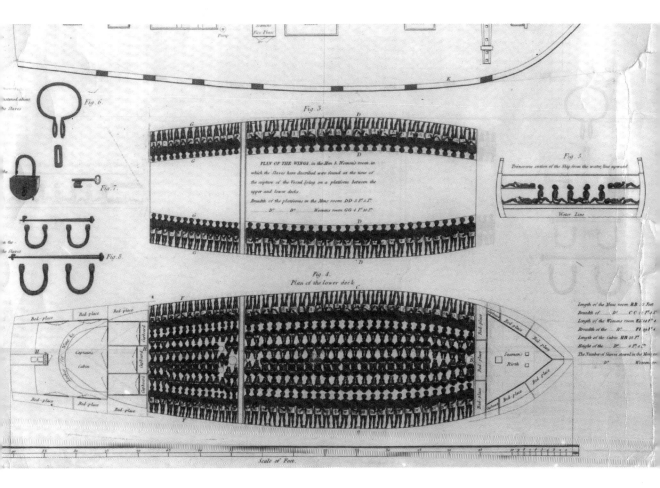

Diagram of the lower deck of a slave ship

These meals occur twice daily – at ten in the morning and four in the after-noon – and are terminated by another ablution. Thrice in each twenty-four hours they are served with half a pint of water. Pipes and tobacco are circulated eco-nomically among both sexes; but as each negro cannot be allowed the luxury of a separate bowl, boys are sent round with an adequate supply, allowing a few whiffs to each individual. On regular days – probably three times a week – their mouths are carefully rinsed with vinegar, while, nearly every morning, a dram is given as an antidote to scurvy.

Although it is found necessary to keep the sexes apart, they are allowed to con-verse freely during day while on deck. Corporal punishment is never inflicted save by order of an officer, and, even then, not until the culprit understands exactly why it is done. Once a week, the ship's barber scrapes their chins without assistance from soap; and, on the same day, their nails are closely pared, to ensure security from harm in those nightly battles that occur, when the slave contests with his neighbour every inch of plank to which he is glued. During afternoons of serene weather, men, women, girls, and boys are allowed to unite in African melodies, which they always enhance by an extemporaneous *tom-tom* on the bottom of a tub or tin kettle.

A Fundamentalist Prayer Meeting, America

FANNY TROLLOPE

Trollope's mother reserved some of her most biting comment for the American way of religion. Here she attends a 'born again' prayer meeting which would be wholly familiar to the modern viewer of American religious television.

I N EVERY part of the church a movement was perceptible, slight at first, but by degrees becoming more decided. Young girls arose, and sat down, and rose again; and then the pews opened, and several came tottering out, their hands clasped, their heads hanging on their bosoms, and every limb trembling, and still the hymn went on; but as the poor creatures approached the rail their sobs and groans became audible. They seated themselves on the 'anxious benches;' the hymn ceased, and two of the three priests walked down from the tribune, and going, one to the right, and the other to the left, began whispering to the poor tremblers seated there. These whispers were inaudible to us, but the sobs and groans increased to a frightful excess. Young creatures, with features pale and distorted, fell on their knees on the pavement, and soon sunk forward on their faces; the most violent cries and shrieks followed, while from time to time a voice was heard in convulsive accents, exclaiming, 'Oh Lord!' 'Oh Lord Jesus!' 'Help me, Jesus!' and the like.

Meanwhile the two priests continued to walk among them; they repeatedly mounted on the benches, and trumpet-mouthed proclaimed to the whole congregation, 'the tidings of salvation', and then from every corner of the building arose in reply, short sharp cries of 'Amen!' 'Glory!' 'Amen!' while the prostrate penitents continued to receive whispered comfortings, and from time to time a mystic caress. More than once I saw a young neck encircled by a reverend arm. Violent hysterics and convulsions seized many of them, and when the tumult was at the highest, the priest who remained above, again gave out a hymn as if to drown it.

It was a frightful sight to behold innocent young creatures, in the gay morning of existence, thus seized upon, horror struck, and rendered feeble and enervated for ever. One young girl, apparently not more than fourteen, was supported in the arms of another, some years older; her face was pale as death; her eyes wide open, and perfectly devoid of meaning; her chin and bosom wet with slaver; she had every appearance of idiotism. I saw a priest approach her, he took her delicate hand, 'Jesus is with her! Bless the Lord!' he said, and passed on.

An Encounter with a Virtuoso, Paris

WILHELM VON LENZ

Franz Liszt's total virtuosity on the piano and magnetic personality bewitched Parisian audiences in a quite unprecedented fashion. Something of his egomania comes across in the following account written by Wilhelm von Lenz, a devoted amateur who was fortunate enough to meet several great piano masters.

I N LISZT I found a pale, haggard young man, with unspeakably attractive features. He was reclining on a broad sofa, smoking a long Turkish pipe, and apparently lost in deep meditation. Three pianos stood near. He made not the slightest sign when I entered – he did not even seem to notice me.

When I explained to him, in French – at that time no one presumed to address him in any other language – that my family had sent me to Kalkbrenner, but that I had come to him because he dared to play a Beethoven concerto in public – he seemed to smile. His smile, however, was like a glitter of a dagger in the sunlight.

'Play me something,' he said, with indescribable sarcasm, which nevertheless, did not hurt my feelings – any more, for instance, than one feels insulted when it thunders.

'I will play the Kalkbrenner Sonata for the left hand,' said I, feeling that I had chosen well.

'That I will not hear. I do not know it, and I do not care to know it!' he answered with even stronger sarcasm, and hardly concealed scorn.

I felt that I was making a very poor impression. Perhaps I was expiating the sins of someone else, of some Parisian. However, I said to myself, as I looked at this young Parisian – for in appearance at least he was thoroughly Parisian – that he must surely be a genius, and thus, without any further skirmishing, I did not care to be driven from the field by any Parisian. With modest, but firm step, I approached the nearest piano.

'Not that one!' cried Liszt, without in the least changing his half-recumbent position on the sofa. 'There, at the other one.'

I walked to the second piano. At that time I was absorbed in Weber's 'Invitation to the Dance.' I had married it out of pure love two years before, and we were still on our honeymoon,

I had studied with good masters. But when I tried to strike the three first A flats, I found it quite impossible to make the instrument give forth a sound!

A Thug Foray, India   KHAIMRAJ

The cult of Thugee was dedicated to the goddess Kali and flourished in India from the late 16th century until it was suppressed by the British in the 1830s. Its adherents murdered travellers as a sacrifice to Kali and lived on the money plundered from their victims. This is part of a confession by a captured Thug to Captain W. H. Sleeman who was responsible, almost single-handed, for its suppression. It is the origin of the word 'thug' in English.

I AM AN INHABITANT of Mullaitra and for four years have been on an intimate footing with Oomrao Sing and his gang of Thugs, but it was not until last year that I actually joined them and accompanied them until the present expedition. Previous to setting out upon it, the several gangs assembled at the Oomrao Sing's residence at Mullaitra. From here Dirkpal and Mundun Jemadar, with their

OPPOSITE PAGE 146 Wellington signals the general advance of the British in the Battle of Waterloo 1815

OPPOSITE PAGE Floral tributes for Diana at Kensington Palace.

1831

Brahman and Mussulman gangs, preceded Oomrao Sing's and Makhun's by twenty days.

Of their acts and proceedings since I have been associated with them, I speak from personal knowledge. Six stages brought us to Seronge, where we murdered a traveller, and next morning continued our journey without doing anything. The stage following we came to a river where we found four sepoys cooking, whom we murdered. This occupied some time and was not effected without difficulty, for they seem to have entertained suspicion and, having in a hurried manner got through their meal, they quickly recommenced their journey. They stopped at a village where our spies saw them fairly lodged; we halted a short distance away, and at night sent a select party of Thugs to effect our object. The sepoys commenced their journey next morning, followed by our party, who, watching their opportunity and when remote from any village, fell upon them and murdered them as they walked along the road. One of the sepoys must have perceived the design of the party and made such extraordinary efforts to save his life that he got away a few paces and raised his spear in defence, but was instantly overpowered and murdered; 2,000 rupees was the amount of plunder obtained on this occasion. As we were resting close to where the sepoys had just met their fate, four strolling players joined us. We spoke kindly to them, promising to hear their *ras*, at our next halting place, and to give them a rupee for their performance; they were persuaded to accompany us and take up their quarters with us at a well-known shrine near Bhopal, where we murdered them that night and plundered them of all they had, something about fifty rupees.

1832

Delacroix Visits Morocco EUGENE DELACROIX

The painter Delacroix was one of the finest of the Orientalist school of painters and an early exponent of photography. This extract from his journal of a visit to North Africa is clearly intended as an aide-mémoire for a painting with its evocative description of colour, shade and shape at a Jewish wedding.

THE JEWISH WEDDING. Moors and Jews at the entrance. The two musicians. The violinist with his thumb in the air, the underneath part of his other hand very much in shadow, the light behind him; the *haik* on his head transparent in places; white sleeves, background in shadow. The other violinist squatting on his heels, and his *gelabia*. Blackness between them down below. The guitar case lying on the knees of the musician; very dark towards the waist, red waistcoat, brown trimmings, blue at the back of the neck. Shadow thrown from the left arm, which is at right angles, on to the *haik* over his knee. Shirtsleeves rolled up so as to show the arm as far as the biceps; green woodwork beside him; wart on the neck, short nose.

Beside the violinist, a pretty Jewish girl; waistcoat and sleeves, gold and purple. She stands out, half against the door, half against the wall. Nearer in the foreground, an older woman with a great deal of white about her which almost entirely conceals her. Shadows full of reflections; white in the shadows.

A pillar stands out dark against the foreground. The women on the left rise in tiers one above the other like pots of flowers. Gold and white predominate; yellow handkerchiefs. Children sitting on the ground in front.

Sitting beside the guitar player, the Jew playing the tambourine. His face is a dark silhouette hiding part of the guitarist's hand. The lower part of the head stands out sharply against the wall; one end of the *gelabia* under the guitar player. In front of him, sitting cross-legged, a young Jew holding a plate; clothes, grey. Leaning against his shoulder, a young Jewish boy about ten years old.

Bodysnatchers, England 'Lord' George Sanger

c.1834

The theft of dead bodies for use in medical schools was common in the 18th and early 19th centuries and aroused widespread disgust until the position was regulated by the Anatomy Act. George Sanger, the English showman, became famous along with his brother for his travelling circuses.

M Y FATHER and I walked on by the horses while our passengers on the front of the wagon laughed and talked, and one of them started singing a coarse song, but stopped when my father objected. Then for some reason I fell a bit behind the wagon, and as I did so I noticed the parcel the men had put on the back showing out in the strong moonlight. It was a bulky long shapeless sort of bundle contained in a big sack, and it wobbled in a fashion that made it seem, to my boyish eyes, as though it had something alive in it. This roused my curiosity, though at the same time it gave me a creepy kind of feeling.

After travelling for some half a mile farther I let the wagon again pass me, and fell behind it, my eyes once more fixed on the mysterious parcel at the back. This time my curiosity overcame me. I swung myself up to the wagon rail and took a close look at the bundle. I could see the neck of the sack was unloosed, as though somebody had recently untied it, and pulling the sack aside I peeped in.

Oh! my God, the horror of that moment! I hung to the rail paralysed with fear. The moonlight shone clearly through the loosened sack, and I saw a naked human arm and the pallid wax-like face of a dead woman!

Why I did not scream out I cannot tell from that day to this. But I did not. I simply dropped off the back of the wagon shaking with fear, my knees giving way under me so that I could not walk. Indeed, when I recovered myself the wagon was some distance ahead, and I had to run to catch it.

When I got to my father's side he evidently saw by my white face and shaking form that I had discovered what we were carrying, for he caught hold of my shoulder, and stooping down said in a stern whisper, 'Don't speak, Georgie, not a word! Keep on by the side of the horses!'

I obeyed him, and walked on as if in a dream, with the face of the dead woman before my eyes seeming to bob at me with every movement of the animals. I walked mechanically, seeing nothing except that awful face, nor did I rouse out of my stupor until we were within two miles of Reading.

1835

Darwin in the Galapagos Islands

CHARLES DARWIN

Darwin's world voyage in HMS Beagle *from 1832 to 1836 was the foundation of many of his theories on evolution and the origin of species. His visit to Galapagos was particularly fruitful because its isolation and unique fauna and flora enabled him to study an ecology unaffected by outside influences.*

I WILL FIRST describe the habits of the tortoise, which has been so frequently alluded to. Some grow to an immense size: Mr Lawson, an Englishman, and vice-governor of the colony, told us that he had seen several so large, that it required six or eight men to lift them from the ground; and that some had afforded as much as two hundred pounds of meat. The old males are the largest, the females rarely growing to so great a size: the male can readily be distinguished

Darwin testing the speed of an elephant tortoise in the Galapagos Islands

from the female by the greater length of its tail. The tortoises which live on these islands where there is no water, or in the lower and arid parts of the others, feed chiefly on the succulent cactus. Those which frequent the higher and damp regions, eat the leaves of various trees, a kind of berry (called guayavita) which is acid and austere, and likewise a pale green filamentous lichen, that hangs in tresses from the boughs of the trees.

The tortoise is very fond of water, drinking large quantities, and wallowing in the mud. The larger islands alone possess springs, and these are always situated towards the central parts, and at a considerable height. The tortoises, therefore, which frequent the lower districts, when thirsty, are obliged to travel from a long distance. Hence broad and well-beaten paths branch off in every direction from the wells down to the sea-coast; and the Spaniards by following them up, first discovered the watering-places. When I landed at Chatham Island, I could not imagine what animal travelled so methodically along well-chosen tracks. Near the springs it was a curious spectacle to behold many of these huge creatures, one set eagerly travelling onwards with outstretched necks, and another set returning, after having drunk their fill. When the tortoise arrives at the spring, quite regardless of any spectator, he buries his head in the water above his eyes, and greedily swallows great mouthfuls, at the rate of about ten in a minute. The inhabitants say each animal stays three or four days in the neighbourhood of the water, and then returns to the lower country; but they differed respecting the frequency of these visits. The animal probably regulates them according to the nature of the food on which it has lived. It is, however, certain that tortoises can subsist even on those islands, where there is no other water than what falls during a few rainy days in the year.

Première of Berlioz's *Requiem*, Les Invalides, Paris   HECTOR BERLIOZ

1837

The première of the Requiem *was given in December 1837 to commemorate the death of General Damrémont. At the last minute, Berlioz, who normally conducted his own works, was asked by the mysterious 'X' to allow François-Antoine Habeneck – an aged state conductor with whom Berlioz did not get on – to direct the performance. The authenticity of the curious events described below has been disputed.*

M Y FORCES had been divided into several groups spread over a wide area; necessarily so because of the four brass bands which I use in the Tuba mirum, and which have to be placed beyond the main body of performers, one at each corner. At the point where they enter, at the beginning of the Tuba mirum – which follows the *Dies irae* without a pause – the music broadens to a tempo twice as slow. First, all four groups break in simultaneously – at the new tempo – then successively, challenging and answering one another from a distance, the entries piling up, each a third higher than the one before. It is therefore of the utmost importance to indicate the four beats of the slower tempo very clearly the moment it is reached; otherwise the great cataclysm, a musical representation of the Last Judgment, prepared for with such deliberation and employing an exceptional combination of forces in a manner at the time unprecedented and not attempted since – a passage which will, I hope, endure as a landmark in music – is mere noise and pandemonium, a monstrosity.

With my habitual mistrust I had stayed just behind Habeneck. Standing with my back to him, I supervised the group of timpani (which he could not see), as the moment approached for them to join in the general tumult. There are perhaps a thousand bars in my *Requiem*. In the very bar I have been speaking of, the bar in which the tempo broadens and the brass proclaim their tremendous fanfare – the one bar, in fact, in which the conductor's direction is absolutely indispensable – Habeneck laid down his baton and, calmly producing his snuff-box, proceeded to take a pinch of snuff. I had been keeping my eye on him. In a flash I turned on my heel, sprang forward in front of him and, stretching out my arm, marked out the four great beats of the new tempo. The bands followed me and everything went off in order. I conducted the piece to the end. The effect I had dreamed of was attained. When, at the final words of the chorus, Habeneck saw that the Tuba mirum was saved, he said, 'God! I was in a cold sweat. Without you we would have been lost.'

'I know,' I replied, looking him straight in the eye. I did not say another word. Had he done it deliberately? Was it possible that this man, in collusion with X (who hated me) and with Cherubini's friends, had actually planned and attempted to carry out an act of such base treachery? I would rather not think so. Yet I cannot doubt it. God forgive me if I do an injustice!

Chartist Riots, Newport, Wales

1839

'LORD' GEORGE SANGER

The famous showman recalls the serious riots in Newport which eventually had to be dispersed by the army, killing several of the rioters. The Chartists were an early socialist movement which, among other things, sought to extend the vote to working-class men and women.

WHEN WE got about a mile from the town we saw a tremendous crowd of people coming down the road, and there was nothing for it but to pull up close to the roadside to let them pass, and to pray that they might be peaceable in their passage.

They were the Chartist colliers, whose coming we had so dreaded, and I doubt if it is possible for any of you who read this to conceive our feelings as they drew near. If they attacked our wagon and broke it up it meant utter hopeless ruin to us; moreover, there was the awful fear of personal outrage and even murder at their hands. So we sat and waited, and trembled.

On they came, many of them half drunk, yelling, swearing, and waving great cudgels, a terrifying mass of men. It was estimated afterwards that they numbered about thirty thousand, and I should think that for quite two hours they were tramping by our caravan. Perhaps we were too insignificant for their attention. Anyhow, beyond flinging an occasional volley of oaths at us, we were not interfered with. But it was not until the main body had passed that we drew our breaths freely, and father put down the loaded blunderbuss that, with grim determination to protect his family and property at all costs, he had taken up when the crowd first came into view.

Some little while after the colliers had gone by we heard the sound of firing in the direction of the town. Father got out an old spy-glass he possessed, to see if he could view anything of what was going on. Presently he said, 'Into the wagon, all of you! Shut up all the windows and the door. Here they come back again!'

They did come. At a much faster pace than they had gone down the hill they raced back again and very soon were passing our wagon in thousands. This time they were in such a hurry that they did not even stop to swear at us. From what was now and again muttered by them, mother said it was evident that the soldiers were after them, and they were afraid of being shot. But we saw no soldiers, only the hurrying crowd, and when that had passed the road lay quiet and peaceful, the only objects on it being the caravans, dotted here and there by the hedge-side, of show-folk, who, like ourselves, had fled the town, and had drawn up to let the mob go by.

Spanish Gypsies   George Borrow

1840

Gypsies were, and are, often supposed to possess occult powers over animals. Here the linguist and expert on gypsy lore, George Borrow, recounts an incident at a horse fair in Leon, and gives a vivid description of gypsy attire.

THERE IS A celebrated cattle-fair held at Leon on St John's or Midsummer Day, and on one of these occasions, being present, I observed a small family of Gitános, consisting of a man of about fifty, a female of the same age, and a handsome young Gypsy, who was their son; they were richly dressed after the Gypsy fashion, the men wearing zamarras with massy clasps and knobs of silver, and the woman a species of riding-dress with much gold embroidery, and having immense gold rings attached to her ears. They came from Murcia, a distance of one hundred leagues and upwards. Some merchants, to whom I was recommended, informed me that they had credit on their house to the amount of twenty thousand dollars.

They experienced rough treatment in the fair, and on a very singular account: immediately on their appearing on the ground, the horses in the fair, which, perhaps, amounted to three thousand, were seized with a sudden and universal panic; it was one of those strange incidents for which it is difficult to assign a rational cause; but a panic there was amongst the brutes, and a mighty one; the horses neighed, screamed, and plunged, endeavouring to escape in all directions; some appeared absolutely possessed, stamping and tearing, their manes and tails stiffly erect, like the bristles of the wild boar – many a rider lost his seat. When the panic had ceased, and it did cease almost as suddenly as it had arisen, the Gitános were forthwith accused as the authors of it; it was said that they intended to steal the best horses during the confusion, and the keepers of the ground, assisted by a rabble of chalans, who had their private reasons for hating the Gitános, drove them off the field with sticks and cudgels. So much for having a bad name.

c.1843

Sioux Sun-Dance, Great Plains, America

GEORGE CATLIN

Ritual self-torture was a common right of passage for young warriors in the plains indian culture. Here the explorer Catlin records the 'sun-dance' in which young warriors inserted hooks into their pectoral muscles and were pulled up by cords attached to a pole, an excruciating ordeal.

AN INCH or more of the flesh on each shoulder, or each breast was taken up between the thumb and finger by the man who held the knife in his right hand; and the knife, which had been ground sharp on both edges, and then hacked and notched with the blade of another, to make it produce as much pain as possible, was forced through the flesh below the fingers, and being withdrawn, was followed with a splint or skewer, from the other, who held a bunch of such in his left hand, and was ready to force them through the wound. There were then two cords lowered down from the top of the lodge, which were fastened to these splints or skewers, and they instantly began to haul him up; he was thus raised until his body was suspended from the ground where he rested, until the knife and a splint were passed through the flesh or integuments in a similar manner on each arm below the shoulder, below the elbow, on the thighs, and below the knees.

In some instances they remained in a reclining position on the ground until this painful operation was finished, which was performed, in all instances, exactly on the same parts of the body and limbs; and which, in its progress, occupied some five or six minutes.

Each one was then instantly raised with the cords, until the weight of his body was suspended by them, and then, while the blood was streaming down their limbs, the bystanders hung upon the splints each man's appropriate shield, bow and quiver, &c; and in many instances, the skull of a buffalo with the horns on it, was attached to each lower arm and each lower leg, for the purpose, probably, of preventing by their great weight, the struggling, which might otherwise have taken place to their disadvantage whilst they were hung up.

Borneo Pirates, Sarawak   SURGEON EDWARD CREE

The suppression of piracy was an important role for the Victorian Royal Navy, particularly in the East Indies. Cree was a naval surgeon on board HMS Vixen *when with other vessels it attacked the lair of the pirate Pangeran Usop.*

As THE REFRACTORY Rajah refused to comply with the demands, and had collected a large force of his friends and dependants, we moved higher up the river, abreast of his stockades. The *Pluto* and *Nemesis* went up a branch of the river which flanks them; the gunboats with the Marines accompanied them. We gave him till 2 p.m. and then fired a shot through the roof of his house, just as a reminder, on which he immediately opened fire from his stockade with five or six of his guns, which was most ridiculous, as a broadside from our 84s and 32s sent his stockades and other defences flying in splinters and dismounted his guns. At the same time the two other ships were giving him a heavy flanking fire. However brave the chief and his followers might be, they soon found this much too hot for them; their places were soon riddled with grapeshot. In about a quarter of an hour they had cleared out, and fled into the jungle at the back. The Marines and small-arm men landed and took possession, and kept up a dropping fire on stragglers. One poor fellow had a narrow squeak as I was watching him swimming across the river under a shower of bullets. The officers had some trouble to make the men cease firing, as is always the case. We had no one hurt, as the enemy's shot went well over us, but one unfortunate man of the *Nemesis* was blown from his gun, through carelessness in loading. I don't think the enemy had many killed, as they did not stop long enough for that.

A Buffalo Hunt, Great Plains, America

FRANCIS PARKMAN

Parkman, a Bostonian with a delicate constitution, went on an expedition to see the peoples and animals of the Great Plains, in 1846. Within forty years the mighty herds that he writes about had been reduced virtually to the point of extinction.

AT LENGTH I was fairly among the buffalo. They were less densely crowded than before, and I could see nothing but bulls, who always run at the rear of a herd to protect their females. As I passed among them they would lower their heads, and turning as they ran, try to gore my horse; but as they were already at full speed there was no force in their onset, and as Pauline ran faster than they, they were always thrown behind her in the effort. I soon began to distinguish cows amid the throng. One just in front of me seemed to my liking, and I pushed close to her side. Dropping the reins I fired, holding the muzzle of the gun within a foot of her shoulder. Quick as lightning she sprang at Pauline; the little mare dodged the attack, and I lost sight of the wounded animal amid the tumult. Immediately after, I selected another, and urging forward Pauline, shot into her both pistols in succession. For a while I kept her in view, but in attempting to load my gun lost sight of her also in the confusion. Believing her to be mortally wounded and unable to keep up with the herd, I checked my horse. The crowd rushed onwards. The dust and tumult passed away, and on the prairie, far behind the rest, I saw a solitary buffalo galloping heavily. In a moment I and my victim were running side by side. My firearms were all empty, and I had in my pouch nothing but rifle bullets, too large for the pistols and too small for the gun. I loaded the gun, however, but as often as I levelled it to fire, the bullets would roll out of the muzzle and the gun returned only a report like a squib as the powder harmlessly exploded. I rode in front of the buffalo and tried to turn her back; but her eyes glared, her mane bristled, and, lowering her head, she rushed at me with the utmost fierceness and activity. Again and again I rode before her, and again and again she repeated her furious charge. But little Pauline was in her element. She dodged her enemy at every rush, until at length the buffalo stood still, exhausted with her own efforts, her tongue lolling from her jaws.

Riding to a little distance, I dismounted, thinking to gather a handful of dry grass to serve the purpose of wadding, and load the gun at my leisure. No sooner were my feet on the ground than the buffalo came bounding in such a rage towards me that I jumped back again into the saddle with all possible despatch. After waiting a few minutes more, I made an attempt to ride up and stab her with my knife; but Pauline was near being gored in the attempt. At length, bethinking me of the fringes at the seams of my buckskin trousers, I jerked off a few of them and, reloading the gun, forced them down the barrel to keep the bullet in its place; then approaching, I shot the wounded buffalo through the heart. Sinking to her knees, she rolled over lifeless on the prairie. To my astonishment, I found that, instead of cow, I had been slaughtering a stout young bull. No longer wondering at his fierceness, I opened his throat, and cutting out his tongue tied it at the back of my saddle. My mistake was one which a more experienced eye than mine might easily make in the dust and confusion of such a chase.

An Eviction in the Great Famine, Ireland

1847

HENRY TUKE

The failure of the Irish potato crop, the staple diet for most of Ireland's poor, resulted in the deaths of over 1,000,000 between 1845 and 1849. Thousands were evicted from their homes and 1,500,000 more emigrated in the aftermath of Ireland's greatest disaster.

EVICTION is in many cases practised, and not a few of the roofless dwellings which meet the eye, have been destroyed at the instance of the landlords, after turning adrift the miserable inmates; and this even at a time like the present, when the charity of the whole world has been turned towards the relief of this starving peasantry. Whilst upon the island of Achill, I saw a memorable instance of this mode of proceeding, at the wretched fishing village of Kiel. Here, a few days previous to my visit, a driver of Sir R. O'Donnells, whose property it is, had ejected some twenty families, making, as I was informed, with a previous recent eviction, about forty. A crowd of these miserable ejected creatures collected around us, bewailing, with bitter lamentations, their hard fate. One old grey-

Irish peasants being evicted during the Great Famine

headed man came tottering up to us, bearing in his arms his bed-ridden wife, and putting her down at our feet, pointed, in silent agony to her, and then to his roof-less dwelling, the charred timbers of which were scattered in all directions around. This man said he owed little more than one year's rent, and had lived in the village, which had been the home of his forefathers, all his life. Another man, with five motherless children, had been expelled, and their 'boiling-pot' sold for 3s. 6d. Another family, consisting of a widow and four young children, had their only earthly possession 'a little sheep', seized, and sold for 5s. 6d.

1847

A Duel in a Bedroom, Mexico

Samuel Chamberlain

The Mexican-American War of 1846–48 produced no more picaresque hero than the author of this piece, as much a warrior in the bedroom as on the battlefield, at least by his own account.

ONE MORNING I stopped at the *casa* of Velasco to make an early call. I fastened my horse in the patio and entered the sleeping apartment of the young ladies with the freedom of an old friend of the house. This was a great mistake of mine – I should have sent in my card! My two charmers were in bed, but not alone! The black shaggy head of a Mexican lay on the pillow between the raven tresses of Rosita and Nina!

I recognized the invader as one Antonio, a renegade who acted as guide to our army. Overcome with my emotions, I was about to retire with becoming modesty when the voluptuous rascal sprang up and drawing a machete from under his pillow, and wrapping his blanket around his left arm, rushed on me like some wild beast. The fastidious young ladies, instead of fainting or screaming, sat up in bed and cried '*Bravo! Bravo! bueno Antonio! matar! matar el grande pendejo!*' (Bravo! Bravo! good Antonio! kill! kill the big fool!)

What charming creatures! I drew my sabre and came to guard in an instant. He was as active as a cat, and I found I had all I could attend to in keeping his ugly knife from getting between my ribs, while all my cuts and points were received on his confounded blanket. More than once his knife glided over my guard, cutting my jacket. I could hear the gentle Nina say, '*Anda! Anda! mia dulce, mia alma!*' (Quick! quick! my sweet, my soul!) while Rosita in her most dulcet tones murmured, '*Antonio, mia amor, punga el gringo, que la cama!*' (Antonio, my love, stick the foreigner and come to bed!)

How cheering to myself were the words of the darlings! But I did not lose heart, and finally succeeded in giving my antagonist an ugly slash across one of his bare legs, causing him to drop his knife, when I gave him a point in a part that made him howl with agony, and would cause him to lose the regards of the '*dos margaritas*'.

Leaving the villain on the floor bleeding profusely, I made a graceful exit, and returned to camp, thoroughly disgusted with the fickleness of womankind, Mexican Señoritas in particular.

The Amazonian Rain Forest

ALFRED RUSSEL WALLACE

1848

Wallace developed the same theories about natural selection as Darwin and at roughly the same time. He is now forgotten, undeservedly, since his extended travels in South America and Indonesia contributed greatly to the development of natural science in the 19th century.

ABOUT TEN o'clock we reached the mouth of the igaripé, or small stream we were to ascend, and I was very glad to get into still water. We stayed for breakfast in a little clear space under a fine tree, and I enjoyed a cup of coffee and a little biscuit, while the men luxuriated on fish and farinha. We then proceeded up the stream, which was at its commencement about two hundred yards wide, but soon narrowed to fifty or eighty. I was much delighted with the beauty of the vegetation, which surpassed anything I had seen before: at every bend of the stream some new object presented itself, – now a huge cedar hanging over the water, or a great silk-cotton-tree standing like a giant above the rest of the forest. The graceful assai palms occurred continually, in clumps of various sizes, some times raising their stems a hundred feet into the air, or bending in graceful curves till they almost met from the opposite banks. The majestic murutí palm was also abundant, its straight and cylindrical stems like Grecian columns, and with its immense fan-shaped leaves and gigantic bunches of fruit, produced an imposing spectacle. Some of these bunches were larger than any I had before seen, being eight or ten feet in length, weighing probably two or three hundredweight: each consisted of several bushels of a large reticulated fruit. These palms were often clothed with creepers, which ran up to the summits, and there put forth their blossoms. Lower down, on the water's edge, were numerous flowering shrubs, often completely covered with convolvuluses, passion-flowers, or big-nonias. Every dead or half-rotten tree was clothed with parasites of singular forms or bearing beautiful flowers, while smaller palms, curiously-shaped stems, and twisting climbers, formed a background in the interior of the forest.

Nor were there wanting animated figures to complete the picture. Brilliant scarlet and yellow macaws flew continually overhead, while screaming parrots and paroquets were passing from tree to tree in search of food. Sometimes from a branch over the water were suspended the hanging nests of the black and yellow troupial, into which those handsome birds were continually entering. The effect of the scene was much heightened by the river often curving to one side or the other, so as to bring to view a constant variety of objects.

1849

Gay Sex in a Cairo Bathhouse, Egypt

GUSTAVE FLAUBERT

In the autumn of 1849 the French novelist Flaubert left for a tour of Egypt with his friend Maxime du Camp. As well as a keen interest in the Orient, fashionable at the time, they were also 'sexual tourists' in a very modern sense.

IT'S AT THE baths that such things take place. You reserve the bath for yourself (five francs including masseurs, pipe, coffee, sheet and towel) and you skewer your lad in one of the rooms. Be informed, furthermore, that all the bath-boys are bardashes. The final masseurs, the ones who come to rub you when all the rest is done, are usually quite nice young boys. We had our eye on one in an establishment very near our hotel. I reserved the bath exclusively for myself. I went, and the rascal was away that day! I was alone in the hot room, watching the daylight fade through the great circles of glass in the dome. Hot water was flowing everywhere; stretched out indolently I thought of a quantity of things as my pores tranquilly dilated. It is very voluptuous and sweetly melancholy to take a bath like that quite alone, lost in those dim rooms where the slightest noise resounds like a cannon shot, while the naked *kellaas* call out to one another as they massage you, turning you over like embalmers preparing you for the tomb. That day (the day before yesterday, Monday) my *kellaa* was rubbing me gently, and when he came to the noble parts he lifted up my *boules d'amour* to clean them, then continuing to rub my chest with his left hand he began to pull with his right on my prick, and as he drew it up and down he leaned over my shoulder and said '*baksheesh, baksheesh.*' He was a man in his fifties, ignoble, disgusting – imagine the effect, and the word '*baksheesh, baksheesh.*' I pushed him away a little, saying '*làh, làh*' ('no, no') – he thought I was angry and took on a craven look – then I gave him a few pats on the shoulder, saying '*làh, làh*' again but more gently –he smiled a smile that meant, 'You're not fooling me – you like it as much as anybody, but today you've decided against it for some reason.' As for me, I laughed aloud like a dirty old man, and the shadowy vault of the bath echoed with the sound.

1849

Sims Perfects a Gynaecological Treatment, America   JAMES MARION SIMS

James Marion Sims was one of America's greatest gynaecologists, who pioneered the celebrated 'Sims position' and 'Sims speculum'. It is ironic, therefore, that on the eve of his great discovery – the positive surgical treatment of vesico-vaginal fistula, developed between 1845 and 1849 – he had no interest in gynaecology. The courageous contribution of Sims' patients – all Negro slaves who were operated on before the advent of anaesthetic – should be borne in mind.

I HAD BEEN three weeks without performing a single operation on either of the half-dozen patients that I had there. They were clamorous, and at last the idea occurred to me about three o'clock one morning. I had been lying awake for an hour, wondering how to tie the suture, when all at once an idea occurred to me to run a shot, a perforated shot, on the suture, and, when it was drawn tight, to compress it with a pair of forceps, which would make the knot perfectly secure. I was so elated with the idea, and so enthusiastic as I lay in bed, that I could not help waking up my kind and sympathetic wife and telling her of the simple and beautiful method I had discovered of tying the suture. I lay there till morning, tying the suture and performing all sorts of beautiful operations, in imagination, on the poor people in my little hospital; and I determined, as soon as I had made my round of morning calls, to operate with this perfected suture. Just as I had got ready to perform my operation I was summoned to go twenty miles into the country, and I did not get back until late in the night. I looked upon it as a very unfortunate thing, and one of the keenest disappointments of my life, because it kept me from seeing all the beautiful results of my method. However, the next day, in due time, the operation was performed on Lucy. When it was done, I said, 'Could anything be more beautiful? Now I know that she will be cured very soon, and then all the rest must be cured.' It was with great impatience that I waited a whole week to see what the result of the operation would be. When I came to examine it, it was a complete failure. Just in this time of tribulation about the subject, I was walking from my house to the office, and picked up a little bit of brass wire in the yard. It was very fine, and such as was formerly used as springs in suspenders before the days of India-rubber. I took it around to Mr Swan, who was then my jeweler, and asked him if he could make me a little silver wire about the size of the piece of brass wire. He said Yes, and he made it. He made it of all pure silver. Anarcha was the subject of this experiment. The operation was performed on the fistula in the base of the bladder, that would admit of the end of my little finger; she had been cured of one fistula in the base of the bladder. The edges of the wound were nicely denuded, and neatly brought together with four of these fine silver wires. They were passed through little strips of lead, one on one side of the fistula, and the other on the other. The suture was tightened, and then secured or fastened by the perforated shot run on the wire, and pressed with forceps. This was the thirtieth operation performed on Anarcha. She was put to bed, a catheter was introduced, and the next day the urine came from the bladder as clear and as limpid as spring water, and so it continued during all the time she wore the catheter. In all the preceding operations, where the silk was used for a suture at the base of the bladder, cystitis always resulted. The urethra was swollen continually, and the urine loaded with a thick, ropy mucus. With the use of the silver suture there was a complete change in these conditions.

Problems of Photography, Egypt

MAXIME DU CAMP

Flaubert's travelling companion to Egypt, Maxime du Camp, was an enthusiastic and accomplished photographer who later published an album of his photographs to considerable public interest.

EVERY TIME I visited a monument I had my photographic apparatus carried along and took with me one of my sailors, Hadji Ismael, an extremely handsome Nubian, whom I had climb up on to the ruins which I wanted to photograph. In this way I was always able to include a uniform scale of proportions. The great difficulty was to get Hadji Ismael to stand perfectly motionless while I performed my operations; and I finally succeeded by means of a trick whose success will convey the depth of naiveté of these poor Arabs. I told him that the brass tube of the lens jutting from the camera was a cannon, which would vomit a hail of shot if he had the misfortune to move – a story which immobilised him completely, as can be seen from my plates.

The day I was returning from Dendera I overheard the following conversation between him and Raïs Ibrahim – a curious account of a photographic expedition:

'Well, Hadji Ismael, what news?' asked the *raïs* as we boarded the *cange*.

'None,' the sailor answered. 'The Father of Thinness ('Abu Muknaf,' as I was always called by my crew) ordered me to climb up on a column that bore the huge face of an idol; he wrapped his head in the black veil, he turned his yellow cannon towards me, then he cried: "Do not move!" The cannon looked at me with its little shining eye, but I kept very still, and it did not kill me.'

'God is the greatest,' said Raïs Ibrahim, sententiously.

'And our Lord Mohammed is his prophet,' replied Hadji.

A Mob Murder in Lancashire, England

'LORD' GEORGE SANGER

Mob violence and random brutality were as much part of Victorian England as they are perceived to be today – as this extract from the autobiography of a fairground impresario demonstrates.

NEARLY OPPOSITE our show was a large ginger-bread stall kept by a man whose name I am almost sure was Sheppard, a big, good-humoured fellow, and a well-known fair-goer. I was on the platform with John outside our show just getting ready to call the people up when we noticed a row at Sheppard's gingerbread stall.

He seemed to be expostulating with a crowd of miners about something, when all at once over went his stall, and the next minute he himself was under their feet with all of them kicking at him anywhere and everywhere as hard as they could. From our position on the platform we could see the poor fellow's body with the heavy clogs battered into it as though it was a stuffed sack instead of a human thing.

I wanted to go down to interfere, but John held me back, saying, 'It's no use, boy! They'd only serve you the same!' And so they would have done, I have no doubt. At any rate, though the crowd formed a sort of ring, nobody stirred a hand to save the man who was being kicked to pulp in the centre of it.

'Kicked to pulp' is by no means too strong an expression, for that is what literally happened to the poor ginger-bread seller. When the crowd with the kickers suddenly melted away there lay the body – I can see it now – a ghastly, shapeless thing in the clear sunlight, with the white dust of the roadway blotched here and there about it with purple stains. It was one of those things that a man once seeing carries for ever after as a shuddering recollection, and I never hear the name Stalybridge but the picture of that battered, awful object lying prone in the sunlight comes before me.

Some little time after the brutal deed had been done one or two constables made a leisurely appearance, looked at the body as though such sights were common to their ordinary day's work, and the corpse was removed. I never learned what verdict the coroner's jury returned concerning Sheppard's death, or whether any attempt was ever made to bring any of his assailants to justice.

The Charge of the Light Brigade, Crimea

1854

GEORGE LOY SMITH

The invasion of the Crimea by British and French forces was an unmitigated disaster. The objective was to besiege and capture the naval port of Sebastopol. The famous charge of the Light Brigade took place during the Battle of Balaclava, between the Allied forces and a Russian relieving army. Due to a breakdown in communications the British light cavalry charged entrenched Russian positions at the end of a valley completely dominated by Russian artillery. This account comes from a sergeant in the 11th Hussars.

THE TRUMPETS now sounded the advance. The 13th and 17th moved off and the 11th were ordered to support them as soon as they had advanced about one hundred yards. We moved off, soon breaking into a gallop, but did not actually cover the 17th the whole way down, consequently we swept down the valley much nearer to the Fedioukine Hills than any other regiment. As we moved off, the Russians opened fire from all their batteries. The round shot passed through us and the shells burst over and amongst us, causing great havoc. The first man of my troop that was struck was Private Young, a cannon ball taking off his right arm. I, being close on his right rear, fancied I felt the wind from it as it passed me. I afterwards found I was bespattered with his flesh. To such a nicety were the enemy's guns elevated for our destruction that, before we had advanced many hundred yards, Private Turner's left arm was also struck off close to the shoulder and Private Ward was struck full in the chest. A shell too burst over us, a piece of which struck Cornet Houghton in the forehead and mortally wounded him.

When Private Young lost his arm, he coolly fell back and asked me what he was to do. I replied, 'Turn your horse about and get to the rear as fast as you can.' I had scarcely done speaking to him when Private Turner fell back, calling out to me for help. I told him too to go to the rear. I then galloped after the regiment. Happening at this moment to look to the rear, I saw the Chasseurs d'Afrique charging up the Fedioukine Hills at the battery that was taking us in flank.

As we neared the battery, a square of infantry that had been placed a little in advance of the guns, gave us a volley in flank. The very air hissed as the shower of bullets passed through us; many men were now killed or wounded. I, at this moment, felt that something had touched my left wrist. On looking down I saw that a bullet, which must have passed close in front of my body, had blackened and cut the lace on my cuff. Private Glanister had his lower jaw shattered by a bullet entering on the right side, and a bullet passed through the back of Private

The Light Brigade
charges the Russian
cavalry

Humphries' neck, just missing the spinal cord. At this time we were at a sweeping gallop. In another moment we passed the guns, our right flank brushing them, when about a hundred yards in rear Colonel Douglas halted us.

Charlotte Brontë's Honeymoon, Ireland

1854

CHARLOTTE BRONTË

After her marriage to an Irish curate at Haworth Church in June 1854, Charlotte Brontë left immediately for a picturesque honeymoon in Ireland, the following account of which is taken from a letter she wrote to a friend. It appears her feelings for her new husband were more those of platonic affection and respect than of genuine love.

YES, I AM married. A month ago this very day I changed my name. The same day we went to Conway – stayed a few days in Wales – then crossed from Holyhead to Dublin. After a short sojourn in the capital went to the coast. Such a wild, iron-bound coast, with such an ocean-view as I had not yet seen, and such battling of waves with rocks as I had never imagined.

My husband is not a poet or a poetical man, and one of my grand doubts before marriage was about 'congenial tastes' and so on. The first morning we went out on to the cliffs and saw the Atlantic coming in all white foam. I did not know whether I should get leave or time to take the matter in my own way. I did not want to talk, but I *did* want to look and be silent. Having hinted a petition, licence was not refused. Covered with a rug to keep off the spray I was allowed to sit where I chose, and he only interrupted me when he thought I crept too near the edge of the cliff. So far he is always good in this way, and this protection which does not interfere or pretend is, I believe, a thousand times better than any half sort of pseudo sympathy. I will try with God's help to be as indulgent to him whenever indulgence is needed.

We have been to Killarney. I will not describe it a bit. We saw and went through the Gap of Dunloe. A sudden glimpse of a very grim phantom came on us in the Gap. The guide had warned me to alight from my horse as the path was now very broken and dangerous. I did not feel afraid, and declined. We passed the dangerous part. The horse trembled in every limb, and slipped once, but did not fall. Soon after she (it was a mare) started, and was unruly for a minute. However I kept my seat. My husband went to her head and led her. Suddenly, without any apparent cause, she seemed to go mad – reared, plunged. I was thrown on the stones right under her. My husband did not see that I had fallen, he still held her. I saw and felt her kick, plunge, trample round me. I had my thoughts about the moment – its consequences – my husband – my father. When my plight was seen, the struggling creature was let loose. She sprang over me. I was lifted off the stones, neither bruised by the fall nor touched by the mare's hoofs. Of course the only feeling left was gratitude for more sakes than my own.

1855

Florence Nightingale in the Crimean War, Balaclava

FLORENCE NIGHTINGALE

Amid a prevailing spirit of philanthropy in which many Britons volunteered to help the wounded in war-torn Crimea, Florence Nightingale became head of a large group of government-sponsored nurses. After encountering appalling conditions and inadequate resources, she launched a ferocious tirade against the Medical Department. Throughout, however, she was deeply moved by the courage of the soldiers.

Florence Nightingale
(1820–1910)

WHEN I consider what the work has been this winter, what the hardships, I am surprised – not that the army has suffered so much but – that there is any army left at all, not that we have had so many through our hands at Scutari, but that we have not had all as Sir John McNeill says. Fancy working 5 nights out of 7 in the trenches, fancy being 36 hours in them at a stretch – as they were, all December, lying down or half lying down – after 48 hours without food but *raw* salt pork sprinkled with sugar – & their rum & biscuits – nothing hot – because the *exhausted* soldier *could not* collect his own fuel, as he was expected, to cook his own ration. And fancy, thro' all this, the army preserving their courage & patience – as they have done – & being now eager, the old ones more than the young ones, to be led even into the trenches. There was something sublime in the spectacle. The brave 39th, whose Regimental Hospitals are the best I have ever seen, turned out & gave Florence Nightingale three times three, as I rode away. There was nothing empty in that cheer nor in the heart which received it. I took it as a true expression of true sympathy – the sweetest I have ever had. I took it as a full reward of all I have gone through. I promised my God that I would not die of disgust or disappointment, if he would let me go through this. In all that has been said against & for me, no one soul has appreciated what I was really doing, none but the honest cheer of the brave 39th.

Nothing which the 'Times' has said has been exaggerated of Hardship.

It was a wonderful sight looking down upon Sevastopol – the shell whizzing right & left. I send you a Miniè bullet I picked up on the ground which was ploughed with shot & shell – & some little flowers. For this is the most flowery place you can imagine – a beautiful little red Tormentilla which I don't know, yellow Jessamine & every kind of low flowering shrub. A Serjt of the 97th picked me a nosegay. I once saved Serjt —'s life by finding him at 12 o'clock at night lying – wounds undressed – in our Hosp*l*. with a bullet in his eye & a fractured skull. And I pulled a stray Surgeon out of bed to take the bullet out. But you must not tell this story. For I gave evidence against the missing Surgeon – & have never been forgiven.

An English Lady at the Siege of Lucknow, India
Mrs G. Harris

The outbreak of the Indian mutiny in 1857 quickly resolved itself into a war of sieges, with the mutineers besieging troops and civilians at Lucknow, Cawnpore and other military posts. Lucknow was the most celebrated and was eventually relieved in November. The author was the wife of a British officer.

THE ENEMY made a very strong attack to-day; it began at 10 o'clock and lasted three hours, when they gave it up. Two 18-pounders came through the room Em. B. and I used to sleep in, and where we have since always gone to perform an alarmed and hurried toilet; it was impossible to wash and dress down in the Tye Khana, so we have hitherto braved the danger. J. was in the room this morning at his ablutions when the round-shots came through; he was quite smothered with dust, as a great piece of wall and ceiling came down, but was most mercifully saved from hurt. I was dreadfully frightened when I heard the noise, for I knew he was in the room. I really felt paralyzed with terror, till I heard him call out he was 'all right!' He was obliged to creep out of the rubbish almost in a state of nature, as he was just in the act of bathing when the shot struck the room.

We have by degrees crept upstairs during the day and sat in the little entrance-hall, which is considered tolerably safe; but this morning we were all hurried down to the lower regions in double-quick time. We dress now in a tiny barricaded closet out of the dining-room, where no balls have come yet.

We had two killed and nine wounded this morning during the attack. There were nine funerals to-night — the largest number since the battle of Chinhut. Mrs Polehampton has left the hospital and gone to a room at the Begum Kotee, which she shares with Mrs Barbor and Mrs Galle, both widows, whose husbands were murdered by the mutineers.

We have had no less than eight round-shot through this house to-day.

A Sewer-Hunter, London   Henry Mayhew

Victorian London, capital of a mighty empire, was a harsh and unforgiving environment for the poor. As in developing countries today, they had to eke out a living in any way they could.

I GOES DOWN to Cuckold's P'int and there I sits near half the day, when who should I see but the old un as had picked me up out of the mud when I was a sinking. I tells him all about it, and he takes me home along with hisself, and gits me a bag and an o, and takes me out next day, and shows me what to do, and shows me the dangerous places, and the places what are safe, and how to rake in the mud for rope, and bones, and iron, and that's the way I comed to be a shore-worker. Lor' bless you, I've worked Cuckold's P'int for more no twenty year. I know places where you'd go over head and ears in the mud, and jist alongside on 'em you may walk as safe as you can on this floor. But it don't do for a stranger to try it, he'd wery soon git in, and it's not so easy to git out agin, I can tell you. I stay'd with the old un a long time, and we used to git lots o' tin, specially when we'd go to work the sewers. I liked that well enough. I could git into small places where the old un couldn't, and when I'd got near the grating in the street, I'd search about in the bottom of the sewer; I'd put down my arm to my shoulder in the mud and bring up shillings and half-crowns, and lots of coppers, and plenty other things. I once found a silver jug as big as a quart pot, and often found spoons and knives and forks and every thing you can think of. Bless your heart the smell's nothink; it's a roughish smell at first, but nothing near so bad as you thinks, 'cause, you see, there's sich lots o' water always a coming down the sewer, and the air gits in from the gratings, and that helps to sweeten it a bit.

1862

Tothill Fields Prison, London HENRY MAYHEW

The shocking state of London's prisons gave continued cause for concern throughout the first half of the 19th century. This account by Henry Mayhew, journalist and social observer, is of the prison for boys at Tothill Fields.

AT A LATER part of the day we accompanied the warder to the airing-yard, to see the boys exercising. This was done much after the fashion of other prisons, the lads circling round and round, and each walking some six or seven feet apart from those next him. There were about forty boys altogether in the yard. 'They exercise', said the warder, 'in detachments, for about an hour each; we keep them walking briskly, and in cold mornings we make them move along in double quick time.'

As the little troop paced over the flag-stones, their heavy prison boots sounded very differently from what their naked feet are wont to do when outside the prison gates; and we could tell, by their shuffling noise and limping gait, how little used many of them had been to such a luxury as shoe leather. Then each boy had a small red cotton pocket-handkerchief tied to the button-hole of his jacket (for no pockets are allowed in the prison garb), and we could not help wondering how many of the forty young 'offenders' there had ever before known the use of such an article.

While the lads kept on filing past us, the chief warder, at our request, called over the number of times that those who had been recommitted had been previously in prison. This he did merely by quoting to us the red figures stitched to the arms of the 'known' delinquents.

The following cyphers indicate the number of recommittals among the band:- 4, 3, 2, 4, 2, 10, 3, 3, 10, 7, 6, 3, 4, 3, 4, 4, 2, 4, 6, 4, 3, 9, 2, 4, 2. Thus we see that out of the 40 exercising in the yard, there were no less than 25 who had paid many previous visits to the prisons.

After this, one of the lads, who had been ten times recommitted, was called from out of the ranks, and questioned as to his age and antecedents.

'How old are you, boy?'

'Thirteen years, please, sir.'

'What are you in for?'

'Coat and umbereller, sir. This makes seven times here and three times at Coldbath Fields, please, sir.'

'How long have you got now?'

'Three calendar months, and I've had two two-monthses as well – one of the two monthses here, and one at Coldbath Fields; and I've done one six weeks, and one two days besides, sir. It's mostly been for prigging,' added the young urchin.

'What did you take?'

'I took a watch and chain once, sir, and a pair of goold bracelets another time. I did a till twice, and this time it's for the coat and umbereller as I told you on afore. The two days I had was for a bottle of pickles, but that there was three or four years ago.'

A Confederate Soldier in Battle, Virginia, America WILLIAM H. MORGAN

1864

Morgan was Captain in a Virginia infantry regiment. He fought throughout the civil war until his capture in May 1864, which he describes here.

THE MEN OF the companies were scattered around on the hill, among the trees, embracing about an acre in area, without any regard to lines, fighting on the Indian style, some protecting themselves behind trees, some lying down, while most of them stood out in the open, watching for and shooting at every Yankee who showed himself within range. The Yankees, too, were under cover as much as possible with longer range guns than ours, slipping around behind trees, bushes and fences, and at every opportunity popping away at the Confederates, all the while getting a little closer and extending their lines around the hill. They were not very good shots, however.

Captain Horton and myself consulted, or held a small council of war, upon the situation. It was beyond question that if we remained on the hill, all would be killed or made prisoners in a short time. Some, or all of us, might escape by beating a hasty retreat. We agreed to try the latter, orders or no orders. Turning to the men who were by this time pretty close together about the center of the hill, with the Yankees still closing in, we told them we would all make a break and attempt to escape. Many of the men so earnestly demurred to this, saying, 'We will all be killed as we run across the bottom,' that Captain Horton and myself concluded not to make the attempt. I said to the men, 'We will stay with you then.' Near the top of the hill there was a ditch leading from what appeared to be an old ice-house, and in this ditch we made the last stand and fought the Yankees until they were close up. I remember Marion Seay, of Company E, who still lives in Lynchburg, was at the upper end of the ditch, shooting at a Yankee not thirty steps away, and then calling out and pointing his finger, saying, 'D—n you, I fixed you,' repeating it several times. Seay was then a little tow-headed boy, but he was game to the backbone.

Pretty soon our men ceased firing, as all knew that the inevitable had come. The Yankees then rushed up to the ditch, and all the Confederates dropped their guns – the seventy-five men left were prisoners of war.

As the Yankees came up, one of their men was shot through the head, and fell dead into the ditch; killed, I think, by one of his own men who was some distance off, firing. as he thought, at the Rebels. Some of the Confederates were bespattered with the brains of the dead Yankee.

1865

A Visit to Brigham Young, Utah, America

ALBERT D. RICHARDSON

The Mormon sect was founded by Joseph Smith in the 1830s. After his death he was succeeded by Brigham Young, by which time the Mormons had emigrated westwards and were firmly established in what is now the State of Utah.

BRIGHAM YOUNG, who succeeded Joseph Smith in the 'first presidency' of the church, was also born in Vermont. He is six feet high, portly, weighing about two hundred, in his sixty-sixth year, and wonderfully well-preserved. His face resembles that of the late Thomas H. Benton, though with a suggestion of grossness about the puffed cheeks and huge neck which Old Bullion never gave. His cheek is fresh and unwrinkled, his step agile and elastic; his curling, auburn hair and whiskers untinged with gray. Is he a new Ponce de Leon, who has found in polygamy the fountain of perpetual youth?

His inclosure of ten acres in the very heart of the city is surrounded by a wall, eleven feet high, of bowlders laid in mortar. It contains his two chief dwellings, the Lion House and the Bee-hive House. In them reside most of his wives, though a few favorite ones occupy separate dwellings outside. The inclosure contains various other buildings for his domestic and business purposes, and ample, well-kept gardens abounding in flowers and fruits.

Babies seem indigenous to Salt Lake. Their abundance through all the streets causes wonder till one remembers that they are the only product of the soil which does not require irrigation.

By Brigham's invitation I spent an hour in his school. Its register bore the names of thirty-four pupils; three, Brigham's grandchildren; all the rest his own sons and daughters. There were twenty-eight present, from four to seventeen years old, on the whole looking brighter and more intelligent than the children of any other school I ever visited.

With three of the prophet's daughters I had some conversation. Their language is good, and their manners graceful. One has a classic face; and another is so pretty that half the young men of the church are in love with her. Afterward, I visited the ward schools of the city. There, the foreheads are narrow and the average intelligence low. Tuition costs from four to ten dollars a quarter. *There are no free schools in Utah.*

Though Brigham has buried eight sons and two daughters, he has fifty surviving children and several grandchildren. His wives number about thirty; he increases the list by one or two additions yearly. The first and eldest is matronly and well-looking; all the later ones I saw are exceedingly plain and unattractive. Among the present generation of Mormons, the men are far more intelligent and cultivated than the women.

The Assassination of Lincoln, Washington, America   DANIEL DEAN BEEKMAN

1865

On 14 April 1865, President Abraham Lincoln was shot dead by a disaffected former Confederate, John Wilkes Booth, at Fords Theatre, Washington, where he had gone to see Our American Cousin. *Booth was later tried and executed. The narrator gave this version of events in a magazine article.*

I WAS IN MY seat at 7:30 facing the President's box when he came at 8:30 with his wife, Miss Harris (Senator Harris' daughter), and Major Henry R. Rathbone – Grant and his wife leaving the city at six o'clock that night. As the President walked along the gallery to his box, the orchestra played 'Hail to the Chief' and the audience arose and cheered him. I remarked to my friend, 'He is the homeliest man I have ever seen,' but when he acknowledged the applause by bowing and smiling, it so changed his countenance, that I said, it was the most heavenly smile I ever saw on a man's face. He sat in the right-hand corner of the box, in a rocking chair, his head resting on his hand, elbow leaning on the arm of his chair, looking utterly worn out and apparently in deep thought.

Upon the closing of the second scene in the third act of the play, about twenty minutes past ten, I heard the report of a pistol, and I said to my friend, 'that is

Abraham Lincoln (1809–65)

strange, there is no shooting in this play,' and just as I said that, Wilkes Booth, whom I took to be Edwin Booth, (the actor), threw one leg over the President's box, brandishing his dagger, crying out in a loud voice, 'Sic Semper Tyrannis,' Virginia's motto, which means, 'Thus always with Tyrants.' Booth's spur caught in the flag which decorated the President's box, and he fell on his knee, a distance of nine feet, causing him to limp as he ran across the stage, still theatrically brandishing his dagger, then disappeared behind the curtain before anyone in the audience realised what had happened.

Then I heard a woman scream, and some one called out, 'The President is shot' – and then, there was an uproar. The man sitting ahead of me was on the stage second, and I was the third one. I noticed a surgeon of the army, standing beside me, whom I knew by his straps, (having two brothers in the war, both Lieutenants, serving under Sherman, in the 135th N.J. Regiment) looking anxiously up to the President's box, and I said to him, 'Do you want to get up

Newspaper headlines announcing the death of the President

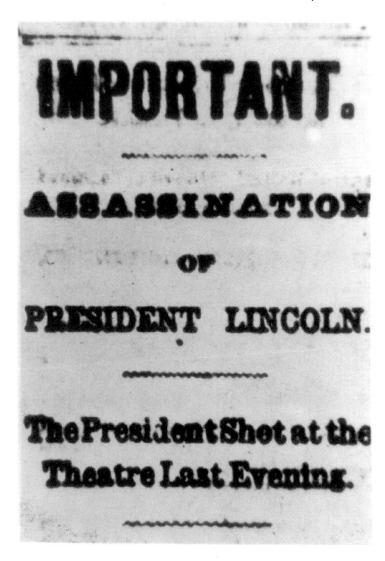

IMPORTANT.

ASSASSINATION

OF

PRESIDENT LINCOLN.

The President Shot at the Theatre Last Evening.

there?' and he said, 'Yes.' I told him to put his foot on my hand, the other foot on my shoulder, and I boosted him up into the President's box, which was about nine feet from the stage. No one could get in the box from the back, as Booth had barricaded the door after he got in by putting a piece of plank across, one end of which was secured in the wall, the other against the door.

The President was shot in the head, back of the left ear, so the surgeon told me after.

Everyone rushed out of the theatre as the report was circulated around that there were conspirators in Washington, and that all the Cabinet were killed. I told my friend, I was going to stay to see the President carried out which I did, taking hold of his elbow, lifting up his arm and putting my other hand on his wrist. I knew by his pulse, which was very irregular and weak, that he was fatally shot, which remark I made to my friend. They carried him across the street, where he died twenty minutes past seven the next morning just nine hours after he was shot.

A Victorian Picnic, Snodhill Castle, England

1870

REVD FRANCIS KILVERT

It would be difficult to better this lyrical description of a typical Victorian picnic in the Welsh border country 120 years ago – and the participants certainly had nothing to learn from us when it came to food and drink. The author, Kilvert, was an English clergyman whose diary is now an important social historical document.

TWENTY minutes passed, during which the gentlemen stood round the fire staring at the pot, while the ladies got flowery wreaths and green and wild roses to adorn the dishes and table cloth spread under an oak tree and covered with provisions. Then the pot hook was adjusted, the pot heaved and swung off the fire, a fork plunged into the potatoes and they were triumphantly pronounced to be done to a turn. Then there was a dispute how they should be treated. 'Pour away the water', said one. 'Let the water stay in the pot', said another. 'Steam the potatoes', 'Pour them out on the ground', 'Hand them round in the pot', 'Fish them out with a fork'. They were, however, poured out on the ground and then the pot fell upon them, crushing some and blackening others. Eventually the potatoes were handed round the table cloth, every one being most assiduous and urgent in recommending and passing them to his neighbour. There was plenty of meat and drink, the usual things, cold chicken, ham and tongue, pies of different sorts, salads, jam and gooseberry tarts, bread and cheese. Splendid strawberries from Clifford Priory brought by the Haigh Allens. Cup of various kinds went round, claret and hock, champagne, cider and sherry, and people sprawled about in all attitudes and made a great noise – Henry Dew was the life of the party and kept the table in a roar. After luncheon the gentlemen entrenched themselves upon a fragment of the Castle wall to smoke and talk local news and politics and the ladies wandered away by themselves. At last we all met upon the mount where Mary Bevan and someone else had been trying to sketch the Keep, and sat in a great circle whilst the remains of the cup, wine, and soda water were handed round. Then we broke up, the roll of the carriages was heard coming through the lanes below and everyone seized upon something to carry down the steep slippery grass slopes.

1870

An Awkward Funeral, Worcester, England

Revd Francis Kilvert

The burial of Kilvert's aunt, Maria, gives the diarist an opportunity to exercise his mordant wit on this most solemn of occasions!

So the clergy and choir came to meet us at the door, then turned and moved up the Cathedral nave chanting in solemn procession, 'I am the Resurrection and the Life saith the Lord'. But meanwhile there was a dreadful struggle at the steps leading up from the Cloisters to the door. The bearers were quite unequal to the task and the coffin seemed crushingly heavy. There was a stamping and a scuffling, a mass of struggling men swaying to and fro, pushing and writhing and wrestling while the coffin sank and rose and sank again. Once or twice I thought the whole mass of men must have been down together with the coffin atop of them and some one killed or maimed at least. But now came the time of the fat chief mourner. Seizing his opportunity he rushed into the strife by an opening large and the rescued coffin rose. At last by a wild effort and tremendous heave the ponderous coffin was borne up the steps and through the door into the Cathedral where the choristers, quite unconscious of the scene and the fearful struggle going on behind, were singing up the nave like a company of angels. In the Choir there was another dreadful struggle to let the coffin down. The bearers were completely overweighted, they bowed and bent and nearly fell and threw the coffin down on the floor. When it was safely deposited we all retired to seats right and left and a verger or beadle, in a black gown and holding a mace, took up his position at the head of the coffin, standing. The Psalm was sung nicely to a very beautiful chant. The Dean had the gout and could not appear, so Canon Wood read the lesson well and impressively in a sonorous voice. The Grave Service was intoned by the Sacristan Mr Raisin and sung by the choir, standing on the planking round the vault whilst a crowd of people looked in through the cloister windows.

Chinese Punishment of Criminals

REVD. E. D. G. PRIME

1870

Unusual and cruel methods of judicial punishment frequently shocked visitors to the Orient, as in this account by an American pastor.

AT SEVERAL points as I was passing along I came upon police-stations, where criminals of different grades were undergoing different degrees of punishment. Some were simply confined in large cages, the sport of the passers-by. Others wore immense collars made of two wide boards brought together at their edges, with a hole large enough for the neck. The collar is so wide that the prisoner cannot reach his head with his hands, and is dependent upon his friends or upon charity not only for his food, but for getting it to his mouth. Others had their heads jutting out of the tops of cages which were so high that they could not sit down, and so low that they could not stand up, or in which they stood on tip-toe, and they were condemned to pass days and nights in this uncomfortable and even torturing position.

A short time before, several criminals who had been guilty of a capital offense were condemned to death, and placed in these cages, where they died from starvation before the eyes of the people, no one being allowed to furnish them with food. Torture, as I subsequently learned by witnessing it at Canton, enters largely into the idea of punishment among the Chinese, and is freely resorted to for the purpose of extorting confession from the accused.

The Paris Commune EDMOND DE GONCOURT

1871

The defeat of France in the Franco-Prussian War of 1870 led directly, in the following year, to a communist insurrection in the capital which was savagely put down by the Federal authorities with heavy loss of life.

ALARGE BAND of National Guards appeared with their officers, falling back slowly and in good order. Others followed, marching faster. And finally some more came rushing along in a general stampede, in the midst of which we saw a dead man with his head covered in blood, whom four men were carrying by his arms and legs like a bundle of dirty washing, taking him from door to door without finding a single one open.

On the other side of the boulevard there was a man stretched out on the ground of whom I could see only the soles of his boots and a bit of gold braid. These were two men standing by the corpse, a National Guard and a lieutenant. The bullets were making the leaves rain down on them from a little tree spreading its branches over their heads. I was forgetting a dramatic detail: behind them, in front of the closed doors of a carriage entrance, a woman was lying flat on the ground, holding a peaked cap in one hand.

Soup kitchen during the Paris commune

At last our boulevard was in the hands of the Versailles troops. We had ventured out on to our balcony to have a look at them when a bullet struck the wall just above us. It was a fool of a tenant who had taken it into his head to light his pipe at his window.

The shells started falling again – this time shells fired by the Federates at the positions captured by the Versailles troops. We camped in the anteroom. Renée's little iron bed was pulled into a safe corner. Madeleine lay down on a sofa near her father, her face lit up by the lamp and silhouetted against the white pillow, her thin little body lost in the folds and shadows of a shawl. Mme Burty sank into an armchair. As for myself, I kept listening to the heart-rending cries of a wounded infantryman who had dragged himself up to our door and whom the concierge, out of a cowardly fear of compromising herself, refused to let in.

Now and then I went to the windows overlooking the boulevard, to look out at that black night of Paris, unrelieved by a gleam of gaslight or lamplight, and whose deep, fearful darkness concealed those of the day's dead who had not been collected.

c.1874 Lister Operating with Carbolic Acid, Edinburgh, Scotland   JOHN RUDD LEESON

Joseph Lister was the first surgeon to establish the need for antiseptics in surgical operations, following his successful use of carbolic acid to disinfect wounds as early as 1865. The following passage reveals that there were not yet attempts to exclude germs from wounds, merely to kill those that were present. Furthermore, carbolic acid itself

*attacked tissue as well as microbes. Lister saw in its use a delicate balance of 'evil'. John
Rudd Leeson worked with Lister.*

THE OPERATING theatre was grimed with the filth of decades; I suppose it
was occasionally cleaned, but such process was never in evidence. There was
but one window, the large one to the north, which lighted it, but it was never
opened. The frayed old wooden floor was browny-red, telling its tale of the scenes
it had witnessed. Many of the students came straight from the dissecting room.
The operating table looked as though it was never washed and around its base
sawdust was sprinkled.

No one dreamt of washing his hands before commencing work. I have seen
dressers assisting who wore 'mourning' beneath their nails. No one ever took off
his coat; occasionally the professor would turn up his cuffs, but the assistants
never; probably they would have considered it a breach of etiquette as assuming
an unwarranted importance.

When one thinks of the modern operating theatre, with its impermeable walls
and tesselated floor, the ritual of the officiating priests, their hand-washings,
scrubbings, boiled rubber gloves, sterilised overalls and face-pieces, one marvels
that early antiseptic surgery survived at all, but it was saved by carbolic; everything
was soaked in 1 in 20, hands, instruments, and patients' skins; huge Winchester
quarts of the precious fluid were everywhere around, and it was Lister's delight to
say again and again that carbolic acid penetrated grease, and its capacity was certainly tested to the uttermost, and it lived up to its reputation; we could not have
done without it.

Moreover, the whole scene of an operation or dressing was enveloped in its
spray, which dispersed its globules into every nook and cranny of the wound, and
our faces and coat-sleeves often dripped with it.

Towels soaked in 1 in 20 figured largely in the scene, and were placed around
the wound. I never remember them so used in London, but Lister never worked
without them; he would pin them carefully with (carbolised) safety-pins around
the part, leaving a window in which he worked; he was very fond of safety-pins.

Death of a Whale, South Pacific   FRANK T. BULLEN

c.1875

*From the 1750s onwards, whaling was an important industry to the expanding
European nations, particularly Britain, Holland and the Scandinavian countries, and
later America. Bullen was the first mate on a two year voyage to the South Seas on the
Cachalot, a New Bedford whaling ship.*

DURING A momentary lull in the storm, I took the opportunity to load my
bomb-gun, much as I disliked handling the thing, keeping my eye all the
time on the water around where I expected to see mine enemy popping up mur-
derously at any minute. Just as I had expected, when he rose, it was very close, and

on his back, with his jaw in the first biting position, looking ugly as a vision of death. Finding us a little out of reach, he rolled right over towards us, presenting as he did so the great rotundity of his belly. We were not twenty feet away, and I snatched up the gun, levelled it, and fired the bomb point-blank into his bowels. Then all was blank. I do not even remember the next moment. A rush of roaring waters, a fighting with fearful, desperate energy for air and life, all in a hurried, flurried phantasmagoria about which there was nothing clear except the primitive desire for life, life, life! Nor do I know how long this struggle lasted, except that, in the nature of things, it could not have been very long.

When I returned to a consciousness of external things, I was for some time perfectly still, looking at the sky, totally unable to realise what had happened or where I was. Presently the smiling, pleasant face of Samuel bent over me. Meeting my gratified look of recognition, he set up a perfect yell of delight. 'So glad, so glad you blonga life! No go Davy Jonesy dis time, hay?' I put my hand out to help myself to a sitting posture, and touched blubber. That startled me so that I sprung up as if shot. Then I took in the situation at a glance. There were all my poor fellows with me, stranded upon the top of our late antagonist, but no sign of the boat to be seen.

1876

An Indian Account of the Battle of the Little Big Horn, Montana, America TWO MOON

This interesting account of one of the greatest victories of the 19th century by Native Americans against the US army is recounted by a Cheyenne who was present.

INDIANS KEEP swirling round and round, and the soldiers killed only a few. Many soldiers fell. At last all horses killed but five. Once in a while some man would break out and run toward the river, but he would fall. At last about a hundred men and five horsemen stood on the hill all bunched together. All along the bugler kept blowing his commands. He was very brave too. Then a chief was killed. I hear it was Long Hair [Custer], I don't know; and then the five horsemen and the bunch of men, may be so forty, started toward the river. The man on the sorrel horse led them, shouting all the time. He wore a buckskin shirt, and had

long black hair and mustache. He fought hard with a big knife. His men were all covered with white dust. I couldn't tell whether they were officers or not. One man all alone ran far down toward the river, then round up over the hill. I thought he was going to escape, but a Sioux fired and hit him in the head. He was the last man. He wore braid on his arms [sergeant].

All the soldiers were now killed, and the bodies were stripped. After that no one could tell which were officers. The bodies were left where they fell. We had no dance that night. We were sorrowful.

Next day four Sioux chiefs and two Cheyennes and I, Two Moon, went upon the battlefield to count the dead. One man carried a little bundle of sticks. When we came to dead men, we took a little stick and gave it to another man, we

General Custer's death struggle at the Battle of Little Big Horn counted the dead. There were 388. There were thirty-nine Sioux and seven Cheyennes killed, and about a hundred wounded.

Some white soldiers were cut with knives, to make sure they were dead; and the war women had mangled some. Most of them were left just where they fell. We came to the man with big mustache; he lay down the hills towards the river. The Indians did not take his buckskin shirt. The Sioux said, 'That is a big chief. That is Long Hair.' I don't know. I had never seen him. The man on the white-faced horse was the bravest man.

1881

Pasteur's Public Demonstration of the Germ Theory, Pouilly le Fort, France   Louis Pasteur

One of Louis Pasteur's great scientific achievements was to show that infectious diseases are caused by germs. In the following extract from a letter to his children, Pasteur relates a critical stage in his celebrated public demonstration of the vaccination against anthrax in sheep. Amid incredible public and media interest, he injected twenty-four sheep with a mild culture of anthrax and later injected the same sheep, plus another twenty-four, with a fatal dose of anthrax microbes. Two days later, the twenty-four vaccinated sheep were alive and well, whereas the others had all died.

IT IS ONLY Thursday, and I am already writing to you; it is because a great result is now acquired. A wire from Melun has just announced it. On Tuesday last, 31st May, we inoculated all the sheep, vaccinated and non-vaccinated, with very virulent splenic fever. It is not forty-eight hours ago. Well, the telegram tells me that, when we arrive at two o'clock this afternoon, all the non-vaccinated subjects will be dead; eighteen were already dead this morning, and the others dying. As to the vaccinated ones, they are all well; the telegram ends by the words '*stunning success*'; it is from the veterinary surgeon, M. Rossignol.

It is too early yet for a final judgment; the vaccinated sheep might yet fall ill. But when I write to you on Sunday, if all goes well, it may be taken for granted that they will henceforth preserve their good health, and that the success will indeed have been startling. On Tuesday, we had a foretaste of the final results. On Saturday and Sunday, two sheep had been abstracted from the lot of twenty-five vaccinated sheep, and two from the lot of twenty-five non-vaccinated ones, and inoculated with a very virulent virus. Now, when on Tuesday all the visitors arrived, we found the two unvaccinated sheep dead, and the two others in good health. I then said to one of the veterinary surgeons who were present, 'Did I not read in a newspaper, signed by you, à propos of the virulent little organism of saliva, "There! one more microbe; when there are 100 we shall make a cross"?' 'It is true,' he immediately answered, honestly. 'But I am a converted and repentant sinner.' 'Well,' I answered, 'allow me to remind you of the words of the Gospel: Joy shall be in heaven over one sinner that repenteth, more than over ninety and nine just persons which need no repentance.' Another veterinary surgeon who was present said, 'I will bring you another, M. Colin.' 'You are mistaken,' I replied. 'M. Colin contradicts for the sake of contradicting, and does not believe because he will not believe. You would have to cure a case of neurosis, and you cannot do that!' Joy reigns in the laboratory and in the house.

Eruption of Mount Krakatoa, East Indies

SEAMAN DALBY

1883

On 27 August 1883 the volcano of Krakatoa in the Sunda Strait between Java and Sumatra exploded with extraordinary ferocity. The destruction of the cone is believed to have been the loudest natural noise in recorded history. Here a seaman on board the barque Hope *gives his account.*

THE RUMBLINGS got louder; they seemed all round us. The gusts of wind increased to a hurricane such as no man aboard had ever experienced. The wind seemed a solid mass pushing everything before it, and roaring like a huge steam-engine, shrieking through the rigging like demons in torment.

It became absolutely pitch dark, with flashes of vivid lightning which almost blinded us. The thunder was deafening. We followed the officers around to make sure of anything that looked like breaking away. We let go the other anchor, and officers and seamen were watching the cables all the day. We were fearful of our anchors, but they held. When we got a glimpse of the heavens we could see a terrible commotion going on. The clouds were whirling round at terrific speed. Most of us thought we were in the vortex of a cyclone, but, as the noise became louder and louder, I at any rate reckoned it was something volcanic, especially when about noon it rained a continuous downpour of dust. This seemed a sulphurous gritty sort of stuff, and as we had only about two cotton garments on, everyone was smothered all over, burned, choked and almost blinded.

Visibility at this time was about a yard. I seemed isolated, and felt my way about the deck, never loosing my hold of anything handy. No one could imagine the force of the wind. Occasionally I met others on the same lay as myself, but quite unrecognisable, just moving grey objects. Ropes and lines were lashing across the decks like whips. Once I noticed two terrified eyes belonging to a poor old coolie peeping from under a boat.

The noise was terrible, especially one great bang about noon, which is supposed to have been the loudest noise ever heard on earth. It shook the people out of their beds at Batavia, ninety miles away. It was the top of Krakatoa blowing up into the skies. Not that we knew or cared what it was. The whole heavens seemed a blaze of fire and the clouds formed such fantastic shapes as to look startlingly unnatural; at times they hung down like ringlets of hair, some jet black, others dirty white.

Death of General Gordon, Khartoum, Sudan

1885

RUDOLPH C. SLATIN PASHA

In 1885 General Gordon, commanding a garrison of Egyptian troops, was killed when Khartoum was stormed and captured by the Mahdi's dervishes. This account is by European mercenary in Egyptian pay who had been captured by Mahdist forces at Dara. There are no eyewitness accounts of Gordon's death, apart from a rather suspect one by a dervish who was present.

THE SUN WAS now rising red over the horizon; what would this day bring forth? Excited and agitated, I awaited the result with intense impatience. Soon shouts of rejoicing and victory were heard in the distance; and my guards ran off to find out the news. In a few minutes, they were back again, excitedly relating how Khartum had been taken by storm, and was now in the hands of the Mahdists. Was it possible the news was false? I crawled out of my tent, and scanned the camp; a great crowd had collected before the quarters of the Mahdi and Khalifa, which were not far off; then there was a movement in the direction of my tent; and I could see plainly they were coming towards me. In front, marched three Black soldiers; one named Shatta, formerly belonging to Ahmed Bey Dafalla's slave body-guard, carried in his hands a bloody cloth in which something was wrapped up, and behind him followed a crowd of people weeping. The slaves had now approached my tent, and stood before me with insulting gestures; Shatta undid the cloth and showed me the head of General Gordon!

The blood rushed to my head, and my heart seemed to stop beating; but, with a tremendous effort of self-control, I gazed silently at this ghastly spectacle. His blue eyes were half-opened; the mouth was perfectly natural; the hair of his head, and his short whiskers, were almost quite white.

'Is not this the head of your uncle the unbeliever?' said Shatta, holding the head up before me.

'What of it?' said I, quietly. 'A brave soldier who fell at his post; happy is he to have fallen; his sufferings are over.'

Tchaikovsky Meets Brahms, Leipzig, Germany

1888

ANNA LVOVNA BRODSKY

The following passage describes a fascinating encounter between two great, though very different, composers of the romantic era, Johannes Brahms and Piotr Ilyich Tchaikovsky. Anna Lvovna Brodsky was the wife of Adolph Brodsky, the Russian violinist who gave the first performance of Tchaikovsky's Violin Concerto.

WE INVITED Tschaikovsky to dinner, but, knowing his shyness with strangers, did not tell him there would be other guests. Brahms was having a rehearsal of his trio in our house that morning with Klengel and A. B. – a concert being fixed for the next day. Brahms was staying after the rehearsal for early dinner. In the midst of the rehearsal I heard a ring at the bell, and expecting it would be Tschaikovsky, rushed to open the door. He was quite perplexed by the sound of music, asked who was there, and what they were playing. I took him into the room adjoining and tried to break, gently, the news of Brahms' presence. As we spoke there was a pause in the music; I begged him to enter, but he felt too nervous, so I opened the door softly and called my husband. He took Tschaikovsky with him and I followed.

Tschaikovsky and Brahms had never met before. It would be difficult to find two men more unlike. Tschaikovsky, a nobleman by birth, had something elegant and refined in his whole bearing and the greatest courtesy of manner. Brahms with his short, rather square figure and powerful head, was an image of strength and energy; he was an avowed foe to all so-called 'good manners'. His expression was often slightly sarcastic. When A. B. introduced them, Tschaikovsky said, in his soft melodious voice: 'Do I not disturb you?'

'Not in the least,' was Brahms' reply, with his peculiar hoarseness. 'But why are you going to hear this? It is not at all interesting.'

Tschaikovsky sat down and listened attentively. The personality of Brahms, as he told us later, impressed him very favourably, but he was not pleased with the music. When the trio was over I noticed that Tschaikovsky seemed uneasy. It would have been natural that he should say something, but he was not at all the man to pay unmeaning compliments. This situation might have become difficult, but at that moment the door was flung open and in came our dear friends – Grieg and his wife, bringing, as they always did, a kind of sunshine with them. They knew Brahms, but had never met Tschaikovsky before. The latter loved Grieg's music, and was instantly attracted by these two charming people, full as they were of liveliness, enthusiasm and unconventionality, and yet with a simplicity about them that made everyone feel at home.

Despair of Vincent Van Gogh, Arles, France

1889

VINCENT VAN GOGH

The life of Vincent van Gogh hit a sudden, ultimately tragic, crisis in December 1888. After a dispute with Paul Gauguin, in a state of feverish excitement, he cut off a piece of his own ear and took it as a gift to a woman in a brothel. Following the incident he spent some time in hospital. Returning home in 1889, in an attempt to rebuild his life, he was hounded by local people who considered him a lunatic. Van Gogh committed suicide in 1890.

A NUMBER OF people here addressed to the mayor a petition (there were more than eighty signatures) describing me as a man not fit to be at liberty. The inspector of police then gave the order to shut me up again. So here I am shut up the livelong day under lock and key, and with keepers in a cell, without my guilt being proved, or even capable of proof. Needless to say, in the secret tribunal of my soul I have much to reply to all that. Needless to say, I cannot be angry, and to excuse myself I think is to accuse myself in such a case. Only I want to let you know.

You understand what a staggering blow between the eyes it was to find so many people here cowardly enough to join together against one man, and that man ill. And since I had really done my best to be friendly with people, and had no suspicion of it, it was rather a bad knock.

As far as my mental state is concerned, I am greatly shaken, but I am recovering a sort of calm in spite of everything. Strong emotion can only aggravate my case; while I am absolutely calm at the present moment, I may easily relapse into a state of overexcitement on account of fresh mental emotion. And if I did not restrain my indignation I should at once be thought a dangerous lunatic. Besides, humility becomes me after the experience of repeated attacks. So I am being patient. I am myself rather afraid that if I were at liberty outside I should not always keep control of myself if I were provoked or insulted, and then they would be able to take advantage of that. Here, except for liberty, I am not too badly off.

Meanwhile, I do beg you to leave me here quietly. I am persuaded that the mayor as well as the inspector are really rather friendly, and that they will do what they can to settle all this. I told the mayor that I was quite prepared to chuck myself into the water if that would please these good folk once for all; but that in any case if I had in fact inflicted a wound on myself, I had done nothing of the sort to them.

It is a shame – and all, so to speak, for nothing. I will not deny that I should rather have died than have caused and suffered such trouble.

1890

Prison Conditions in a Russian Penal Colony

ANTON CHEKHOV

Chekhov is perhaps the most popular Russian author outside his own country. The main reason for Chekhov's journey was to investigate the conditions in which prisoners were forced to live – and to try and publicise the brutalities of prison life in order to effect an improvement.

VOYEVODSK prison consists of three main buildings and one small one containing individual cells. Naturally, there is nothing good to say about the cubic content of air or the ventilation. When I entered the prison, they were just finishing washing down the floors, and the humid foul air had not yet dissipated from the night and it hung there heavily. The floors were wet and unpleasant to look at. The first thing I heard was complaints about bugs. You cannot live with them. At one time they were killed with chlorated lime, or they were frozen to death during intensely cold weather, but now nothing helps. The prison guards' quarters smell of latrines and sourness; they also complain about the bugs.

In the Voyevodsk prison convicts are fettered with balls and chains. There are eight fettered convicts here. They live in the common ward with the other prisoners and pass their time in absolute idleness. In any event, in the *Report on Assigning Various Kinds of Work to the Forced Labour Convicts*, those who are kept in balls and chains are numbered among the unemployed. Each is chained with manacles and fetters. From the middle of the manacles there hangs a long chain about three to four arshins long which is attached to the bottom of a small iron ball. The chains and ball constrain the prisoner and he moves as little as possible, which undoubtedly affects his musculature. Their hands become so accustomed to this that each slightest move-ment is made with a feeling of heaviness and when the prisoner finally is released from his ball and chain his hands retain their clumsiness and he makes excessively strong, sharp movements. When he takes a cup, for example, he spills his tea as though he were suffering from St Vitus's dance. At night, while sleeping, the prisoners keep the ball under the plank bed. To facilitate this, the prisoner is usually placed at the end of the bed

Anton Chekhov
(1860–1904)

A Description of the Ainu, Sakhalin, Russia

1890

Anton Chekhov

The Russian writer and physician Anton Chekhov travelled to the Island of Sakhalin in the far east of Russia to examine and report on the lives of the inhabitants. The Ainu were the aboriginal peoples of the area and can still be found in northern Japan. They are now close to extinction.

THE AINU are as dark as gypsies. They have tremendous beards and mustaches, and thick, wiry black hair. Their eyes are dark, expressive and gentle. They are of medium height and have a strong, stocky physique. Their features are massive and coarse but, in the words of the sailor V. Rimsky-Korsakov, they have neither the flat faces of the Mongols nor the slit eyes of the Chinese. It would appear that the bearded Ainu closely resemble Russian peasants. Actually, when an Ainu dons his *khalat*, which is similar to our farmer's short coat, and belts it, he resembles a merchant's coachman.

The Ainu's body is covered with dark hair which at times grows quite thick and in bunches on his chest, although it is far from being hirsute. This chest hair, and his heavy beard and thick wiry head of hair, is so rare in aboriginals that it astounded travellers, who returned home and spoke of 'the hairy Ainu'. Our Kazakhs who exacted tribute in furs from them on the Kurile Islands during the last century also called them 'hairy ones'.

c.1890

A Japanese Childhood, Tokyo JUNICHIRO TANIZAKI

This vivid account of Japanese dress and manners in late 19th-century Tokyo is by the eminent writer Tanizaki, one of the giants of Japanese literature.

THE STUDENTS all wore Japanese dress. The boys' kimonos had to be narrow-sleeved, though *haori* coats could be worn over them. In Shitamachi schools at any rate, *hakama* skirts were not part of the students' outfit. The girls wore nothing over their kimonos while the boys had a kind of apron to protect their clothes from dirt. Japan was not as sanitary a place then as it is now, and there were often many children with discharges from the ears and runny noses. (There were actually some teachers who would suck up the mucus running from their pupils' noses!) The boys' kimonos were for the most part made of cotton, either solid dark blue or with a splashed pattern, with sons of richer families wearing silk, including especially thin silk in the summer. The cleats attached to the soles of the boys' sandals made a characteristic metallic sound as they walked along. The narrow waistbands that held the kimonos together were usually of crepe de Chine, but some of the boys wore real *mousseline de soie*, dyed black so as not to be quite so conspicuous. I remember one day as I was being carried along on Granny's back, wearing a broad sash of *mousseline de soie*, a street thief sneaked up from behind and, with a single slash of his razor-sharp knife, cut through my sash and made off with it. (It must have been white, and so very conspicuous.) At any rate, I was always dressed in a stylish, rather showy manner, like a child actor in the Kabuki theatre; and I stood out from most of the other children at the Sakamoto school for this reason as well.

1892

An Anarchist Attempts to Murder Henry Clay Frick, Pennsylvania, America

ALEXANDER BERKMAN

The narrator, a Russian-born anarchist, tried to murder the steel magnate Henry Clay Frick during the bitter Homestead strike of 1892, and served fourteen years in prison for his crime. He committed suicide in 1936.

For an instant the sunlight, streaming through the windows, dazzles me. I discern two men at the further end of the long table.

'Fr—,' I begin. The look of terror on his face strikes me speechless. It is the dread of the conscious presence of death. 'He understands,' it flashes through my mind. With a quick motion I draw the revolver. As I raise the weapon, I see Frick clutch with both hands the arm of the chair, and attempt to rise. I aim at his head. 'Perhaps he wears armor,' I reflect. With a look of horror he quickly averts his face, as I pull the trigger. There is a flash, and the high-ceilinged room reverberates as with the booming of cannon. I hear a sharp, piercing cry, and see Frick on his knees, his head against the arm of the chair. I feel calm and possessed, intent upon every movement of the man. He is lying head and shoulders under the large armchair, without sound or motion. 'Dead?' I wonder. I must make sure. About twenty-five feet separate us. I take a few steps toward him, when suddenly the other man, whose presence I had quite forgotten, leaps upon me. I struggle to loosen his hold. He looks slender and small. I would not hurt him: I have no business with him. Suddenly I hear the cry, 'Murder! Help!' My heart stands still as I realise that it is Frick shouting. 'Alive?' I wonder. I hurl the stranger aside and fire at the crawling figure of Frick. The man struck my hand, – I have missed! He grapples with me, and we wrestle across the room. I try to throw him, but spying an opening between his arm and body, I thrust the revolver against his side and aim at Frick, cowering behind the chair. I pull the trigger. There is a click – but no explosion! By the throat I catch the stranger, still clinging to me, when suddenly something heavy strikes me on the back of the head. Sharp pains shoot through my eyes. I sink to the floor, vaguely conscious of the weapon slipping from my hands

An Encounter with the Ona, Tierra del Fuego, South America   E. Lucas Bridges

1894

The Ona indians of Tierra del Fuego, at the southernmost tip of South America, had virtually no outside contacts until sheep farmers moved into the area in the 1890s. They were greatly feared by the other tribes as warlike and ruthless killers. Within twenty years they had been virtually exterminated by disease and a deliberate policy of genocide.

One lovely evening at Cambaceres, towards the end of 1894, two tall Indians appeared on the crest of a hill some four hundred yards away from the house. My sisters, Bertha and Alice, were with me at the time. They could both use a rifle, so I left mine with them and went out to speak to these strangers. I had a small revolver hidden on my person and carried a handkerchief full of biscuits.

To show their peaceable intentions, the men had placed their bows and quivers on some nearby bushes. They were both well-grown, powerful, resolute-looking fellows, and their guanaco-skin robes, triangular head-dress and paint made them look even larger than they really were. The taller, about six feet high, was, I learnt later, called Chalshoat. Although his companion was two inches shorter, there could be no doubt that it was he whom I should address, for I guessed at once that this was the famous Kaushel. Though he smiled in an amiable way in answer to my manifestations of friendship, there was a dignity about the man that one could not help feeling.

We sat down together. I started eating a biscuit, then offered them a share. Having heard stories of Ona being poisoned, I made a rule always to consume some of any food I gave them, in case anyone might be taken ill afterwards and then blame it on me. We tried hard to talk but the only thing that emerged clearly was that we all wanted to be friends. Kaushel's voice, considering the harsh, guttural language he spoke, was gentle. At last I intimated that the sun was down, that it was time for sleep and that they should return the following morning. I do not know how much they understood, but we all rose, and they, adjusting their robes with a fling quite inimitable and as natural as it was graceful, turned and went back to pick up their bows and quivers from the bushes.

Queen Victoria's Diamond Jubilee, London

1897

ERNEST H. SHEPARD

One of the defining moments of the Victorian age, this sparkling account is given by the writer and illustrator E H Shepard, illustrator of A A Milne's Winnie-the-Pooh.

A STRANGE hush fell upon the crowds. First rode a solitary officer in the uniform of the 2nd Life Guards, the tallest man in the British Army. It was so quiet as he passed that the sound of his horse's hooves could be heard clip, clop, but from the distance came a muffled roar of cheering telling us that the Queen's carriage was drawing near. The waves of sound grew gradually louder until the State carriage, drawn by eight cream-coloured horses with purple trappings, and moving at a steady walk, came in sight. It was an open carriage on 'C-springs' and it seemed to rock slightly though the pace was slow and stately. The little old lady, a bonnet with a white osprey feather on her head and a black-and-white parasol in her hand, kept bowing to left and right. She looked pale. We learned afterwards that she was overcome more by the warmth of her reception south of the river than by the heat of the day. Indeed she nearly broke down, the tears streaming down her face. There could be no doubt what she meant to her people.

The carriage was followed by a glittering array of Emperors, Kings and Princes, Grand Dukes and Heads of State in uniforms of all colours. I was particularly impressed by a magnificent old Hussar, and also by a Guard Cuirassier

Queen Victoria's
Diamond Jubilee

from Germany. The Indian Princes who followed were splendidly mounted and their turbans and swords shone with precious stones.

It was all over before two o'clock. The Queen must have arrived back at Buckingham Palace and had her luncheon by that time and was no doubt being called on by the crowds outside to appear on the balcony in her wheeled chair. It was much later when we were able to leave our room and make our way home. The streets were thronged with people. Indeed, this was the case for the rest of the day and most of the night. We were very tired by the time we reached our own house.

1898

Cavalry Charge at Omdurman, Sudan

WINSTON CHURCHILL

The Sudan campaign of 1898 was planned and carried out to re-capture the Sudan from the dervishes who had controlled it since the death of General Gordon and the capture of Khartoum in 1885. Churchill was present at the final battle as a Lieutenant in the 21st Lancers.

THE WHOLE event was a matter of seconds. The riflemen, firing bravely to the last, were swept head over heels into the *khor*, and jumping down with them, at full gallop and in the closest order, the British squadrons struck the fierce brigade with one loud furious shout. The collision was prodigious. Nearly thirty Lancers, men and horses, and at least two hundred Arabs were overthrown. The shock was stunning to both sides, and for perhaps ten wonderful seconds no man heeded his enemy. Terrified horses wedged in the crowd, bruised and shaken men, sprawling in heaps, struggled, dazed and stupid, to their feet, panted, and looked about them. Several fallen Lancers had even time to remount. Meanwhile the impetus of the cavalry carried them on.

Stubborn and unshaken infantry hardly ever meet stubborn and unshaken cavalry. Either the infantry run away and are cut down in flight, or they keep their heads and destroy nearly all the horsemen by their musketry. On this occasion two living walls had actually crashed together. The Dervishes fought manfully. They tried to hamstring the horses. They fired their rifles, pressing the muzzles into the very bodies of their opponents. They cut reins and stirrup-leathers. They flung their throwing-spears with great dexterity. They tried every device of cool, determined men practised in war and familiar with cavalry; and, besides, they swung sharp, heavy swords which bit deep. The hand-to-hand fighting on the further side of the *khor* lasted for perhaps one minute. Then the horses got into their stride again, the pace increased, and the Lancers drew out from among their antagonists. Within two minutes of the collision every living man was clear of the Dervish mass. All who had fallen were cut at with swords till they stopped quivering.

1899

Winston Churchill is Captured by Boers, South Africa   WINSTON CHURCHILL

The young Winston Churchill went to South Africa in 1899 to cover the Boer war as a correspondent for the Morning Post. *He was captured when the armoured train on which he was travelling was ambushed.*

SUDDENLY there appeared on the line at the end of the cutting two men not in uniform. 'Platelayers,' I said to myself, and then, with a surge of realisation,

'Boers.' My mind retains a momentary impression of these tall figures, full of animated movement, clad in dark flapping clothes, with slouch, storm-driven hats poising on their rifles hardly a hundred yards away. I turned and ran between the rails of the track, and the only thought I achieved was this, 'Boer marksmanship.' Two bullets passed, both within a foot, one on either side. I flung myself against the banks of the cutting. But they gave no cover. Another glance at the figures, one was now kneeling to aim. Again I darted forward. Movement seemed the only chance. Again two soft kisses sucked in the air, but nothing struck me. This could not endure. I must get out of the cutting – that damnable corridor. I scrambled up the bank. The earth sprang up beside me, and something touched my hand, but outside the cutting was a tiny depression. I crouched in this, struggling to get my wind. On the other side of the railway a horseman galloped up, shouting to me and waving his hand. He was scarcely forty yards off. With a rifle I could have killed him easily. I knew nothing of white flags, and the bullets had made me savage. I reached down for my Mauser pistol. 'This one at least,' I said, and indeed it was a certainty; but alas! I had left the weapon in the cab of the engine in order to be free to work at the wreckage. What then? There was a wire fence between me and the horseman. Should I continue to fly? The idea of another shot at such a short range decided me. Death stood before me, grim sullen Death without his light-hearted companion, Chance. So I held up my hand, and like Mr Jorrocks's foxes, cried 'Capivy'. Then I was herded with the other prisoners in a miserable group, and about the same time I noticed that my hand was bleeding, and it began to pour with rain.

An Incident in the Boxer Rebellion, China

1900

Frank Richards

Chinese resentment at foreign interference led to a nationalist uprising and the siege of the diplomatic quarter in Peking which was eventually relieved in 1900 by a mixed force of European and Japanese troops including elements of the Royal Welch Fusiliers.

During the evening when the looting was at its height Robb and another man entered the house of an old Chinaman whom they found shivering with fright in a corner; not coming across anything of value they concluded that he had his valuables concealed somewhere. They made him understand that if he unearthed his treasure they would not kill him, but if he was obstinate they would. The old Chinaman shook his head, saying that he was a very poor man and that he had no valuables to hide. Robb's mate lost his temper and was just about to drive the bayonet home when Robb stopped him saying: 'No, not that way! I'm going to shoot him. I've always had a longing to see what sort of a wound a dum-dum will make and by Christ, I am going to try one on this blasted Chink!' He raised his rifle and shot the old man through the head. He fell dead at their feet. To satisfy his longing Robb examined the back of the head where the bullet had come out and what he saw caused him to remark: 'Christ, the dum-dum has blown out the back of his bloody nut!'

We were at Agra when Robb applied to be transferred to the home establishment. He was sent back and joined the First Battalion in Ireland. There on the Curragh one day he went with a lot of other men to bathe in a large pool. He dived into the water, where no doubt the ghost of the murdered Chinaman was lurking in wait for him. He did not come up from his dive and when his chums came to miss him they found him lying at the bottom near a big stone on which he had apparently struck his head. They pulled him out half-drowned and uncon-scious, with a big bruise on his head, and carried him to hospital. The injury left half of his body permanently paralysed. I never heard what became of him in the end, but the doctors did not hold out much hope for his recovery.

1902

Breaking Through the Blockhouse Line, South Africa   DENEYS REITZ

The defeat of the main Boer armies in 1900 was followed by two years of guerrilla warfare. The British Commander, Lord Kitchener, tried to limit the mobility enjoyed by the Boer commandos by dividing the country into sectors with lines of blockhouses built along the railways.

A S IS THE case with most railways in South Africa, a fence ran on either side of the line, composed of thick strands of wire which had to be cut before the horses could be led through. The only implement we possessed was a large file, and with this a young fellow named Verster and I tried to saw the wires, while the others waited a hundred yards back. The file grating across the taut wires made a tremendous noise, and before we had cut even one strand, we were again challenged and fired at by a sentry, who sounded not twenty yards away. We hur-riedly mounted to rejoin our companions, but our horses began to plunge and flounder over obstructions staked along the ground. In approaching the railway we had somehow or other missed these entanglements, but now we were in the thick of them, and the tins always attached to them were clanging and jangling, and increasing the terror of our animals. To this din was added a blaze of musketry from a block-house standing only a few yards away, which in the darkness we had mistaken for a mound of rocks.

Rifle-fire at point-blank range is unpleasant at the best of times, but when one is on a maddened horse staggering amid wire loops, it is infinitely more so, and had there been even a glimmer of light to guide the soldiers we should both have been shot. It was so dark, however, that they were firing at the sounds, and not at us, and Verster managed to wrench his horse free, but mine was hit and I was nearly pinned underneath him. I undid the buckles of the girth, and dragged my saddle from under the prostrate animal and, stumbling over the rest of the obstructions, we got clear away to where the others stood whistling and shouting to us and anxiously watching, not daring to shoot for fear of killing us. I had left the Shetland pony with them when I went forward to the fence, so I now put my saddle on him, and we galloped off, leaving the soldiers firing blindly into the night. We made a half-moon, until we again reached the railway-line, intending to have another try, but as soon as I began to use the file, we heard the sound of men running along the track towards us, so we lost no time in decamping, and abandoned all thought of crossing that night.

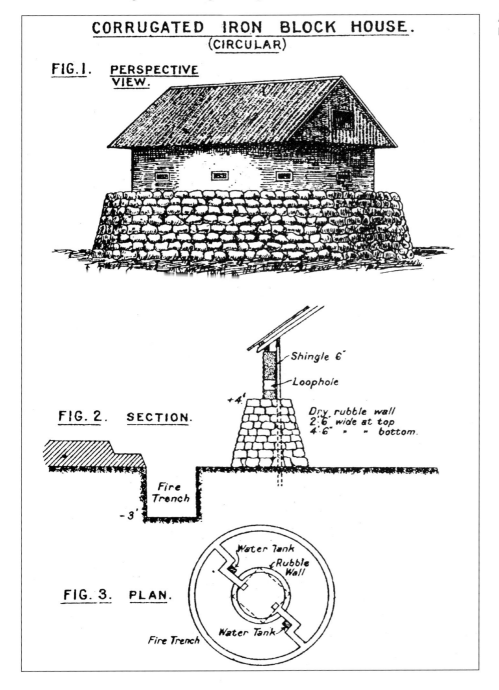

A typical Boer War blockhouse

1902

Renoir Battles with Arthritis, Essoyes, France

JEAN RENOIR

Pierre Auguste Renoir was one of the most successful and best-loved of the French Impressionists. His long battle against arthritis is here movingly recounted by his son.

RENOIR'S MALADY grew worse at irregular intervals. I should say that his condition changed radically after my brother Claude was born in 1902. The partial atrophy of a nerve in his left eye became more apparent. It had been caused by a bad cold caught some years before while he was out painting a landscape. His rheumatism made this semi-paralysis worse. Within a few months his face took on the fixed expression which so startled people who met him for the first time. All of us in the family, however, soon got used to his changed appearance, and except for the attacks of pain, which grew steadily worse, we completely forgot he was so ill.

Each year his face became more emaciated, his hands more twisted. One morning he decided to give up juggling the three balls, at which he had been so expert. He was no longer able to pick them up. He threw them as far away as he could, saying in an irritated tone, 'The devil take it, I'm going gaga!' He had to fall back on the game of *bilboquet*, played with a ball and peg, 'just like the one Henri III used in Alexandre Dumas!' He also tried juggling with a small log. He asked our coal and wood dealer to cut one for him very evenly, about eight inches long and two inches thick. He scraped it with a knife himself and sandpapered it till it was perfectly smooth. He would toss it into the air, making it turn round and round, and catch it adroitly, being careful to change hands from time to time. 'One paints with one's hands,' he would say. And in this way his fight to save his hands went on.

1905

At the Opera, Covent Garden, London

GEORGE BERNARD SHAW

THE IRISH-BORN dramatist and critic, George Bernard Shaw, came to London in 1876. After an unsuccessful career as a novelist, he became a celebrated critic of literature, art and music. His musical writings provide a vivid and often amusing impression of the place of music in London society. A freethinker and supporter of equality for women, this philosophy finds a rather curious extension in the following anecdotal plea.

NOW LET me describe what actually happened to me at the Opera. At 9 o'clock (the Opera began at 8) a lady came in and sat down very conspicuously in my line of sight. She remained there until the beginning of the last act. I do not complain of her coming late and going early; on the contrary, I wish she had come later and gone earlier. For this lady, who had very black hair, had stuck over her right ear the pitiable corpse of a large white bird, which looked exactly as if someone had killed it by stamping on its breast, and then nailed it to the lady's temple, which was presumably of sufficient solidity to bear the operation. I am not, I hope, a morbidly squeamish person, but the spectacle sickened me. I presume that if I had presented myself at the doors with a dead snake round my neck, a collection of blackbeetles pinned to my shirtfront, and a grouse in my hair, I should have been refused admission. Why, then, is a woman to be allowed to commit such a public outrage? Had the lady been refused admission, as she should have been, she would have soundly rated the tradesman who imposed the disgusting headdress on her under the false pretence that 'the best people' wear such things, and withdrawn her custom from him; and thus the root of the evil would be struck at; for your fashionable woman generally allows herself to be dressed according to the taste of a person whom she would not let sit down in her presence.

Dreyfus is Honoured at the *École Militaire*, Paris ALFRED DREYFUS

1906

In the following extract from his memoirs, Alfred Dreyfus describes a ceremony which took place on 20 July 1906, in which he was promoted to the rank of Chevalier of the Légion d'honneur, a decoration that completed his transformation from villain to hero of the French Republic. He had previously been reinstated in the Army, with the rank of major, and on 15 October 1906 resumed service, exactly twelve years after his false arrest on charges of treason.

ON THE afternoon of the same day, the ceremony of the investiture of my decoration took place in the Artillery Court of the *École Militaire.*

At five minutes to two the trumpets sounded. General Gillain, commanding the First Division of Cavalry, a man with white moustache and a martial bearing, entered the courtyard on foot. With swift strides he passed in front of the troops. The silence was heavy, impressive, and in that silence my thoughts flew back and lost themselves in suppressed memories of twelve years ago – the shouts of the crowd, the humiliating ceremony, my decorations unjustly torn off, my sword broken and falling at my feet in scattered fragments. . . . My heart beat as though it would burst. The blood rushed to my temples. Sweat broke on my forehead. . . . I had to make a tremendous effort of will to control myself and not to weep aloud for my past sufferings.

The command: 'Sound the drum!' tore me from my sorrowful reverie and brought me back to the reality of reparation. With a noble gesture, General Gillain drew his sword and pinned the Cross of an Officer of the *Légion d'honneur*, first upon Major Targe. Then the drums rolled again, immediately, for me. This time General Gillain pronounced the regular formula in a voice broken with emotion, and as he pinned the insignia of the order on my breast, he said to me, gently: 'Major Dreyfus, I am happy to have been charged with the duty of decorating you. I know what excellent memories you left behind you in the First Division of Cavalry.' Then he embraced me with all his heart, and his eyes were wet. The troops were then massed at one end of the Court. The command: 'Forward March!' rang out. And with the Lieutenant-Colonel at their head, preceded by a fanfare of trumpets, the troops marched past in front of General Gillain, Major Targe, and me. The officers saluted with their swords as they marched past. The trumpets sounded out, loud and clear, on this joyful day.

The troops vanished from sight. Immediately a crowd surrounded me, crying: 'Vive Dreyfus!' 'No,' I exclaimed: 'Vive la République, vive la vérité.' Hands were stretched out towards me, eagerly. I shook them, with a trembling grip. I embraced my friends. And it was all so moving that no words of mine can describe it.

1906

The San Francisco Earthquake, America

JOHN BARRYMORE

In the following extract, John Barrymore, of the famous Barrymore acting dynasty, describes his somewhat surreal experience of the San Francisco Earthquake. One night in April 1906, he along with (in his words) 'all of San Francisco and his wife' had heard a performance of Carmen, *with Caruso in a lead role, at the Grand Opera House – the first and, due to events in the small hours of the following morning, only night of what was intended to be a short season.*

I HAD ONLY been in bed a few minutes when the earthquake – the first great shock – occurred. It all but threw me out of bed. I put on my evening clothes again and went out into the hall, where I found the valet trying to wake his master, without success. An earthquake or the fact that his house was all askew did not disturb him, but when I went into his room and shouted at him, 'Come and see what has happened to the Ming Dynasty,' he jumped out of bed, for he was a true collector. The collection in which he had taken so much pride had been shaken into little more than a mere powder of glass.

There was nothing for us to do there, so we walked toward town. Everywhere whole sides of houses were gone. The effect was as if someone had lined the streets with gigantic dolls' houses of the sort that have no fronts. People were hurriedly dressing and at the same time trying to gather and throw out what seemed most valuable to them. More prudent persons, who couldn't too readily shake off the habits of shyness nor too quickly forget their decorum, were putting up sheets to shield themselves from the passers-by.

As I was getting very sleepy I went back to the St Francis and went to the desk to get my key. The clerk started to talk to me and to tell me that there was a split in the front of the hotel. I asked him if it was safe to go up to my room.

'Perfectly,' he said, with the trained assurance of a Californian. 'There isn't the slightest chance in the world of it ever happening again.'

Just then the second version, which was a little before eight o'clock, shook the whole place angrily, and the clerk jumped across the desk and, with what seemed to me like one motion, was out in Union Square. It was not so much a jump as it was a dive. It reminded me greatly of the old extravaganza, *Superba*, in which the Hanlon Brothers, of pleasing memory, used to make the most surprising entrances and diving exits from the stage.

Force-Feeding a Suffragette, Liverpool, England

1910

CONSTANCE LYTTON

The Women's Suffrage Movement produced many martyrs. Their campaign of civil disobedience resulted in many women being sent to prison where they frequently used hunger strikes as a protest. The government reacted by forcibly feeding them – a horrific experience as this extract shows.

TWO OF THE wardresses took hold of my arms, one held my head and one my feet. One wardress helped to pour the food. The doctor leant on my knees as he stooped over my chest to get at my mouth. I shut my mouth and clenched my teeth. I had looked forward to this moment with so much anxiety lest my identity should be discovered beforehand, that I felt positively glad when the time had come. The sense of being overpowered by more force than I could possibly resist was complete, but I resisted nothing except with my mouth. The doctor offered me the choice of a wooden or steel gag; he explained elaborately, as he did on most subsequent occasions, that the steel gag would hurt and the wooden one not, and he urged me not to force him to use the steel gag. But I did not speak nor open my mouth, so that after playing about for a moment or two with the wooden one he finally had recourse to the steel. He seemed annoyed at my resistance and he broke into a temper as he plied my teeth with the steel implement. He found that on either side at the back I had false teeth mounted on a bridge which did not take out. The superintending wardress asked if I had any false teeth, if so, that they must be taken out; I made no answer and the process went on. He dug his instrument down on to the sham tooth, it pressed fearfully on the gum. He said if I resisted so much with my teeth, he would have to feed me through the nose. The pain of it was intense and at last I must have given way for he got the gag between my teeth, when he proceeded to turn it much more than necessary until my jaws were fastened wide apart, far more than they could go naturally. Then he put down my throat a tube which seemed to me much too wide and was something like four feet in length. The irritation of the tube was excessive. I choked the moment it touched my throat until it had got down. Then the food was poured in quickly; it made me sick a few seconds after it was down and the action of the sickness made my body and legs double up, but the wardresses instantly pressed back my head and the doctor leant on my knees. The horror of it was more than I can describe.

1912

Escape from the *Titanic*, North Atlantic

Colonel Archibald Gracie

Archibald Gracie was one of the last to leave the sinking Titanic *and, before his death towards the end of 1912, left a detailed account of what happened from the moment the liner struck the iceberg. The following, eerie passage describes his remarkable escape from the sinking ship.*

As I was rising, I came in contact with ascending wreckage, but the only thing I struck of material size was a small plank, which I tucked under my right arm. This circumstance brought with it the reflection that it was advisable for me to secure what best I could to keep me afloat on the surface until succor arrived. When my head at last rose above the water, I detected a piece of wreckage like a wooden crate, and I eagerly seized it as a nucleus of the projected raft to be constructed from what flotsam and jetsam I might collect. Looking about me, I could see no *Titanic* in sight. She had entirely disappeared beneath the calm surface of the ocean and without a sign of any wave. That the sea had swallowed her up with all her precious belongings was indicated by the slight sound of a gulp behind me as the water closed over her. The length of time that I was under water can be estimated by the fact that I sank with her, and when I came up there was no ship

Sketches of the sinking of the *Titanic* made by a survivor while he was on one of the vessel's collapsible rescue boats

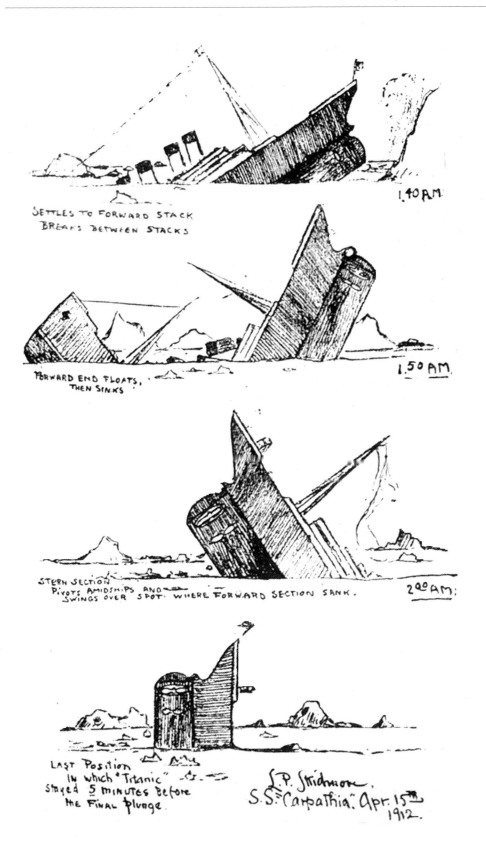

1.40 A.M.

SETTLES TO FORWARD STACK
BREAKS BETWEEN STACKS

1.50 A.M.

FORWARD END FLOATS,
THEN SINKS

2.00 A.M.

STERN SECTION
PIVOTS AMIDSHIPS AND
SWINGS OVER SPOT WHERE FORWARD SECTION SANK.

LAST POSITION
IN WHICH "TITANIC"
STAYED 5 MINUTES BEFORE
THE FINAL PLUNGE.

L.P. Skidmore.
S.S. "Carpathia" Apr. 15th
1912.

in sight. The accounts of others as to the length of time it took the *Titanic* to sink afford the best measure of the interval I was below the surface.

What impressed me at the time that my eyes beheld the horrible scene was a thin light-gray smoky vapor that hung like a pall a few feet above the broad expanse of sea that was covered with a mass of tangled wreckage. That it was a tangible vapor, and not a product of imagination, I feel well assured. It may have been caused by smoke or steam rising to the surface around the area where the ship had sunk. At any rate it produced a supernatural effect, and the pictures I had seen by Dante and the description I had read in my Virgil of the infernal regions, of Charon, and the River Lethe, were then uppermost in my thoughts. Add to this, within the area described, which was as far as my eyes could reach, there arose to the sky the most horrible sounds ever heard by mortal man except by those of us who survived this terrible tragedy. The agonising cries of death from over a thousand throats, the wails and groans of the suffering, the shrieks of the terror-stricken and the awful gaspings for breath of those in the last throes of drowning, none of us will ever forget to our dying day. 'Help! Help! Boat ahoy! Boat ahoy!' and 'My God! My God!' were the heart-rending cries and shrieks of men, which floated to us over the surface of the dark waters continuously for the next hour, but as time went on, growing weaker and weaker until they died out entirely.

1913

Scandalous Première of Stravinsky's *Rite of Spring*, Paris IGOR STRAVINSKY

The première of the controversial Rite of Spring *by Diaghilev's Ballets Russes produced one of the most violent reactions in the history of classical music. Indeed, the orchestra was scarcely audible amid the whistling, shouting and laughter of an indignant audience. Stravinsky here recalls the occasion, playing down the effect it had on himself, Monteux (the conductor) and Nijinsky (the choreographer).*

I WAS SITTING in the fourth or fifth row on the right and the image of Monteux's back is more vivid in my mind today than the picture of the stage. He stood there apparently impervious and as nerveless as a crocodile. It is still almost incredible to me that he actually brought the orchestra through to the end. I left my seat when the heavy noises began – light noise had started from the very beginning – and went backstage behind Nijinsky in the right wing. Nijinsky stood on a chair, just out of view of the audience, shouting numbers to the dancers. I wondered what on earth these numbers had to do with the music for there are no 'thirteens' and 'seventeens' in the metrical scheme of the score.

From what I heard of the musical performance it was not bad. Sixteen full rehearsals had given the orchestra at least some security. After the 'performance' we were excited, angry, disgusted, and . . . happy. I went with Diaghilev and Nijinsky to a restaurant. So far from weeping and reciting Pushkin in the Bois de Boulogne as the legend is, Diaghilev's only comment was: 'Exactly what I wanted.' He certainly looked contented. No one could have been quicker to understand the publicity value and he immediately understood the good thing that had happened in that respect. Quite probably he had already thought about the possibility of such a scandal when I first played him the score, months before, in the east corner ground room of the Grand Hotel in Venice.

Shackleton and his Crew Abandon Ship, Weddell Sea, Antarctic   SIR ERNEST SHACKLETON

1915

The following passage relates a celebrated episode from Sir Ernest Shackleton's courageous, though ill-fated, attempt to cross the Antarctic continent from sea to sea. The entire crew of twenty-eight men were marooned on the desolate, floating ice of the Weddell Sea, after turbulent ice floes had surrounded and crushed their ship Endurance. *As a result, most had to face several months of desperate hunger and cold while Shackleton sailed in a lifeboat in search of help from the island of South Georgia.*

THE PRESSURE was increasing steadily, and the passing hours brought no relief or respite for the ship. The attack of the ice reached its climax at 4 p.m. The ship was hove stern up by the pressure, and the driving floe moving laterally across the stern, split the rudder and tore out the rudder-post and stern-post. Then, while we watched, the ice loosened and the *Endurance* sank a little. The decks were breaking upwards and the water was pouring in below. Again the pressure began, and at 5 p.m. I ordered all hands on to the ice. The twisting, grinding floes were working their will at last on the ship. It was a sickening sensation to feel the decks breaking up under one's feet, the great beams bending and then snapping with a noise like heavy gun-fire. The water was overmastering the pumps, and to avoid an explosion when it reached the boilers I had to give orders for the fires to be drawn and the steam let down. The plans for abandoning the ship in case of emergency had been made well in advance, and men and dogs descended to the floe and made their way to the comparative safety of an unbroken portion of the floe without a hitch. Just before leaving, I looked down the engine-room skylight as I stood on the quivering deck, and saw the engines dropping sideways as the stays and bed-plates gave way. I cannot describe the impression of relentless destruction that was forced upon me as I looked down and around. The floes, with the force of millions of tons of moving ice behind them, were simply annihilating the ship.

A Day in the Trenches, France   Robert Graves

1915

This is as vivid a description of trench life in the First World War as one is likely to find, written by the poet and writer Robert Graves who served with the Royal Welch Fusiliers. He became friends with Siegfried Sassoon who served in the same battalion.

I JUMPED up on the fire-step beside the sentry and cautiously raised my head, staring over the parapet. I could see nothing except the wooden pickets supporting our protecting barbed-wire entanglements, and a dark patch or two of bushes beyond. The darkness seemed to move and shake about as I looked at it; the bushes started travelling, singly at first, then both together. The pickets did the same. I was glad of the sentry beside me; he gave his name as Beaumont. 'They're quiet tonight, sir,' he said. 'A relief going on; I think so, surely.'

I spent the rest of my watch in acquainting myself with the geography of the trench-section, finding how easy it was to get lost among culs-de-sac and disused alleys. Twice I overshot the company frontage and wandered among the Munster Fusiliers on the left. Once I tripped and fell with a splash into deep mud. My watch ended when the first signs of dawn showed. I passed the word along the line for the company to stand-to-arms. The N.C.O.s whispered hoarsely into the dug-outs: 'Stand-to, stand-to,' and out the men tumbled with their rifles in their hands. Going towards company headquarters to wake the officers I saw a man lying on his face in a machine-gun shelter. I stopped and said: 'Stand-to, there!' I flashed my torch on him and saw that one of his feet was bare.

The machine-gunner beside him said: 'No good talking to him, sir.'

I asked: 'What's wrong? Why has he taken his boot and sock off?'

'Look for yourself, sir!'

I shook the sleeper by the arm and noticed suddenly the hole in the back of his head. He had taken off the boot and sock to pull the trigger of his rifle with one toe; the muzzle was in his mouth.

'Why did he do it?' I asked.

'He went through the last push, sir, and that sent him a bit queer; on top of that he got bad news from Limerick about his girl and another chap.'

A Zeppelin is Shot Down, London

1916

Charles Ricketts

London was the first city in the world to suffer sustained aerial bombardment. From 1915 onwards the Germans flew regular airship raids across the Channel, and 556 people were killed as a result.

MY EYES FELT strained with watching the sky, and I was bathing them with eye-lotion when Shannon, who was by the stove, cried, 'Look! look!' and the room became filled with a salmon-pink glow. I imagined a searchlight breaking into the window, the Zepps being overhead. In the time it took to get to the window Shannon had guessed at a burning Zeppelin, and there it was, hanging perpendicularly above and to the right of the steeple of the church, looking at once detailed and unreal, like a twist of burning paper in the sky. The light increased and the flames billowed out at the base. The sky became like a sunset, pieces became detached, one larger than the others, obviously the gondola. Slowly the thing descended, breaking into different shapes, leaving the skeleton visible in the rack of the smoke. By it, seemingly immobile, stood a fixed light in the sky, from which dropped two bluish flames: this we imagined to be an aeroplane; and to the east a red light flashed up and out in mid-sky. Shannon and I, who watched breathless, exclaimed automatically, 'How splendid! How smart! How slowly she descends! How long has she been?' Shannon looked at his watch by the glow of his cigarette, it was five to 12. Then the flames grew amazingly less, the thing seeming half its size as it sank behind the church at the horizon, the afterglow rose in the sky; this was less than I imagined in effect. The cheering spread towards us, to be taken up hoarsely by the old road-watcher who crouched at his charcoal stove below.

The First Day of the Somme, an Aerial View, France, CECIL LEWIS

1916

This account, by a pilot in the Royal Flying Corps, combines all the lyricism of early flying literature, with a sharply observed account of the opening of the Battle of the Somme. The mine craters he describes may still be seen and are now official war cemeteries.

NOW THE watch in the cockpit, synchronised before leaving the ground, showed a minute to the hour. We were over Thiepval and turned south to watch the mines. As we sailed down above it all, came the final moment. Zero!

At Boisselle the earth heaved and flashed, a tremendous and magnificent column rose up into the sky. There was an ear-splitting roar, drowning all the guns, flinging the machine sideways in the repercussing air. The earthy column rose, higher and higher to almost four thousand feet. There it hung, or seemed to hang, for a moment in the air, like the silhouette of some great cypress tree, then fell away in a widening cone of dust and debris. A moment later came the second mine. Again the roar, the upflung machine, the strange gaunt silhouette invading the sky. Then the dust cleared and we saw the two white eyes of the craters. The barrage had lifted to the second-line trenches, the infantry were over the top, the attack had begun.

Storming of the Winter Palace, St Petersburg, Russia JOHN REED

1917

This must be one of the most famous accounts of the Russian Revolution ever written – by an American journalist covering the events in Russia on behalf of a radical newspaper 'The Masses.' He decided to live in Russia after the Revolution and died there of typhus in 1920.

AFTER A FEW minutes huddling there, some hundreds of men, the Army seemed reassured and without any orders suddenly began again to flow forward. By this time, in the light that streamed out of all the Winter Palace windows, I could see that the first two or three hundred men were Red Guards, with only a few scattered soldiers. Over the barricade of fire-wood we clambered, and leaping down inside gave a triumphant shout as we stumbled on a heap of rifles thrown down by the *yunkers* who had stood there. On both sides of the main gateway the doors stood wide open, light streamed out, and from the huge pile came not the slightest sound.

Carried along by the eager wave of men we were swept into the right-hand entrance, opening into a great bare vaulted room, the cellar of the east wing, from which issued a maze of corridors and staircases. A number of huge packing cases stood about, and upon these the Red Guards and soldiers fell furiously, battering them open with the butts of their rifles, and pulling out carpets, curtains, linen, porcelain, plates, glass-ware. . . . One man went strutting around with a bronze clock perched on his shoulder; another found a plume of ostrich feathers, which he stuck in his hat. The looting was just beginning when somebody cried, 'Comrades! Don't take anything. This is the property of the People!' Immediately twenty voices were crying, 'Stop! Put everything back! Don't take anything! Property of the People!' Many hands dragged the spoilers down. Damask and tapestry were snatched from the arms of those who had them; two men took away the bronze clock. Roughly and hastily the things were crammed back in their cases, and self-appointed sentinels stood guard. It was all utterly spontaneous. Through corridors and up staircases the cry could be heard growing fainter and fainter in the distance, 'Revolutionary discipline! Property of the People. . . .'

We crossed back over to the left entrance, in the west wing. There order was also being established. 'Clear the Palace!' bawled a Red Guard, sticking his head through an inner door. 'Come, comrades, let's show that we're not thieves and bandits. Everybody out of the Palace except the Commissars, until we get sentries posted.'

Two Red Guards, a soldier and an officer, stood with revolvers in their hands. Another soldier sat at a table behind them, with pen and paper. Shouts of 'All out! All out!' were heard far and near within, and the Army began to pour through the door, jostling, expostulating, arguing. As each man appeared he was seized by the self-appointed committee, who went through his pockets and looked under his coat. Everything that was plainly not his property was taken away, the man at the table noted it on his paper, and it was carried into a little room. The most amazing assortment of objects were thus confiscated; statuettes, bottles of ink, bedspreads worked with the Imperial monogram, candles, a small oil-painting, desk blotters, gold-handled swords, cakes of soap, clothes of every description, blankets. One Red Guard carried three rifles, two of which he had taken away from *yunkers*; another had four portfolios bulging with written documents. The culprits either sullenly surrendered or pleaded like children. All talking at once the committee explained that stealing was not worthy of the people's champions; often those who had been caught turned around and began to help go through the rest of the comrades.

Ambush at Kilmichael, Ireland TOM BARRY

1920

From 1919 to 1921 Irish nationalist guerrillas (the Irish Republican Army) fought a bitter guerrilla war against British troops. One of the most successful was Tom Barry, commander of the West Cork Flying Column who gives his own account of a typical ambush of British forces.

FIFTEEN seconds later, the first lorry came around the bend into the ambush position at a fairly fast speed. For fifty yards it maintained its speed and then the driver, apparently observing the uniformed figure, gradually slowed it down until at fifty yards from the Command Post, it looked as if it were about to stop. But it still came on slowly and, as it reached thirty-five yards from the small stone wall, the Mills bomb was thrown, an automatic barked and the whistle blew.

The bomb sailed through the air to land in the driver's seat of the uncovered lorry. As it exploded the rifle shots rang out. The lorry lurched drunkenly, but still came on impelled by its own weight, the foot brake no longer pressed as the driver was dead. On it came, the Auxiliaries firing their revolvers at the I.R.A. who were pouring lead into them, and then the lorry stopped a few yards from the small stone wall. Some of the Auxiliaries were now fighting from the road and the fight became a hand-to-hand one. Revolvers were used at point blank range, and at times, rifle butts replaced rifle shots. So close were the combatants that in one instance the pumping blood from an Auxiliary's severed artery struck one attacker full in the mouth before the Auxiliary hit the ground. The Auxiliaries were cursing and yelling as they fought, but the I.R.A. were tight lipped, as ruthlessly and coldly they outfought them.

It was not possible to see the efforts of the I.R.A. except those near me. There Jim (Spud) Murphy, John (Flyer) Nyhan and Mick O'Herlihy were fighting splendidly. Once I got a side glance of Flyer's bayonet being driven through an Auxiliary, whom I had thought dead as I passed him, but who had risen to fire and miss me at four yards' range. There was no surrender called by those Auxiliaries and in less than five minutes they had been exterminated. All nine

Auxiliaries were dead or dying, sprawled around the road near the little stone wall, except the driver and another, who with the life smashed out of them were huddled in the front of the lorry.

1921

Fighting the Riffs, Spanish Morocco

ARTURO BAREA

The rebellion of the Riff tribes against Spanish and French rule in Morocco escalated into the biggest colonial war since the conquest of North Africa in the mid 19th century. It involved the virtual annihilation of a Spanish army of 12,000 at Anual.

THE HANDLING of explosives was one of my specialities. That afternoon they came to fetch me. A sergeant of the Legion came together with one of our officers. They explained the case to me. They were just burying the dead. A legionary had bayoneted a Moor and stabbed him through the chest, but with such barbaric force that the rifle had penetrated up to the bolt. It was impossible to pull out the weapon except by sawing the corpse in two. But the rifle was still fit for use. So they had thought of introducing explosive into the rifle and blowing it up.

I organised the explosion as best I could. I poured a few percussion caps of mercury fulminate, such as we used for blowing up bore-holes in the quarry, down the rifle barrel which stuck out from the Moor's back. His was a skeleton-like body, wrapped in a torn grey burnous soaked in blood.

The mulatto, his lips still inflamed, his hands idle, watched me with curiosity while I dropped the golden little percussion caps with much care into the barrel. He stood back when I gave the order. I set fire to the fuse in the rifle mouth and ran away. The Moor's stomach burst open.

The mulatto laughed like an animal, with a twist to the lip that still smarted.

Back in my tent, I drank a large glass of brandy and stopped myself from being sick.

1922

A Chinese Wedding   NORA WALN

The writer of this piece was a member of an American Quaker family which had trading interests in China. She went there to live with a traditional Chinese family in 1920. Here she describes the wedding of the daughter of the house.

THE WEDDING dress was slipped over Mai-da's head, adjusted. It was admired by all the women and children who were now clustered in the room, in the doorway, and around the window. Mai-da had been a quiet doll to paint and dress, but suddenly she began to laugh with shrill hysteria. No one could stop her. The Elder's wife sent word that everyone, excepting Shun-ko, who 'has sense', and Faithful Duck, were to leave the Springtime Bower. Uncle Keng-lin came with his table lute and played lullabies to quieten Mai-da's nerves.

It was noon when Mai-da came to the Hall of Dignity. She bowed to the guests. She knelt in farewell to the Elders and to her parents. Her father fastened the groom's cloak about her shoulders. Her mother dropped his handkerchief as a veil over her face. The Family cried 'May you be as happy as the maid from Canton!' Crackers were fired in loud explosion. Mai-da was lifted into the bride's chair. The chair was closed. The sealing papers were fastened.

Kuei-tzu, Lady of First Authority in the Lin homestead, put her name on the seals. The drums rapped the call to start. The cymbals clanged assent. Flutes gave the 'Wail of Departure'. The groom's aunt and Faithful Duck got into the two green chairs. Lifting poles creaked. The bride's procession passed out of the House of her girlhood. The To and From the World Gate was locked behind her.

The clan of Lin gathered from far and near, feasting and talking and playing table games to pass the time, waited until the invitation should come from the clan of Tseng inviting the bride's mother to the 'After the Rites of the Marriage Bed Breakfast', which is assurance that the groom's family are satisfied. Thus Mai-da went to her husband.

Howard Carter Discovers Tutankhamun's Tomb, Egypt HOWARD CARTER

Howard Carter's exploration of the Valley of the Kings, where he hoped to find the tomb of the boy-pharaoh, Tutankhamun, bore little fruit between 1917 and the summer of 1922. Indeed he almost gave up the search. That he persevered was a great act of fate, for on 26 November 1922 he was to make the greatest archaeological discovery of modern times, described in the following passage.

Slowly, desperately slowly it seemed to us as we watched, the remains of passage debris that encumbered the lower part of the doorway were removed, until at last we had the whole door clear before us. The decisive moment had arrived. With trembling hands I made a tiny breach in the upper left-hand corner. Darkness and blank space, as far as an iron testing-rod could reach showed that whatever lay beyond was empty, and not filled like the passage we had just cleared. Candle tests were applied as a precaution against possible foul gases, and then, widening the hole a little, I inserted the candle and peered in, Lord Carnarvon, Lady Evelyn and Callender standing anxiously beside me to hear the verdict. At first I could see nothing, the hot air escaping from the chamber causing the candle flame to flicker, but presently, as my eyes grew accustomed to the light, details of the room within emerged slowly from the mist, strange animals, statues, and gold – everywhere the glint of gold.

Howard Carter
discovers the Tomb of
King Tutankhamun

Surely never before in the whole history of excavation had such an amazing
sight been seen as the light of our torch revealed to us.

First, right opposite to us – we had been conscious of them all the while, but
refused to believe in them – were three great gilt couches, their sides carved in
the form of monstrous animals, curiously attenuated in body, as they had to be to
serve their purpose, but with heads of startling realism. Uncanny beasts enough to
look upon at any time: seen as we saw them, their brilliant gilded surfaces picked
out of the darkness by our electric torch, as though by limelight, their heads
throwing grotesque distorted shadows on the wall behind them, they were almost
terrifying. Next, on the right, two statues caught and held our attention; two life-
sized figures of a king in black, facing each other like sentinels, gold kilted, gold
sandalled, armed with mace and staff, the protective sacred cobra upon their
foreheads.

These were the dominant objects that caught the eye at first. Between them,
around them, piled on top of them, there were countless others – exquisitely
painted and inlaid caskets; alabaster vases, some beautifully carved in openwork

designs; strange black shrines, from the open door of one a great gilt snake peeping out; bouquets of flowers or leaves; beds; chairs beautifully carved; a golden inlaid throne; a heap of curious white oviform boxes; staves of all shapes and designs; beneath our eyes, on the very threshold of the chamber, a beautiful lotiform cup of translucent alabaster; on the left a confused pile of overturned chariots, glistening with gold and inlay; and peeping from behind them another portrait of a king.

An Execution by Guillotine, French Guiana

KRARUP NIELSON

c.1925

For over a hundred years, French Guiana was a penal colony with an extremely harsh regime. The most hardened prisoners were sent to the notorious Devil's Island. The death penalty was frequently carried out, often by the prisoners themselves who were forced to act as executioners.

IMMEDIATELY before daybreak everything was ready for the execution. In the square round the guillotine the highest officials of the administration were present in uniform, according to regulation, as well as the Catholic priest, and a number of warders and officers.

In a circle outside all this were ranged the prisoners. According to the regulations all prisoners who are at the time in solitary confinement or Blockhaus, as well as the convicts of Class Two and Three have to be present at the execution. In front knelt the prisoners from the cells and Blockhaus in their chains; behind them stood the prisoners of Classes Two and Three.

The three condemned men were brought into the square and taken to their places beside the guillotine. Hespel had been granted the favour of being executed last, so that he might have the opportunity of making sure that 'the widow' was functioning properly, as he was responsible for having set her up. For his last meal he had been given a bottle of wine and a box of sardines. He drank the wine himself, and presented the condemned Chinese with the sardines.

The first of the two Chinese was calm and quiet up to the end, but when the knife had severed his head from his body his comrade collapsed and had to be dragged to the guillotine.

Hespel lit his last cigarette while the executioner lashed the Chinese on to the plank of the guillotine and cold-bloodedly felt for the exact spot where the 'widow' did her work. The cigarette was not finished when his turn came. He kept the end in his mouth, lay down on the plank, and murmured to his successor: 'See that I am lying right.'

A few seconds later the guillotine whirred and dropped on Hespel's neck. His head fell into the basket with the cigarette-end still between his lips.

In 'le Bagne' no one can afford to throw away a cigarette, and Hespel was in this respect a true 'bagnard'.

1927

Howling Dervishes, Syria   W. B. SEABROOK

Dervishes are one of the mystical sects of Islam who seek to achieve a state of hypnotic trance ('melboos') by various forms of dancing, self-torture and mortification. The Rufai or Howling Dervishes are here described. W. B. Seabrook was an American adventurer and travel writer active in the 1920s and 30s.

WE TRAVERSED a bare corridor, mounted a short flight of steps, passed several closed doors in a second corridor, and came to one which the sheikh opened.

On the stone floor, in the centre of a drab cell, whose only furniture was a worn pallet, a man sat hunched like an Aztec mummy. A broad leather strap, blackened and greasy, was fastened tightly round his body and across his back just beneath the armpits, then crossed again over the base of his neck and buckled under his drawn-up knees, so that his head was held down between them. His arms hung free and limp. He was naked to the waist, barefooted, with only a ragged pair of baggy drawers. He was motionless, except for his slow, steady breathing, and seemed unconscious. The Rufai sheikh told us that he had fastened himself in this position and would remain so for a day and a night, perhaps even a little longer, when he would return to a normal state of consciousness and probably release himself, but if he were too numb or exhausted he would call out, and one of his brothers would come and release him. He had already been there for about ten hours, and had long since passed into *melboos*, so that we entered the cell and spoke without the need of lowering our voices.

1927

Lindbergh Flies the Atlantic: Crossing the French Coast   CHARLES A. LINDBERGH

On 20 May 1927, Charles Lindbergh set off from New York in his plane the Spirit of St Louis. *He landed in Paris thirty-four hours later, thus completing the first non-stop airplane flight between the continents of America and Europe, a touchstone in aviation history.*

THE SEA is calm. Southward, just out of gliding range, lies the dusk-touched coast of Normandy. Little boats sail in toward shore, apparently motionless on the surface, leaving only their wakes as signs of movement to an airman's eye. A faint point of land, far ahead on my left, marks the location of Le Havre. The expanse of water, extending on eastward below it, is the estuary of the Seine.

I cross the coast again exactly on course, over Deauville. All the east foreshadows night. Day now belongs only to the western sky, still red with sunset. What more I see of France, before I land, will be in this long twilight of late spring. I nose the *Spirit of St Louis* lower, while I study the farms and villages – the signs I can't read, the narrow, shop-lined streets, the walled-in barnyards. Fields are well groomed, fertile, and peaceful – larger than those of England. It's not hard to

see how French farmers make a living; and there are plenty of places where I could land in emergency without cracking up.

People come running out as I skim low over their houses – blue-jeaned peasants, white-aproned wives, children scrambling between them, all bareheaded and looking as though they'd jumped up from the supper table to search for the noise above their roofs. Four-twenty on the clock. That's nine-twenty here. Why, it's past suppertime! I hold the stick with my knees, untwist the neck of the paper bag, and pull out a sandwich – my first food since take-off. The *Spirit of St Louis* noses up. I push the stick forward, clamp it between my knees again, and uncork the canteen. I can drink all the water I want, now – plenty more below if I should be forced down between here and Paris. But how flat the sandwich tastes! Bread and meat never touched my tongue like this before. It's an effort even to swallow. I'm hungry, because I go on eating, but I have to wash each mouthful down with water.

One sandwich is enough. I brush the crumbs off my lap, I start to throw the wrapping through the window – no, these fields are so clean and fresh it's a shame to scatter them with paper. I crunch it up and stuff it back in the brown bag. I don't want the litter from a sandwich to symbolise my first contact with France.

Lynching of a Black Prisoner, Indiana, America

1930

JAMES CAMERON

In the America of the 1930s the Ku Klux Klan became a powerful and malign influence. In this horrifying account, a young Black man then aged sixteen, describes the lynching of a friend for the alleged rape of a White woman – a crime for which the author himself had also been arrested.

THEY WALKED back to the cell where Tommy stood. No questions were asked. They reached in and grabbed him with violent and merciless hands.

He was beaten and kicked until he reeled and sagged to the floor in physical exhaustion. They dragged his senseless limp body out of the cell block.

From my cell block upstairs on the second floor, I could see the bloodthirsty crowd come to life the moment Tommy's body was dragged into view. It seemed to me as if all of those 10 to 15 thousand people were trying to hit him all at once. They surged forward in grim determination. In a matter of seconds, Tommy was a bloody mass and bore no resemblance to any human being. The mob kept beating on him just the same. Even after the long, thick rope had been placed around his neck, fists and clubs still mauled him, and sticks and stones continued to pummel his body. It was terrifying and sickening to watch, yet I couldn't turn my eyes away. Some irresistible force held my gaze to the scene being enacted in the streets below me. I watched them drag Tommy's body, around to the side of the jail where the mob hung him from the bars of the windows of the cell block where Abe was incarcerated.

I was told that despite all of that inhuman beating, Tommy had regained consciousness just before they hung him from the window. He had actually returned from the dead. In that brief instant, the instinct of life flickered like a hurricane wind. He fought the mob, savagely, for a few seconds, only to be knocked out for good. The rope, looped through the bars of the window, did the rest.

The crowd cheered wildly, jumping up and down in an insane and intense excitement as Tommy feebly writhed at the end of the rope. For all of 20 minutes, they pushed and shoved among themselves to get a closer look at the 'dead nigger'. The spectacle whetted their murderous appetite. They began chanting for 'another nigger!'

1931

Pierrepoint's First Hanging, Ireland

Albert Pierrepoint

Albert Pierrepoint was a public executioner from 1931 to 1956 and wrote an extraordinary account of his life. This was his first execution.

At nine o'clock we went to bed in a room in the prison officers' quarters. I slept right through until six, when I was awakened with the offer of a cup of tea. We had a good breakfast of ham and eggs, and I went with my uncle to the execution chamber to make the final adjustment to the drop which he had decided on the previous night. We brought up the trap doors, and by a few minutes before eight we were waiting outside the condemned cell.

My uncle stood, relaxed, sucking a sweet, with the arm-pinion in his hand. I never saw him otherwise at any execution, very calm, with a flat sweet in his mouth, the white cap folded in his breast pocket and the strap in his left hand.

At eight o'clock an official gave us the signal. I followed my uncle into the cell. I noticed that a priest was there, and saw little else. I followed my uncle the short distance on to the scaffold, strapped the legs, moved back, and had hardly time to get my balance, let alone look up, when there was a bang and then a space of complete silence. The traps were open, the rope was straight and motionless, the man was dead.

My uncle went into the pit by some side steps to open the prisoner's shirt for the doctor's stethoscope. The doctor confirmed death, and I suddenly realised that the chief prison officer was holding a glass of whisky out towards me. He had somehow produced a full bottle and some glasses, and was pouring drinks for all the witnesses.

'No thanks!' said my uncle quite evenly, but very firmly. I looked at him and saw that he was speaking for me as well as himself. 'No thanks,' I said, and the others stood savouring their drink for a few moments and then went away. The execution chamber was locked, and we followed the engineer to our quarters.

We had an hour to wait. I cannot say that I experienced any strong reaction. I was neither stunned nor relieved. My principal impression was of the astonishing speed of the operation.

An Air Crash in the Libyan Desert

ANTOINE DE SAINT-EXUPÉRY

1936

Antoine de Saint-Exupéry was one of the early pioneers of air flight and wrote lyrical accounts of his journeys across the Sahara and the Andes. In 1936 he and a companion crashed in the desert and only narrowly escaped death.

AT SUNSET, we decide to make camp. I know full well that we should keep moving: this night without water will be the end of us. But we have brought along the pieces of parachute cloth, and if the poison is not in the coating we might be able to drink something in the morning. Once more we must stretch out our dew-traps under the stars.

But to the north, the evening sky is cloudless. And the taste of the wind is different. So is its direction. Already the warm breath of the desert is touching us. The beast awakes! I can feel it licking our hands and our faces . . .

Yet if I keep walking I won't even manage six miles. In the last three days, with nothing to drink, I have already walked more than a hundred . . .

But as we come to a halt, Prévot says:

'I swear to you there's a lake there.'

'You're crazy!'

'How can it be a mirage at this time, at twilight?'

I don't answer, having long since given up any trust in my eyes. Perhaps it isn't a mirage, but then it's an invention of our madness. How can Prévot go on believing? He persists:

'It's only twenty minutes away, I'm going to have a look . . .'

His stubbornness is getting on my nerves:

'Go and see then, go and take a stroll . . . very good for your health. But let me tell you, if your lake does exist it's salt. And salt or not, it's out in hell somewhere. And it doesn't exist anyway.'

Prévot, staring straight ahead, is already on his way. I know all about these irresistible forces of attraction! And the thought occurs to me: 'There are sleepwalkers who throw themselves straight under trains.' I know that Prévot will not come back. Gripped by the vertigo of empty space, he will not be able to turn around. A little further, and he will fall. And he will die where he is, as I will where I am. How unimportant it all is!

1937

George Orwell is Wounded, Spain

GEORGE ORWELL (pen name of Eric Blair)

Like many other socialists at the time, Orwell viewed the Spanish Civil War as a clash between good and evil in which he felt compelled to take a part. He was wounded near Huesca while fighting with the POUM Trotskyist militia.

George Orwell
(1903–50)

IT WAS at the corner of the parapet, at five o'clock in the morning. This was always a dangerous time, because we had the dawn at our backs, and if you stuck your head above the parapet it was clearly outlined against the sky. I was talking to the sentries preparatory to changing the guard. Suddenly, in the very middle of saying something, I felt – it is very hard to describe what I felt, though I remember it with the utmost vividness.

Roughly speaking it was the sensation of being *at the centre* of an explosion. There seemed to be a loud bang and a blinding flash of light all round me, and I felt a tremendous shock – no pain, only a violent shock, such as you get from an electric terminal; with it a sense of utter weakness, a feeling of being stricken and shrivelled up to nothing. The sand-bags in front of me receded into immense distance. I fancy you would feel much the same if you were struck by lightning. I knew immediately that I was hit, but because of the seeming bang and flash I thought it was a rifle nearby that had gone off accidentally and shot me. All this happened in a space of time much less than a second. The next moment my knees crumpled up and I was falling, my head hitting the ground with a violent bang which, to my relief, did not hurt. I had a numb, dazed feeling, a consciousness of being very badly hurt, but no pain in the ordinary sense.

The American sentry I had been talking to had started forward. 'Gosh! Are you hit?' People gathered round. There was the usual fuss – 'Lift him up! Where's he hit? Get his shirt open!' etc., etc. The American called for a knife to cut my shirt open. I knew that there was one in my pocket and tried to get it out, but discovered that my right arm was paralysed. Not being in pain, I felt a vague satisfaction. This ought to please my wife, I thought; she had always wanted me to be wounded, which would save me from being killed when the great battle came.

One of Stalin's Executioners, Russia   LEV RAZGON

c.1938

The 17th Party Conference of 1934 was the start of the terrible period of mass purges in which perhaps five million people died. This chilling interview is with one of the NKVD guards who carried out executions in the labour camps.

'THEY SCRAMBLED down and there was already a trench dug in front of them. They clambered down, clung together and we got to work . . .'

'They didn't make a noise?'

'Some didn't, others began shouting. "We're Communists, we are being wrongly executed", that type of thing. But the women would only cry and cling to each other. So we just got on with it . . .'

'Did you have a doctor with you?'

'What for? We would shoot, those that kept wriggling got another bullet and then we were off back to the van. The work team from the Dalag camps was already nearby, waiting.'

'What work team was that?'

'There was a team of criminal inmates from Dalag who lived in a separate compound. They were the trusties at Bikin and they also had to dig and fill in the pits. As soon as we left they would fill in that pit and dig a new one for the next day. When they finished their work, they went back to the compound. They got time off their sentence for it and were well fed. It was easy work, not like felling timber.'

'And what about you . . . ?'

'We would arrive back at the camp, hand in our weapons at the guardhouse and then could have as much to drink as we wanted. The others used to lap it up: it didn't cost them a kopeck. I always had my shot, went off to the canteen for a hot meal, and then back to sleep in the barracks.'

'And did you sleep well? Didn't you feel bad or anything?'

'Why should I?'

'Well, that you had just killed other people. Didn't you feel sorry for them?'

'No, not at all. I didn't give it a thought. No, I slept well and then I'd go for a walk outside the camp. There are some beautiful places around there. Boring, though, with no women.'

1939

The Holocaust: Mass Arrests in Nazi-occupied Lódź, Poland DAVID SIERAKOWIAK

After the outbreak of the Second World War and the Nazi occupation of Lódź, the young David Sierakowiak and his family were among the city's 200,000 Jews who were rounded up and segregated in the notorious Lódź Ghetto, where hunger and disease were rife. Sierakowiak died, it is thought from tuberculosis, in 1943.

IT'S BEEN three days since the mass arrests began. Thousands of teachers, doctors, and engineers, Jews and Poles, have been taken from their homes, together with their families (infants have not been spared), and hurried to the market halls, and from there to various German jails. All old activists, former legionnaires, even simply rich people share the same fate. Groups of more prominent people are often dispatched immediately into the next world. The repairman who came to fix the faucet said that his wife and some engineers have been arrested. They could not touch the engineer because he's sick (the last phase of tuberculosis). So the Germans sealed the apartment with him and his servant inside. They were, for all practical purposes, condemned to death from hunger. His merciful neighbours lowered a string with bread (challah) so the servant could catch it through the window.

In the evening Mrs Pomeranc came for a visit. She had been to the Jewish Community Council and learned what's really going on. It's true that Lódź is to be cleared of Jews. All the poor who register at the Jewish Community Council receive 50 złotys per person and are literally thrown out of the city: they are taken to Koluszki by train, and are let loose into the world from there. Mrs Pomeranc was advised at the Jewish administration to wait. We, too, considered various plans for departure, but in the end nothing came of them, and we have to wait. Either they will throw us out, or they will not . . . In any case, the Hitlerjugendpartei [German; Hitler Youth Party] leader gave a huge speech, and what he said could be summed up in one sentence: 'We will exterminate the Jews because there is no place for them in the Reich!'

1942

The Holocaust: On the Run from Nazi Terror, Poland CHAIM PRINZENTAL

The following extract is taken from a farewell letter written by a Polish Jew to his children in Palestine, in anticipation of his murder by the Nazis. The desperate cry of somebody facing death, the letter forms part of the Yad Vashem Archives, a collection of hundreds of letters and postcards written by Jews under Nazi oppression.

I AM ALONE now in my misfortune, my comrade in distress was caught by the murderers on the second day of Rosh Hashana [the Jewish New Year], in full daylight; he had not been cautious enough. They tortured and then shot him. They searched for me, too, they even trod on me in the stack of straw where I was hiding. Yet, for the time being, they have not succeeded. Since then I have been wandering alone at night from village to village, from tent to tent, from forest to forest. But the forest, unfortunately, has started balding, and I also am naked and barefoot, hungry and sleepy. I am walking like a sleepwalker without seeing my own shadow, I am wandering – where to, I myself do not know. Shall I succeed in staying alive? I am not at all sure, it is very improbable.

A Secret Hiding Place, Holland   ANNE FRANK

1942

In 1942, the German-born Anne Frank and her family, who were Jewish, went into hiding in a secret part of their office building in Amsterdam. They remained there until their discovery and capture in 1944. Anne died in Belsen concentration camp. This is an extract from her diary, kept throughout this period.

O NLY WHEN we were on the road did Mummy and Daddy begin to tell me bits and pieces about the plan. For months as many of our goods and chat-

Anne Frank
(1929–45)

tels and necessities of life as possible had been sent away and things were sufficiently ready for us to have gone into hiding of our own accord on 16th July. The plan had had to be speeded up ten days because of the call-up, so our quarters would not be so well organised, but we had to make the best of it. The hiding-place itself would be in the building where Daddy has his office. It will be hard for outsiders to understand, but I shall explain that later on. Daddy didn't have many people working for him: Mr Kraler, Koophuis, Miep, and Elli Vossen, a twenty-three-year-old typist, who all knew of our arrival. Mr Vossen, Elli's father, and two boys worked in the warehouse; they had not been told.

The right door leads to our 'Secret Annexe'. No one would ever guess that there would be so many rooms hidden behind that plain grey door. There's a little step in front of the door and then you are inside.

There is a steep staircase immediately opposite the entrance. On the left a tiny passage brings you into a room which was to become the Frank family's bed-sitting-room,

next door a smaller room, study and bedroom for the two young ladies of the family. On the right a little room without windows containing the washbasin and a small W.C. compartment, with another door leading to Margot's and my room. If you go up the next flight of stairs and open the door, you are simply amazed that there could be such a big light room in such an old house by the canal. There is a gas stove in this room (thanks to the fact that it was used as a laboratory) and a sink. This is now the kitchen for the Van Daan couple, besides being general living-room, dining-room and scullery.

A tiny little corridor room will become Peter Van Daan's apartment. Then, just as on the lower landing, there is a large attic. So there you are, I've introduced you to the whole of our beautiful 'Secret Annexe'.

1943

A Poet Deserts, Tunisia   VERNON SCANNELL

The poet Vernon Scannell served in the Gordon Highlanders during the Second World War. He deserted in 1943, was captured and spent several months in a military prison before being released to serve in the Normandy campaign. In his autobiography Arguement of Kings *he calls himself John Bain.*

SOON MORE dead were seen, scattered on the hillside like big broken dolls and when John's platoon reached the now deserted enemy slit-trenches the area was littered with corpses. The rocks and sand had lost their earlier greyness and were now a pale yellowish brown in the morning sun. Already the flesh of the dead soldiers, British and enemy, was assuming a waxy theatrical look, transformed by the maquillage of dust and sand and the sly beginnings of decay.

B Company was ordered to halt and stand easy.

'Can't see any wounded,' Hughie said. 'The meat-wagons must've got them away down one of them tracks on the left flank.'

John did not answer. He could already smell the sweet feculence of the dead.

'You all right, Johnny?'

He nodded. 'Yeah, I'm okay.' But he was feeling strange and Hughie must have seen some outward sign of the sick, slightly feverish condition that seemed to generate an inward shivering and veil his surroundings with a transparent yet elusively transforming tegument of, not so much unreality, as a changed, harder and sharper reality. Then he saw that the other men in his section and from the other platoons must have been given the order to fall out because they were moving among the dead bodies, the Seaforths' corpses as well as the German, and they were bending over them, sometimes turning them with an indifferent boot, before they removed watches, rings and what valuables they could find. They seemed to be moving with unnatural slowness, proceeding from one body to another, stooping, reaching out, methodical and absorbed. Hughie had gone. He must have joined the scavengers.

John Bain watched this scene for a few moments. Then he turned away and started to walk back down the slope towards the foot of the hills where they had dug in on the previous night. No one attempted to stop him. No voice called out, peremptory and outraged. He walked unhurriedly but quite steadily, not looking back, his rifle slung on his right shoulder. And still no one shouted. It was as if he had become invisible. He plodded onwards and downwards. The sun was strong now and he felt the heat biting through his KD shirt. Sweat was soaking his hair under the steel helmet. He did not look back but kept his eyes down, seeing no more than a few yards in front of him. If there were any sounds his ears did not register them. He moved without any sense of physical exertion as if he had been relieved of a great burden and could enjoy an easy, almost floating sense of effortlessness as he walked onwards, down to the level ground and on to a rough track.

Working on the Burma Railway, Thailand

ALFRED ALBURY

1943

The author was captured in the fall of Singapore (February 1942) and worked on the notorious Burma Railway. He escaped when a ship taking him and other prisoners to Japan was torpedoed in 1945.

THOSE NIGHTS in the cutting I found even more hateful than the days. We worked in the fitful glare of hand-powered generators, three men taking it in turn to churn away at the handles. As a man tired and the light began to wane, the rocks would throw out long protecting shadows into the ravine. We squatted idly in the darkness, unseen by the Japanese. Then, as a bamboo fell across the shoulders of the man working the generators, the lamps burned brightly again. We in the cutting, revealed in idleness, were caught in a barrage of stones hurled down on us by the infuriated Japs who squatted on the edge of the cutting – they sat in the shadows just beyond the range of the lamps. Intimation that we had been caught resting was a screamed 'Bugairo' and a rain of flints striking all around us. Flagrant offenders were beaten and either made to stand on a rock holding up a shovel or were consigned to the generator 'hurdy-gurdy'.

I had several all-night sessions on these infernal machines and emerged from them a panting wreck. Bitten all over by swarms of whining mosquitoes, my muscles aching, my head throbbing dully from the fever that was taking hold of me, I used to crawl back to camp in a trance of exhaustion. Those nights seemed neverending. Crouched behind the generator, looking down into the cutting, it was a weird inhuman scene that swam before the operator's eyes. Bearded, silent, near-naked men shuffled along with their litters of stones in an endless column disappearing into the gloom beyond the cutting and returning with a tired reluctance for yet another load. Their arms and shoulders gleamed whitely in the arc-lamp glare; their stomachs were ugly swollen bulges bloated from months of eating rice. The blinding fury of the rains would lash their half-naked bodies and from all around would rise the wild mocking cries of the jungle night.

I sometimes wondered if I really saw this strange fantastic scene, or if it was only a nightmare that had gone on all too long. The momentary dimming of the lamp, the hoarse cursing of the Japanese and the stinging swish of bamboo would soon restore me to a harsh reality.

1944

A German Account of 'D' Day, Normandy, France JOSEPH HAEGER

On 6 June 1944 the biggest amphibious operation in history was successfully launched against the coast of France. By the end of the first day more than 150,000 men were ashore for fewer than 2,500 fatal casualties. The Normandy Campaign had begun.

WE HELD our position in the trenches for more than an hour. It was the most terrible time of my life. We were continually shelled and under fire from snipers. One of our bazookas hit a Canadian tank. We saw the flap opening and a soldier was half-way out when there was another explosion and it burst into flames with the soldier still hanging from the turret. I said to Ferdie, 'I hope we have a better death than that. I'd rather have a bullet.'

After about an hour we were ordered into a bunker, which was a command post almost entirely underground with a small observation hatch on the top. It was already full of wounded men. There were about thirty of them lying on straw blankets, absolutely terrified and crying out all the time. There was hardly any air inside and a man in the observation hole shouted that the Canadians were starting to pile earth up against the ventilators. It started to get very hot and difficult to breathe.

The company commander told us to breathe together: 'Breathe in when I say IN and out when I say OUT.' The battalion commander was firing a machine gun through a small aperture by the door. I will never forget the smell and the heat and noise inside that bunker, the cries of the wounded, the stink of exploding bullets and gases from the machine gun and the company commander yelling, 'IN, OUT, IN, OUT . . .'

Finally the company commander said to the battalion commander: 'Sir, we can't carry on. The wounded are suffocating.' The battalion commander said it was out of the question. 'We'll fight our way out of here if we have to. Count the weapons and the men preparatory to getting out.'

Ferdie said to me: 'You're the only one beside the battalion commander who's got a machine gun. You'll be the first out of here, believe me.' I said: 'No, I'm not going to do it,' and I pulled out the locking pin that held the machine together. Just then the man in the observation post shouted: 'My God, they're bringing up a flamethrower!'

We heard the 'woof' of the flame-thrower, but the flames couldn't get through the staggered sections of the ventilation shaft, although it turned red hot before our eyes. Now there was near panic. One German could speak two words of English and he kept shouting, 'Hello boys, hello boys, hello boys . . .'; eventually we took one of the dirty white sheets from one of the wounded and with the help of a broomstick pushed it out through the observation hatch. A voice from outside shouted, 'All right then, come on out.'

One of the soldiers opened the door and went out carrying the broomstick with a white sheet. Through the opening, we could see Canadian troops standing on either side of the trench. They started to shout, 'Oucha come, oucha come.'

We were made to lay down on the grass at the end of the trench, take off our equipment, boots and tunics. I said to Ferdie, 'Well, it's all over for us now.'

Auschwitz, Poland NATALIA KARPF

1944

Natalia Karpf survived the Płaszów and Auschwitz concentration camps. When she came to Britain with her husband in 1947, they encountered a world that turned a deaf ear to their horrific experiences.

THEY PUT us on trains – we knew we were going to Auschwitz. We were in a cattle wagon, where there was room for twenty or thirty: we were three times as many, we could hardly breathe. But on the way there they opened it up and let us out – we could actually have escaped, but we were terrified that we would be shot so we didn't. It took a few hours. And when we arrived there, there were so many waiting there. It looked much worse than Płaszów enormous. We went to Brzezinka, which was just before Auschwitz and was where the gas chambers were. Barbed wire, towers, barracks, many chimneys.

When we arrived there, they brought us into one barracks. They said, 'Wait here', we didn't know for what – we thought that they will take us to the gas chambers. We were there for twenty-four hours and every few hours there was another rumour: one rumour was that Mengele is coming. This word Mengele meant the biggest threat to your life, because he destroyed everybody, he sent everybody to gas chambers; when we heard Mengele is coming we knew it was our end, but he didn't come. Then another rumour: they are going to shave our heads. And Helunia said to me, 'If they shave my head, I shall commit suicide.' I said to her, 'You idiot – your hair will grow back but your head will not.' I said, 'Wait, don't anticipate anything.' But our hair was never shaved, only cut very short. Another rumour: we are going to the gas chambers. And so it went on for twenty-four hours.

At last they came to fetch us, and took us to the bath and so-called Entlausung – showers to get rid of the lice. We saw water running in the showers so we knew that they weren't gas chambers. And of course they took everything away from us – whatever we had – our own clothes, our toothbrushes. They took everything away from us. All the guards were armed; how could we resist? With our fists? We were so resigned, and so humiliated, that we really didn't care if they took the clothes or not.

1945

VE Day, London   COUNTESS OF RANFURLY

8 May 1945 marked the end of the Second World War in Europe, and was celebrated with scenes of wild rejoicing – but a sombre undertone was also present, a mood caught by the Countess of Ranfurly.

TODAY THE people of London and their children and thousands of visitors took to the streets and parks to celebrate victory in Europe. Flags flew from all the buildings. Shop windows were stuffed with red, white and blue clothes, flowers and materials. Planes flew overhead, and streamers, ticker tape and paper poured out of windows. There was no traffic because people filled the streets and pavements. I walked to the office and found only Air Marshal Slessor there. 'It's a National Holiday – you shouldn't have come,' he said. 'Supposing I stay and help till lunchtime,' I said and added, 'besides it's a brilliant time to throw some of your more boring papers out of our windows.' Before I left I peeled the canvas off one window and emptied the contents of five waste paper baskets on to Kingsway. I longed to be more generous but did not dare.

I eased my way into the Strand and progressed at snail's pace towards Trafalgar Square. It was a good-natured multitude and except for the sounds of feet and voices there was a silence over London – a silence loaded with emotion. A few people were crying and a few were laughing but the majority trudged forward silently. No one pushed. It took ages to reach Trafalgar Square which was already overcrowded – the steps, lions and lamp-posts were coated with people. I looked down on Whitehall which appeared to be paved with heads. Someone said, 'They are waiting for Mr Churchill.'

I drifted with the current along the Mall. As we drew nearer to Buckingham Palace I could hear people shouting, 'We want our King.' Around three o'clock Mr Churchill's voice came over amplifiers announcing that Germany has surrendered and hostilities will end at midnight. The dense crowds cheered and cheered and cheered again, stamped their feet, clapped, waved and threw hats in the air. Around five o'clock the Royal Family and Mr Churchill came out on the balcony and it seemed as if every voice in the world was cheering. I felt desperately sorry Dan was not with me.

Through a giant carnival of dancing, singing and laughing people I slowly made my way home with a thousand thoughts rushing through my head – of the lands, the skies and the seas I'd seen; of the marvellous people I'd met; of the wounded, the dead, the animals, the flowers, of the jokes and the tears; the hopes and the fears; of those terrible, frightening, yet triumphant years.

Bomb-devastated Hiroshima, Japan

1945

KENNETH HARRISON

The first atomic bomb was dropped on Hiroshima on 6 August 1945, killing 78,000 people and gravely wounding some 90,000 more. Kenneth Harrison was an Anti-Tank Gun Sergeant in the Australian army during the Second World War, and fought against the Japanese in the struggle to save Malaya. He spent the last years of the war as a POW in some of the worst Japanese camps, and, after Peace, was among the first non-Japanese to see Hiroshima.

MORNING dawned crisp and sunny. We joined a carriageful of wide-eyed Japanese on the first through train and by ten o'clock we were drawing near to Hiroshima… desolate Hiroshima, with its leaning houses and brooding silence.

At the centre of the city we stopped and looked about us, still unable to believe that one bomb had been responsible for this holocaust. But it was not difficult, standing on this hot road in the heart of the dead city, to imagine the great flash that had first dazzled and then incinerated the shocked people of Hiroshima. Nor was it hard to imagine the immense wave of searing air that had followed and

Hiroshima after the first atomic bomb

blasted down buildings and houses like matchsticks, and that had overturned thousands and thousands of hibachis (charcoal burners), so that all over Hiroshima there sprang countless pinpoints of flame that grew with nightmare speed into the roaring furnace that engulfed the living and the dead.

And, as we stood almost ankle deep in ashes, it was not hard to imagine how those who survived the blast must have run screaming up and down this now silent street. Some would have been carrying their crying, clutching children; others half supporting, half tugging, the shocked older people; all frantically seeking to escape from the blistering, searing heat that had turned their peaceful homes into places of horror, and their familiar streets into crematoriums in which perished possessions, hopes, and, in the end, fear. . . .

But that was imagination.

The reality was the girl with scarred features who passed with averted face. And the listless people who went by so dully; the scarred people; the burnt people; the apathetic people. And the people who even now showed not the slightest sign of hostility or resentment.

Saddened and depressed beyond words at the magnitude of the tragedy, and feeling like ghouls, we decided to leave Hiroshima that same day. There was little to keep us here; nothing to see; no place to rest; nothing to eat; nothing to drink.

Fortunately for our peace of mind we knew nothing of such atomic age refinements as radiation sickness, and although we occasionally picked up a statue or kicked over a strangely fused piece of metal for a closer look, we were never tempted to take a souvenir. One does not rob a tomb.

c. 1952

A Turkish Brothel, Istanbul J. A. CUDDON

The Orient has always been associated with the exotic. This extract gives a marvellously evocative picture of an Istanbul now destroyed by the developer and the onset of tourism.

THERE IS one street in Pera, not far from the main street, where the majority of the brothels are concentrated: perhaps twenty or more. Outwardly there is nothing remarkable about the street, except, of course, the extraordinary number of men in it day and night – but fewest in the mornings.

The houses are large and can be entered through one solid door from the street. In each of these doors, roughly at eye level, there is a small grill. Prospective clients crowd round taking it in turns to see if there is anything which appeals to them: a flesh and blood peep-show; what the butler saw but could not have hoped for.

Being curious, I explored one evening. I felt very self-conscious, nervous even. At last I plucked up enough courage to join a queue and eventually arrived at its head. Beyond the grill lay a salon: a spacious apartment full of sofas, divans and easy-chairs upholstered in more or less gaudy fashion. The boudoirs of lust are always tricked out in some finery.

About the furniture, pneumatic, lolling, sprawling, strolling, were the women. They were usually nine-tenths naked and tended to be large, heavily built, powerful almost; strapping succubae with ponderous, pendulant breasts, hurdler's thighs and discus-thrower's shoulders. Some wore chintz pants: the smallest and most absurd of concessions to modesty. Others were partly draped in transparent negligées; others still minced on high-heeled shoes. They lounged there basking in the harsh electric light and the contracting pupils of the desiring. I was vaguely reminded of alligators on a sandbank. There was a bored and animal lassitude about them and their heavily shadowed eyes were vigilant.

By the door, seated at a desk, was the manager, the pimp: the box-office. Periodically one of the women would throw out a casual remark, light a cigarette or stroll languidly and provocatively across the room, rolling her flaccid buttocks for the benefit of the craning audience which she knew were goggling at her through the grill. I was reminded of something else. It was like looking into a cage full of indolent panthers.

Sooner or later such a voluptuous display of curved and alabaster flesh would be too much for one of the men. There followed a sharp tap at the door. The ready and dexterous hand of the pimp opened it quickly. The man passed in. For a moment or two there was a mild disturbance of choice and transaction. Then the lens cleared and the tableau was as before – but with one fewer in it.

An Indian Hunter, Amazonia, South America

1958

Adrian Cowell

A perfect description of the synthesis between man and nature described by a member of the Oxford and Cambridge expedition to the Xingu.

THE AWETI was certainly an impressive figure. The Indians of the Upper Xingu have a fine eye for proportion and unlike other Indians do not distort their bodies with discs forced into their lips, staves thrust through their noses, or blocks of wood tearing at the lobes of their ears. On Kaluana's shoulders and thighs there were deep scratch marks made with the shark-like teeth of a fish called the *pirara*; but these had been drawn symmetrical to the line and flow of his limbs. In his ears he wore six-inch bamboo pins tipped with a bunch of toucan feathers so that when he turned there was a flash of colour in the forest's drabness; these were as perfectly proportioned to his Indian head as pendant ear-rings to a Marie Antoinette coiffure. And every part of him was in perfect balance to his purpose as a hunter. At the faintest sound, Kaluana could check one leg in the air, an arm half-way through a movement, the whole body frozen in the act of transferring balance from one foot to another, and yet in such perfect poise that the position could be held for minutes on end. He moved like a wraith that, having no substance, can disturb no obstacle, but in his case the secret was a form so supple that it automatically shaped and reshaped itself without conscious thought as it weaved between the bushes. At the end of a day, when I would be cut and marked all over, he would emerge without a single scratch on his naked skin.

A Polish Immigrant Arrives in Montreal, Canada   EVA HOFFMAN

Eva Hoffman was born in Cracow, Poland. At the age of twelve, her family emigrated to Canada, and she had to leave behind the people, places and childhood comforts of home, 'exiled' to the New World. Here she describes her first impressions of an alien environment.

WE ARE IN Montreal, in an echoing, dark train station, and we are huddled on a bench waiting for someone to give us some guidance. Timidly, I walk a few steps away from my parents to explore this terra incognita, and I come back with snippets of amazing news. There is this young girl, maybe my age, in high-heeled shoes and lipstick! She looks so vulgar, I complain. Or maybe this is just some sort of costume? There is also a black man at whom I stare for a while; he's as handsome as Harry Belafonte, the only black man whose face I know from pictures in Polish magazines, except here he is, big as life. Are all black men this handsome, I wonder?

Eventually, a man speaking broken Polish approaches us, takes us to the ticket window, and then helps us board our train. And so begins yet another segment of this longest journey – all the longer because we don't exactly know when it will end, when we'll reach our destination. We only know that Vancouver is very far away.

The people on the train look at us askance, and avoid sitting close to us. This may be because we've brought suitcases full of dried cake, canned sardines, and sausages, which would keep during the long transatlantic journey. We don't know about dining cars, and when we discovered that this train has such a thing, we can hardly afford to go there once a day on the few dollars that my father has brought with him. Two dollars could buy a bicycle, or several pairs of shoes in Poland. It seems like a great deal to pay for four bowls of soup.

The train cuts through endless expanses of terrain, most of it flat and monotonous, and it seems to me that the relentless rhythm of the wheels is like scissors cutting a three-thousand-mile rip through my life. From now on, my life will be divided into two parts, with the line drawn by that train. After a while, I subside into a silent indifference, and I don't want to look at the landscape any-more; these are not the friendly fields, the farmyards of Polish countryside; this is vast, dull, and formless.

The Cuban Missile Crisis, Washington, America ROBERT F. KENNEDY

1962

The following passage describes how President John F. Kennedy decided what action to take against Cuba, following aerial intelligence that Russia was installing ballistic missiles with atomic warheads there. He announced his decision to impose a naval blockade of Cuba on 22 October. Robert F Kennedy (the President's brother) was part of a senior presidential think-tank, though it is the President's own decisiveness which is most striking.

WE MET ALL day Friday and Friday night. Then again early Saturday morning we were back at the State Department. I talked to the President several times on Friday. He was hoping to be able to meet with us early enough to decide on a course of action and then broadcast it to the nation Sunday night. Saturday morning at 10 o'clock I called him at the Blackstone Hotel in Chicago and told him we were ready to meet with him. It was now up to one single man. No committee was going to make this decision. He canceled his trip and returned to Washington.

As he was returning to Washington, our Armed Forces across the world were put on alert. Telephoning from our meeting in the State Department, Secretary McNamara ordered four tactical air squadrons placed at readiness for an air strike, in case the President decided to accept that recommendation.

The President arrived back at the White House at 1:40 p.m. and went for a swim. I sat on the side of the pool, and we talked. At 2:30 we walked up to the Oval Room.

The meeting went on until ten minutes after five. Convened as a formal meeting of the National Security Council, it was a larger group of people who met, some of whom had not participated in the deliberations up to that time. Bob McNamara presented the arguments for the blockade; others presented the arguments for the military attack.

The President made his decision that afternoon in favor of the blockade. There was one final meeting the next morning, with General Walter C. Sweeney, Jr, Commander in Chief of the Tactical Air Command, who told the President that even a major surprise air attack could not be certain of destroying all the missile sites and nuclear weapons in Cuba. That ended the small, lingering doubt that might still have remained in his mind. It had worried him that a blockade would not remove the missiles – now it was clear that an attack could not accomplish that task completely, either.

Jim Garrison Learns of the Assassination of President Kennedy, New Orleans, America

JIM GARRISON

At the time of the Dallas assassination of President John F Kennedy, Jim Garrison was District Attorney of New Orleans. He became involved in the investigation because Lee Harvey Oswald had been resident in New Orleans in the summer of 1963. As the American nation mourned and clamoured for an immediate answer, Garrison began the painstaking work that would result in his implicating the United States government's intelligence community in 1969.

I WAS WORKING at my desk in Criminal Court, as district attorney of New Orleans, when the door flew open and my chief assistant rushed in. 'The President has been shot!' he yelled. It was just past 12:30 p.m., Friday, November 22, 1963.

Today, a quarter of a century later, I remember my shock, my disbelief. After I grasped what Frank Klein was telling me, I clung to the hope that perhaps Kennedy had merely been wounded and would survive.

Frank and I headed for Tortorich's on Royal Street in the French Quarter. It was a quiet, uncrowded place where they kept a television set in the dining room. On the way, the car radio announced that John Kennedy had been killed. The remainder of that trip was spent in absolute silence.

At the restaurant the midday customers were staring solemnly at the television set mounted high in the corner of the room. I felt a sense of unreality as the unending reportage flooded in from Dallas. There was very little conversation at the tables. A waiter came up, and we ordered something for lunch. When it arrived we toyed with our food, but neither of us ate anything.

The information coming from the television was inconclusive. Although the Secret Service, the F.B.I., and the Dallas police, along with an enormous crowd of onlookers, had all been at the assassination scene in Dallas, for at least two hours the crisp voices of the newscasters provided no real facts about who the rifleman or riflemen had been. However, we were hypnotised by the confusion, the unending snippets of trivia, the magic of the communications spectacle. Concerned with what had happened to the President and with our own hurt, no one left the restaurant that afternoon. The business and professional men who had come for lunch cancelled their appointments. Frank and I made our calls to the office and returned to the television set.

Then, well into the middle of the afternoon, the arrest of the accused assassin suddenly was announced. Approximately 15 Dallas police officers had caught him while he was seated in a movie theatre a considerable distance from the assassination scene. The delayed arrest burst like a bomb on the television screen, and the long silence in the restaurant ended. You could feel the sudden explosion of fury, the outburst of hate against this previously unknown young man. His name was Lee Harvey Oswald.

First Arrival on Robben Island, South Africa

1964

NELSON MANDELA

Now President of the Republic of South Africa, Mandela's story is one of the most astonishing come-backs of modern times. Here he tells of his arrival at the notorious prison on Robben Island, having received a thirty-year sentence for treason against the apartheid regime.

Nelson Mandela leaving prison, 1990

THE FOURTH morning we were handcuffed and taken in a covered truck to a prison within a prison. This new structure was a one-storey rectangular stone fortress with a flat cement courtyard in the centre, about one hundred feet by thirty feet. It had cells on three of the four sides. The fourth side was a twenty-foot-high wall with a catwalk patrolled by guards with German shepherds.

The three lines of cells were known as sections A, B and C, and we were put in section B, on the easternmost side of the quadrangle. We were each given individual cells on either side of a long corridor, with half the cells facing the courtyard. There were about thirty cells in all. The total number of prisoners in the single cells was usually about twenty-four. Each cell had one window, about a foot square, covered with iron bars. The cell had two doors: a metal gate or grille with iron bars on the inside and a thick wooden door outside that. During the day, only the grille was locked; at night, the wooden door was locked as well.

The cells had been constructed hurriedly, and the walls were perpetually damp. When I mentioned this to the commanding officer, he told me our bodies would absorb the moisture. We were each issued with three blankets so flimsy and worn they were practically transparent. Our bedding consisted of a single sisal or straw mat. Later we were given a felt mat, and one placed the felt mat on top of the sisal one to provide some softness. At that time of year, the cells were so cold and the blankets provided so little warmth that we always slept fully dressed.

I was assigned a cell at the head of the corridor. It overlooked the courtyard and had a small eye-level window. I could walk the length of my cell in three paces. When I lay down, I could feel the wall with my feet and my head grazed the concrete at the other side. The width was about six feet, and the walls were at least two feet thick. Each cell had a white card posted outside it with our name and our prison service number. Mine read, 'N. Mandela 466/64', which meant I was the 466th prisoner admitted to the island in 1964. I was forty-six years old, a political prisoner with a life sentence, and that small cramped space was to be my home for I knew not how long.

1967

An Incident in the Cultural Revolution, China

JUNG CHANG

1966 saw the start of the Cultural Revolution in China. Orchestrated by Mao Tse Tung it prescribed a state of permanent revolutionary activity and was, in effect, a purge of traditional 'Old Style' communists. An estimated ten million people lost their lives in the period up to 1970.

PHYSICAL abuse finally caught up with my mother. It did not come from people working under her, but mainly from ex-convicts who were working in street workshops in her Eastern District – robbers, rapists, drug smugglers, and pimps. Unlike 'political criminals', who were on the receiving end of the Cultural Revolution, these common criminals were encouraged to attack designated victims. They had nothing against my mother personally, but she had been one of the top leaders in her district, and that was enough.

Several times my mother was paraded through the streets with a dunce cap on her head, and a heavy placard hanging from her neck on which her name was written with a big cross over it to show her humiliation and her demise. Every few steps, she and her colleagues were forced to go down on their knees and kowtow to the crowds. Children would be jeering at her. Some would shout that their kowtowing did not make enough noise and demand that they do it again. My mother and her colleagues then had to bang their foreheads loudly on the stone pavement.

One day that winter there was a denunciation meeting at a street workshop. Before the meeting, while the participants had lunch in the canteen, my mother and her colleagues were ordered to kneel for one and a half hours on grit-covered ground in the open. It was raining and she got soaked to the skin; the biting wind sent icy chills through her wet clothes and into her bones. When the meeting started, she had to stand bent double on the platform, trying to control her shivers. As the wild, empty screaming went on, her waist and neck became unbearably painful. She twisted herself slightly, and tried to lift her head a bit to ease the aching. Suddenly she felt a heavy blow across the back of her head, which knocked her to the ground.

It was only some time later that she learned what had happened. A woman sitting in the front row, a brothel owner who had been imprisoned when the Communists clamped down on prostitution, had fixated on my mother, perhaps because she was the only woman on the platform. The moment my mother lifted her head, this woman jumped up and thrust an awl straight at her left eye. The Rebel guard standing behind my mother saw it coming and struck her to the ground. Had it not been for him, my mother would have lost her eye.

Massacre at My Lai, Vietnam   PHAM THI THUAM

On 16 March 1968 a unit of American soldiers entered a Vietnamese village and massacred some 500 men, women and children. A survivor tells her story in this dead-pan and shocking account.

IN THE DITCH I pushed my daughter down under my stomach and told her not to cry and tried not to move. I pressed my daughter under my tummy while my body was covered with the dead above me. I pretended to be dead and dared not move. The Americans were waiting to see if anyone moved, and then they shot them. I put a hand over my child's mouth to prevent her from crying. She was covered in blood. Long afterwards, when the shooting had completely stopped, I pushed some corpses away to free myself. I looked up and saw dead bodies curled up in the ditch. Then I took hold of my child and ran.

I ran and managed to reach the furthest part of the road, a great distance from the Americans. I run up to the neighbouring hamlet crying. There I washed the blood away from my clothes. The people in the village came to help me and gave me clean clothes to put on.

I don't know why the Americans came and landed here and killed people, we didn't do anything. This was a region where there was security. There was a South Vietnamese military post on Elephant Hill (overlooking My Lai). Down here in the hamlet the people lived and worked normally.

After the massacre life was a struggle, life was very hard. It was a hand-to-mouth existence. We had to hide the things we produced in the field. The soldiers stayed up in their military post. We rebuilt our shelters and put up tents. My daughter is Nguyen Thi Lien. She is married now.

Flight of Apollo 11: First Men on the Moon

EDWIN E ALDRIN

On 21 July, at 0256 hours GMT, Neil Armstrong stepped out of the lunar module, code-named Eagle, and became the first man to set foot on the surface of the moon, followed soon after by Edwin 'Buzz' Aldrin. Over the course of the next thirteen hours that they were on the moon, the pair practised walking, set up scientific experiments, planted an American flag and even received live congratulations from the American President.

THE MOON was a very natural and very pleasant environment in which to work. It had many of the advantages of zero-gravity, but it was in a sense less *lonesome* than zero G, where you always have to pay attention to securing attachment points to give you some means of leverage. In one-sixth gravity, on the moon, you had a distinct feeling of being *somewhere*, and you had a constant, though at many times ill defined, sense of direction and force.

One interesting thing was that the horizontal reference on the moon is not at all well defined. That is, it's difficult to know when you are leaning forward or

Buzz Aldrin
(1930–)

backward and to what degree. This fact, coupled with the rather limited field of vision from our helmets, made local features of the moon appear to change slope, depending on which way you were looking and how you were standing. The weight of the backpack tends to pull you backward, and you must consciously lean forward just a little to compensate. I believe someone has described the posture as 'tired ape' – almost erect but slumped forward a little. It was difficult sometimes to know when you were standing erect. It felt as if you could lean farther in any direction, without losing your balance, than on earth. By far the easiest and most natural way to move on the surface of the moon is to put one foot in front of the other. The kangaroo hop did work, but it led to some instability; there was not so much control when you were moving around

As we deployed our experiments on the surface we had to jettison things like lanyards, retaining fasteners, etc., and some of these we tossed away. The objects would go away with a slow, lazy motion. If anyone tried to throw a baseball back and forth in that atmosphere he would have difficulty, at first, acclimatising himself to that slow, lazy trajectory; but I believe he could adapt to it quite readily.

Technically the most difficult task I performed on the surface was driving those core samplers into the ground to get little tubes of lunar material for study.

Odor is very subjective, but to me there was a distinct smell to the lunar material – pungent, like gunpowder or spent cap-pistol caps. We carted a fair amount of lunar dust back inside the vehicle with us, either on our suits and boots or on the conveyor system we used to get boxes and equipment back inside. We did notice the odor right away.

It was a unique, almost mystical environment up there.

1980

Ted Bundy on Death Row, Florida State Prison, America STEPHEN G MICHAUD

Theodore Robert Bundy, known to have murdered at least twenty-three women, was one of the most notorious mass-killers of modern times. Successful, charming and, in the opinion of unsuspecting friends, 'one of them', he shattered the public stereotypes of the mass-murderer. He was executed in January 1989.

IT WAS INCREASINGLY clear that a child's mind had directed this homicidal rampage. The fantasies were crude, more typical of a sexually innocent twelve-year-old than of an adult sex offender. We knew that by the time he actually started killing, Ted had had several adult sexual encounters, but as he explained it to me, the disordered self, the thing inside him that impelled Ted to kill, knew females through the warp of twisted perception. Only by means of his astounding capacity to compartmentalise had Bundy been able to keep the hunchback from raging through the mask and destroying him. When at last it did, *Ted* became the hunchback. No longer its protector, he and the entity fused.

I felt that I was encountering a wholly novel form of insanity. Rather than being possessed by his illness, Ted appeared to be inhabited by it. The two, man and hunchback, interacted. Above all, I saw elements of will, *conscious* will, taking part in the creation of this entity, as if Ted had wanted to become a killer.

Seeing this, knowing this about him as we sat knee to knee in a cramped and sweltering cubicle buried in the middle of the prison, I myself began to dissociate. A wall, a necessary wall of dispassion, went up in front of me as Bundy spoke in a low voice, holding the tape recorder close to him and darting glances at the guards who periodically looked in on us through a glass pane in the door.

There were times of intense concentration when his features would freeze and a distant, stony quality came into his voice, as if the hunchback had taken corporeal form. More than once, a horizontal white line like a welt appeared across his right cheek. It fascinated me because it did not follow the contour of his face at all.

I wasn't frightened of it, at least no more so than I am at the sight of a shark behind aquarium glass. Far more disconcerting were moments such as the time I pressed Ted for an explanation of how a victim was subdued. Bundy laughed and remarked, 'You, too, Steve, could make a successful mass killer. I really think you have it in you!' Like it or not, I was bound to him, if for no other reason than that I had seen the hunchback. Such distilled horror, once seen, never leaves you.

The Falklands War: the Liberation of Goose Green, Falkland Islands ROBERT FOX

1982

Robert Fox, BBC Radio's correspondent for the land campaign of the Falklands war was one of only two reporters at the Battle of Goose Green, which saw the surrender of 1500 Argentinians.

THE REGIMENTAL Sergeant Major gathered the prisoners together by the stream where we had been mortared for much of the morning. 'I am very proud of the lads,' said the RSM. 'They're doing really well, particularly the young ones. I'll never be able to shout at them again when we get back to Aldershot.' The officers manning the radio, Roger Miller and David Constance, told us to pack up our kit and prepare to move down the track to Darwin. The mortar bombardment had slackened and the sky had cleared. It was a leisurely walk along the path, with puffs of black smoke rising from the horizon before us as the mortars and artillery continued to stonk the Gorse Line. The sea bit into the land before us with a deep curving bay and steep peat banks above the beach. At the end of the coastline, a mile or so off, we could see the white houses, the first glimpse of Port Darwin. Taking a left-hand fork, the track dipped towards the beach and continued to the settlement. We jumped over the peat banks and crunched along the black gravel of the beach, as the men of 'A' Company had done hours before, in the dark.

I remember looking at the flat calm of the sea and the clouds lifting over the mountains, and thinking that the worst seemed to be over. We had not seen much mortar fire for some time, and the sounds of battle were coming from well beyond the Gorse Line from the direction of Goose Green itself. We climbed off the beach towards the nearest clump of gorse at the bottom of the hill outside Darwin. The bushes were blazing, smoke rising in a thick plume and the fire giving off a pungent smell. Men scurried round the bushes carrying drips and field First Aid kits. Three helicopters stood back from the gorse ready to carry the seriously wounded out to San Carlos. Some of them had been unloading the brown metal cases of rifle and machine-gun ammunition. Puffs of smoke, blue and grey, and the clang of metal above spurts of peat announced the renewal of the mortar barrage. The helicopters were ordered back, and we kept going into the gorse to look for cover. Men lay round the clump of bushes at the bottom of the rise; some were on stretchers, others covered with waterproof sheets.

1986

The Meeting of the Beirut Hostages, Lebanon

BRIAN KEENAN

In a week in April 1986 three Europeans, Terry Waite, Brian Keenan and John McCarthy, were kidnapped by Hisbollah Iranian-backed terrorists in the Lebanon. They were later to become famous as the Beirut Hostages. Here Keenan tells of his meeting with McCarthy after some eight weeks blindfolded and in solitary confinement. All the hostages were released by August 1991.

I SAT STILL, then I stood up again, feeling along the edges of the bed to confirm what it was. I stood in silence trying to listen. Was there another person in the room? It was a habit with the guards to stand in silence behind you and wait until you tried to remove your blindfold, which would give them justification for beating or abuse. I stood desperately straining to hear if there was anyone else there. How long I stood I can't remember. Then telling myself that they had left, I slowly raised my hand to my face and very slowly, very cautiously lifted the end of the blindfold from my eye while lifting my head so that I could look from under it without removing it. Nothing happened, no one struck me and as I peered out from beneath the blindfold I could see two feet. Raising my head slowly, I followed the line of the feet along the legs. Whoever was in this room with me was sitting on the floor. It could not possibly be a guard. They would not sit while I was standing. Fascinated, my eye followed along the bodyline. My head tilting ever so slowly backwards to allow myself to see more of this person. A smart blazer filled my gaze and as my eye travelled upwards I saw a man sitting on the floor doing exactly what I was doing. Slowly lifting the corner of his blindfold, taking in every inch of me as I stood looking down at him. Our eyes met from under the blindfolds, looking intensely at one another.

The confirmation that we were both prisoners was a relief to each of us. Both blindfolds were swiftly removed and for a split second we just gazed at one another. Who could this other person be? My companion sitting on the floor and staring up at me suddenly broke the silence and in most eloquent English he said 'Fuck me, it's Ben Gunn.' My mind raced, Ben Gunn, who is Ben Gunn? I didn't know anyone called Ben Gunn. I began to turn over all the names that I had known in Lebanon. Members of staff at the University, friends I had met, wondering: 'Who does he think I am?' He got up from the floor, walked towards me, shook my hand and said 'Hello, my name is John McCarthy, I am a journalist . . . You must be Brian Keenan.'

A Day in Sarajevo, Yugoslavia   ZLATA FILIPOVIC

1992

The siege of Sarajevo, which lasted from 1992 to 1995, was the longest siege in Europe since the Second World War, and was the centre of media attention during the war in the former Yugoslavia. This extract is taken from the diary of a young girl, Zlata Filipovic, who lived through the siege and is now a refugee in France.

DEAR MIMMY,
Today was truly, absolutely the worst day ever in Sarajevo. The shooting started around noon. Mummy and I moved into the hall. Daddy was in his office, under our flat, at the time. We told him on the interphone to run quickly to the downstairs lobby where we'd meet him. We brought Cicko [Zlata's canary] with us. The gunfire was getting worse, and we couldn't get over the wall to the Bobars, so we ran down to our own cellar.

The cellar is ugly, dark, smelly. Mummy, who's terrified of mice, had two fears to cope with. The three of us were in the same corner as the other day. We listened to the pounding shells, the shooting, the thundering noise overhead. We even heard planes. At one moment I realised that this awful cellar was the only place that could save our lives. Suddenly, it started to look almost warm and nice. It was the only way we could defend ourselves against all this terrible shooting. We heard glass shattering in our street. Horrible. I put my fingers in my ears to block out the terrible sounds. I was worried about Cicko. We had left him behind in the lobby. Would he catch cold there? Would something hit him? I was terribly hungry and thirsty. We had left our half-cooked lunch in the kitchen.

When the shooting died down a bit, Daddy ran over to our flat and brought us back some sandwiches. He said he could smell something burning and that the phones weren't working. He brought our TV set down to the cellar. That's when we learned that the main post office (near us) was on fire and that they had kidnapped our President. At around 20.00 we went back up to our flat. Almost every window in our street was broken. Ours were all right, thank God. I saw the post office in flames. A terrible sight. The fire-fighters battled with the raging fire. Daddy took a few photos of the post office being devoured by the flames. He said they wouldn't come out because I had been fiddling with something on the camera. I was sorry. The whole flat smelled of the burning fire. God, and I used to pass by there every day. It had just been done up. It was huge and beautiful, and now it was being swallowed up by the flames. It was disappearing. That's what this neighbourhood of mine looks like, dear Mimmy. I wonder what it's like in other parts of town? I heard on the radio that it was awful around the Eternal Flame. The place is knee-deep in glass. We're worried about Grandma and Grandad. They live there. Tomorrow, if we can go out, we'll see how they are. A terrible day. This has been the worst, most awful day in my eleven-year-old life. I hope it will be the only one.

1997 The End of an Empire, Hong Kong

CHRIS PATTEN

In 1842 Hong Kong was ceded to the British as a result of the First Opium War. The remaining territories were leased for 99 years in 1898 – a period of time that saw the rise and fall of the greatest empire the world had yet seen. Now the colony has been returned to China.

As BRITISH administration ends, we are, I believe, entitled to say our own nation's contribution was to provide the scaffolding that enabled the people of Hong Kong to ascend. The rule of law. Clean and lighthanded government. Values of a free society. The beginnings of representative government and democratic accountability. This is a Chinese city, a very Chinese city, with British characteristics. The dependent territory has been left more properous, none with such a rich fabric of civil society, professions, churches, newspapers, charities, civil servants of the highest probity and most steadfast commitment to the public good. I have no doubt that with people holding on to these values Hong Kong's star will continue to climb.

Hong Kong's values are decent values. They are universal values. They are the values of the future in Asia or elsewhere, a future in which the happiest and the richest communities, and the most confident and the most stable, will be those that best combine political liberty and economic freedom as we do here today.

All of us here tonight, and I am sure all my fellow countrymen and women watching these events from afar, wish the Chief Executive of the Special Administrative Region and his excellent team the very best of luck as they embark on their journey.

The Funeral of Diana, Princess of Wales

1997

CAROL SIMPSON

The unexpected and tragic death of The Princess of Wales gave rise to an unprecedented demonstration of public grief at her funeral. Here, an ordinary member of the public explains how she felt.

FROM THE moment I heard the first bell chiming at eight minutes past nine, my heart just felt so heavy. It made it all seem so final. There were so many people and yet it was so quiet. Everyone was deep in their own thoughts. I was standing at Hyde Park Corner when the police horses came into view. I just felt I was tearing apart inside. In a way it was comforting to know that everyone around about felt the same. I like the way it was done simply: that there wasn't too much pomp and ceremony. I think it's what she would have wanted. As the coffin approached, I kept thinking it was so sad that her life ended so abruptly. She was so young and could have done so much more with her life, in her personal life and her professional life. God works in mysterious ways and He must have had a reason for taking her. When I saw the coffin, it just brought it home, the reality of what's happened. It was over very quickly, but you almost didn't want to go away. You just wanted to stand there, deep in your own thoughts....

When I heard the news on Sunday it was as if something had died inside me. The children and I came to London to lay flowers on Tuesday. I felt simply that I had to do it. As I watched my 12-year-old daughter Claire and my son Kenny, who is nine, put down their bouquet of yellow carnations before the gates of Kensington Palace, my heart went out to William and Harry. I looked at my children and realised I was there to help them through their sadness, but now Diana's boys have no mother to do that for them. We walked quietly to St James's Palace and waited six-and-a-half hours to sign a Book of Condolence. It was the only way I felt I could ever come close to thanking her for what she had done. I wrote: 'A light may have gone out when you passed away, but Heaven has a new star in its midst which will shine down on the world. May God bless your boys and give them peace.' Writing in that book was a celebration of her life. I was saying: 'Take this with you into your next world.' In the corner of the room was a door to the chapel where she lay. I never met Diana but I felt close to her then. I was glad I was there and in some way it gave me a sense of peace. You go through a lot getting married young and I can empathise with Diana. I think many women and young mothers do...

I don't think Diana wasted one minute of life. She lived life to the full and she set us all an example – it doesn't matter who you are or what you are or what you do or how much money you have, there is always someone that you can help. Her death has touched everyone and some good has to come out of it.

Sources of extracts

Vikings reach North America, c.1000 Anon: *The Oxford Book of Exploration*, Robin Hanbury-Tenison, Oxford University Press 1994

Thorfinn Karlsefni Encounters Native Americans, North America, c. 1010 Anon: *The Vinland Sagas: The Norse Discovery of America*, trans. Magnus Magnusson and Hermann Palsson, Penguin Books 1965

Demoniacal Fate of a Witch, Berkeley, Gloucestershire, England 1065 William of Malmesbury: *Witchcraft in Europe 1100–1700: A Documentary History*, ed. Alan C. Kors and Edward Peters, University of Pennysylvania Press 1972

The Battle of Hastings, England 1066 William of Poitiers: *The Norman Conquest: A Documentary History*, ed. R. Allen Brown, Edward Arnold 1948

Henry IV's Penance at Canossa, Tuscany, Italy 1077 Gregory VII: *Select Historical Documents of the Middle Ages*, ed. and trans. Ernest F. Henderson, G. Bell and Sons 1896

Arrival of the Crusaders, Syria 1096–7 Ibn Al-Qalanist: *The Damascus Chronicle of the Crusades*, ed. and trans. A.R. Gibb, Luzac and Co 1932

Death of William Rufus, New Forest, England 1100 William of Malmesbury: *Chronicle of the Kings of the English*, Bohn's Antiquarian Library 1847

The Battle of Tinchebrai, Normandy, France 1106 Anon: *English Historical Documents 1042–1189 (2nd Edition)*, ed. David C. Douglas and George W. Greenaway, Eyre Methuen 1981

Customs and Manners of the Cistercians, England c. 1110 William of Malmesbury: *Chronicle of the Kings of the English*, ed. H.G. Bohn, Bohn's Antiquarian Library 1847

The Crusades, Warfare Against the Franks, Syria 1119 Usamah Ibn-Munqidh: *An Arab-Syrian Gentleman and Warrior in the Period of the Crusades – The Memoirs of Usamah Ibn-Munqidh*, trans. Philip K. Hitti, I.B. Tauris and Co 1987

The Battle of Lincoln, England, 1141 Henry of Huntingdon: *English Historical Documents 1042–1189*, (2nd Edition), ed. David C. Douglas and George W. Greenaway, Eyre Methuen 1981

Hunting in Egypt, c. 1150 Usamah Ibn-Munqidh: *An Arab-Syrian Gentleman and Warrior in the Period of the Crusades – The Memoirs of Usamah Ibn-Munqidh*, trans. Philip K. Hitti, I.B. Tauris and Co 1987

Murder of Thomas à Becket, Canterbury, England, 1170 Edward Grim: *They Saw It Happen 55 B.C. to A.D. 1485*, ed. W.O. Hassall (quoting material for the History of Becket), Basil Blackwell 1957

Beavers on the River Teifi, Wales 1188 Gerald of Wales: *Gerald of Wales – The Journey Through Wales*, trans. Lewis Thorpe, Penguin Books 1978

The Assassins Kill Conrad of Montferrat, Palestine 1192 Anon: (possibly Geoffrey de Vinsauf), *The Third Crusade*, Kenneth Fenwick, The Folio Society 1958

Burning of Constantinople, 1204 Geoffrey de Villehardouin: *Memoirs of the Crusaders* – Villehardouin and De Joinville, trans. Frank T. Marzials, JM. Dent 1908

Satanic Rituals, Stedlinger, Germany 1232 Gregory IX: *Witchcraft in Europe 1100–1700: A Documentary History*, ed. Alan C. Kors and Edward Peters, University of Pennsylvania Press 1972

The Castration of a Knight, England, 1248 Matthew Paris: *The Illustrated Chronicles of Matthew Paris*, trans and ed. Richard Vaughan, Alan Sutton and Corpus Christi College, Cambridge 1993

An Incident from the Seventh Crusade, France 1248 Jean Sire de Joinville: *Memoirs of the Crusaders* – Villehardouin and De Joinville, trans. Frank T. Marzials, JM. Dent 1908

Drunken and Lecherous Priests, Normandy, France 1248 Archbishop Odo of Rigaud: *The Portable Medieval Reader*, James Bruce Ross and Mary Martin McLaughlin, Penguin Books 1981

Vision of a Son's Death, England 1250 Matthew Paris: *The Illustrated Chronicles of Matthew Paris*, trans and ed. Richard Vaughan, Alan Sutton and Corpus Christi College, Cambridge 1993

A Visit to the Great Khan, Mongolia 1253 William of Rubreck: *The Portable Medieval Reader*, James Bruce Ross and Mary Martin McLaughlin, Penguin Books 1981

Kublai Khan and his Concubines, China c. 1280 Marco Polo: *The Travels of Marco Polo the Venetian*, JM. Dent 1926

Handsome Women in Cologne, Germany 1333 Petrarch: *Letters from Petrarch*, ed. and trans. Morris Bishop, Indiana University Press 1966

Charles IV's Temptation at Lucca, Italy 1333 Charles IV: *The Emperor Charles IV*, B. Jarrett, Eyre and Spottiswoode 1935

Lawlessness and Cruelty in Naples, Italy c. 1343 Petrarch: *Letters from Petrarch*, ed. and trans. Morris Bishop, Indiana University Press 1966

English Archers at Crecy, France 1346 Jean Froissant: *Froissart – Chronicles*, trans. and ed. Geoffrey Brereton, Penguin Books 1978

The Black Death Reaches Florence, Italy 1348 Giovanni Boccaccio: *The Black Death*, trans. and ed. Rosemary Horrox, Manchester University Press 1994

Symptoms of the Plague, Italy 1348 Gabriele de Mussis: *The Black Death*, trans. and ed. Rosemary Horrox, Manchester University Press 1994

Flagellants in England, 1349 Robert of Avesbury: *The Black Death*, trans. and ed. Rosemary Horrox, Manchester University Press 1994

The Peasants' Revolt, France 1358 Jean Froissart: *Froissart – Chronicles*, trans. and ed. Geoffrey Brereton, Penguin Books 1978

A Mystical Experience of Severe Illness, Norwich, England 1373 Julian of Norwich: *Showings*, ed. Edmund Colledge and James Walsh, Paulist Press 1978

The Peasants' Revolt, England 1381 Anon (Anonimalle Chronicle): *The Portable Medieval Reader*, ed. James Bruce Ross and Mary Martin McLaughlin, Penguin 1977

Charles VI Goes Mad, France 1392 Jean Froissart: *Froissart – Chronicles*, trans. and ed. Geoffrey Brereton, Penguin Books 1978

Richard II's Capture and Imprisonment in the Tower of London, England 1399 Adam Usk: *Chronicles of the Revolution 1397–1400*, trans and ed. Chris Given-Wilson, Manchester University Press 1993

Execution of Pierre des Essarts, Paris 1413 Journal d'un Bourgeois de Paris: *The Portable Medieval Reader*, ed. James Bruce Ross and Mary Martin McLaughlin, Penguin 1977

Battle of Agincourt, Picardy, France 1415 Jehan de Wavrin: *They Saw It Happen 55 BC to AD 1485*, ed. W.O. Hassall, Basil Blackwell 1957

Wolves in Paris, 1439 Journal d'un Bourgeois de Paris: *The Portable Medieval Reader*, ed. James Bruce Ross and Mary Martin McLaughlin, Penguin 1977

Henry VI's Sickness, Greenwich, England 1454 Edmund Clere: *The Paston Letters (vol. 1)*, ed. John Fenn and re-ed. Mrs. Archer-Hind, JM. Dent 1924

At the Court of King Alfonso V of Portugal, Lisbon c. 1456 Jorg von Ehingen: *The Diary of Jorg von Ehingen*, ed. and trans. Malcolm Letts, Oxford University Press 1929

Single Combat with a Mighty Saracen Knight, Ceuta, Morocco c. 1457 Jorg von Ehingen: *The Diary of Jorg von Ehingen*, ed. and trans. Malcolm Letts, Oxford University Press 1929

The Races at Pienza, Italy 1462 Pius II *Secret Memoirs of a Renaissance Pope – the commentaries of Aeneas Sylvius Piccolomini Pius II*, trans and ed. Florence Gragg and Leona C. Gabel, The Folio Society 1988

Leonardo da Vinci Offers his Services to Ludovico, Milan, Italy c. 1483 Leonardo da Vinci: *Selections from the Notebooks of Leonardo da Vinci*, ed. Irma A. Richter, Oxford University Press 1952

Christopher Columbus Meets Indians, West Indies 1492 Christopher Columbus: *The Four Voyages of Christopher Columbus*, ed. JM. Cohen, Penguin Books 1969

Elephants in India, 1498 Vasco da Gama: *A Journal of the First Voyage of Vasco da Gama 1497–1499*, ed. and trans. E.G. Ravenstein, The Hakluyt Society 1898

The Marriage of Lucrezia Borgia, Rome 1501 Johann Burchard: *At The Court of the Borgia*, trans. Geoffrey Parker, The Folio Society 1963

Martin Luther Enters a Monastery, Erfurt, Germany 1505 Martin Luther: *The Reformation in its Own Words*, Hans J. Hillerbrand, SCM Press Ltd 1964

Michelangelo Finishes Painting the Sistine Chapel, Rome, 1511–12 Giorgio Vasari: *Vasari's Lives of Italian Painters*, ed. Havelock Ellis, Walter Scott Ltd 1895

At the Court of Montezuma, Mexico 1519 Bernal Diaz del Castillo: *The Conquest of New Spain*, ed. and trans. J.M. Cohen, Penguin 1970

A Maya Account of the Spanish Conquest, Mexico 1520 Anonymous Maya Chronicler: *Stolen Continents – the Indian Story*, Ronald Wright, John Murray Ltd 1992

Fate of the German Peasants and Thomas Muntzer, the Battle of Frankenhausen, Germany 1525 Anon: *The Reformation in its Own Words*, ed. Hans J. Hillerbrand, SCM Press Ltd 1964

Blaise de Monluc is Wounded by an Arquebus, Italy 1528 Blaise de Monluc: *Blaise de Monluc – the Hapsburg-Valois Wars and the French Wars of Religion*, ed. Ian Roy, Longman 1971

The Purity of Zwingli's Heart, the Battle of Cappel, Switzerland, 1531 Oswald Myconius: *The Reformation in its Own Words*, ed. Hans J. Hillerbrand, SCM Press Ltd 1964

The Execution of Atahuallpa, King of the Incas, Peru 1533 Pedro Pizarro: *The Discovery and Conquest of Peru*, trans. J.M. Cohen,Penguin 1968

Communism in Anabaptist Munster, Germany 1534 Meister Heinrich Gresbeck: *The Reformation in its Own Words*, ed. Hans J. Hillerbrand, SCM Press Ltd 1964

The Trial and Execution of Sir Thomas More, England 1535 Anthony Castelnau: *Castlenau's Memoirs in Letters and Papers, Foreign and Domestic, of the Reign of Henry*, ed. James Gairdner (also arranged and catalogued by James Gairdner), Her Majesty's Stationery Office 1885

Maya Blood Sacrifice, Yucatan, Mexico c. 1550 Diego de Landa: *The Maya: Account of the Affairs of the Yucatan*, trans. and ed. A. Pagden, O'Hara 1975

The Expulsion of the 'Useless Mouths', Sienna, Italy 1555 Blaise de Monluc: *Blaise de Monluc – the Hapsburg-Valois Wars and the French Wars of Religion*, ed. Ian Roy, Longman 1971

The Burning of Archbishop Cranmer, London 1555 Anon: *They Saw it Happen 1485–1688*, comp. and ed. C.R.N. Routh, Basil Blackwell 1957

A Cannibal Feast, Brazil 1556 Jean de Lery: *A History of a Voyage to the Land of Brazil*, trans. Janet Whateley, University of California Press 1990

An 'Auto-da-fe', Seville, Spain 1559 Anon: *The Reformation in its Own Words*, ed. Hans J. Hillerbrand, SCM Press Ltd 1964

The Usefulness of Camels to Turks, c. 1560 Ogier Ghiselin de Busbecq: *The Turkish Letters of Ogier Ghiselin de Busbecq*, trans. Edward Seymour Forster, Clarendon Press 1927

The Great Turkish Assault, Malta 1565 Francisco Balbi di Correggio: *The Siege of Malta*, trans. Ernle Bradford, The Folio Society 1965

The Murder of David Rizzio, Scotland 1565 Lord Ruthven: *Every One A Witness – The Tudor Age*, compiled by A.F. Scott, Book Club Associates 1975

John Hawkins' Voyage to the West Indies, 1567-8 John Hawkins: *Richard Hakluyt – Voyages and Documents*, ed. Janet Hampden, Oxford University Press 1958

Martin Frobisher Encounters some Eskimos, 1576 Christopher Hall: *Richard Hakluyt - Voyages and Documents*, ed. Janet Hampden, Oxford University Press 1958

A Hutterite Community, Moravia, 1578 Anon: *The Reformation in its Own Words*, ed. Hans J. Hillerbrand, SCM Press Ltd 1964

Search for a Priest Hole, England 1585 Fr William Weston: *Every One A Witness – The Tudor Age*, compiled by A.F. Scott, Book Club Associates 1975

The Torture of a Jesuit Priest, Tower of London, England 1597 Father John Gerard: *John Gerard – the Autobiography of an Elizabethan*, Philip Caraman, Longman Green and Co 1956

Queen Elizabeth in Old Age, Greenwich, England 1598 Paul Hentzner: *The Other Face – Catholic Life under Elizabeth I*, ed. Philip Caraman, Longmans 1960

The Death of Queen Elizabeth, England 1603 Lady Southwell: *The Other Face – Catholic Life under Elizabeth I*, ed. Philip Caraman, Longmans 1960

The Gunpowder Plotters at Holbeach House, England 1605 Father John Gerard: *The Other Face – Catholic Life under Elizabeth I*, ed. Philip Caraman, Longmans 1960

Conditions in Peru after the Spanish Conquest, c. 1605 Huaman Poma: *Letter to a King*, trans. and ed. Christopher Dilke, George Allen and Unwin 1978

Idolatry and Witchcraft in Mayombe, Portuguese Africa c. 1610 Andrew Battell: *The Strange Adventures of Andrew Battell*, ed. EG. Ravenstein, The Hakluyt Society 1901

The Galileo Debate, Tuscany, Italy 1613 Benedetto Castelli: *The Galileo Affair: a Documentary History*, Maurice A. Finocchiaro, University of California Press 1989

An Aristocratic Duel, Holland c. 1615 Edward Sackville, Earl of Dorset: *The World of Adventure*, Cassell and Co Ltd 1891

The Pilgrim Fathers Land in America, 1620 Nathaniel Morton: *New England's Memorial*, N. Hawthorne, JM. Dent 1669

An Indian Chief has a Nosebleed, America c. 1621 Edward Winslow: *Winslow's Relation 1622*

The Collapse of a Church at Blackfriars, England 1623 Thomas Goad: *The Years of Siege – Catholic Life from James I to Cromwell*, Philip Caraman, Longmans 1966

The Battle of Brietenfeld, Germany 1631 Robert Monro: *Monro His Expedition with the Worthy Scots Regiment called MacKeys*, William Jones 1637

Possessed by the Demons of Loudun, France 1636 Jean-Joseph Surin: *Witchcraft in Europe 1100–1700: a documentary history*, ed. Alan C. Kors and Edward Peters, University of Pennsylvania Press 1972

Post-Mortem on an Old Man, England 1636 William Harvey: *The Circulation of the Blood and Other Writings*, Kenneth J. Franklin, JM. Dent 1993, Reprinted by permission of Everyman's Library, David Campbell Publishers Ltd

The Indian Inhabitants of Maryland, America 1634 Father Andrew White: *The Years of Siege – Catholic Life from James I to Cromwell*, Philip Caraman, Longmans 1966

The Siege of Gloucester, England 1643 John Dorney: *A Brief and Exact Relation of the Siege of Gloucester*, Thomas Underhill 1643

The Execution of King Charles I, London 1649 Robert Cotchett: *Derbyshire in the Civil War*, Brian Stone, Scarthin Books 1992

The Great Mogul Prohibits Alcohol, India 1659 Niccolao Manucci: *Memoirs of the Mogul Court*, ed. Michael Edwards, Folio Society

A Boyhood Experiment of Sir Isaac Newton, Grantham, England c. 1660 Dr Stukeley: *Pandaemonium 1660–1886: the coming of the machine as seen by contemporary observers*, ed. Mary-Lou Jennings and Charles Madge, Papermac 1995

Robert Boyle's Classic Experiments with the Air-pump, Oxford, England c. 1660 William Wotton: *Robert Boyle by Himself and his Friends*, ed. Michael Hunter, Pickering and Chatto Ltd 1994

The Smoke of London, 1661 John Evelyn: *Pandaemonium 1660–1886: the coming of the machine as seen by contemporary observers*, ed. Mary-Lou Jennings and Charles Madge, Papermac 1995

The Great Plague, London 1665 Samuel Pepys: *Everybody's Pepys*, ed. OF. Morshead, G. Bell and Sons 1929

The Great Fire of London, 1666 John Evelyn: *The Diary of John Evelyn*, George Newnes Ltd 1818

Newton's Experiments on Light, Cambridge, England 1666 Sir Isaac Newton: *The Ascent of Man*, J. Bronowski, BBC Books 1973

The Buccaneers Sack Panama, Central America 1670 A.O. Exquemelin: *The Buccaneers of America*, trans. Alexis Brown, The Folio Society 1972

Christmas Day at Sea, 1678 Henry Teonge: *The Diary of Henry Teonge*, ed. GE. Manwaring, George Routledge and Sons Ltd 1927

The Great Frost Fair, London 1684 John Evelyn: *The Diary of John Evelyn*, George Newnes Ltd

An Experiment into the Eduction of Light, England 1685 John Evelyn: *The Diary of John Evelyn*, George Newnes Ltd 1818

The Marriage of the Duc de Chartres, Versailles, France 1692 Duc de Saint-Simon: *Saint Simon at Versailles*, trans and ed. Lucy Norton, Book Club Associates 1980

A Surgical Bleeding, Versailles, France 1704 Duc de Saint-Simon: *Saint Simon at Versailles*, trans and ed. Lucy Norton, Book Club Associates 1980

Experimenting with a Live Mare, England, c. 1706 Stephen Hales: *Pandaemonium 1660–1886: the coming of the machine as seen by contemporary observers*, ed. Mary-Lou Jennings and Charles Madge, Papermac 1995

Rescue of Alexander Selkirk, Juan Fernandez Island 1709 Woodes Rogers: *Life Aboard a British Privateer in the Time of Queen Anne*, ed. Robert C. Leslie, Chapman and Hall Ltd 1889

Royal Irish Regiment at the Battle of Malplaquet, Flanders 1709 Robert Parker: *Robert Parker and Comte de Merode-Westerloo*, ed. David Chandler, Longmans 1968

Death of The Sun King, Versailles, France 1715 Duc de Saint-Simon: *Saint Simon at Versailles*, trans and ed. Lucy Norton, Book Club Associates 1980

A Total Eclipse of the Sun, London 1715–16 Dr Edmund Halley: *Pandaemonium 1660-1886: the coming of the machine as seen by contemporary observers*, ed. Mary-Lou Jennings and Charles Madge, Papermac 1995

The Practice of Inoculation, Turkey 1717 Lady Mary Wortley-Montagu: *Chambers Book of Days*, ed. R. Chambers, W&R Chambers Ltd circa 1860

Turkish Baths, Adrianople, Turkey 1717 Lady Mary Wortley-Montagu: *Selected Letters of Lady Mary Wortley-Montagu*, ed. R. Halsband, Longman 1970

Lightning Strikes in Northamptonshire, England 1725 J Wasse: *Pandaemonium 1660–1886: the coming of the machine as seen by contemporary observers*, ed. Mary-Lou Jennings and Charles Madge, Papermac 1995

Farinelli: the Great Castrato, Rome c. 1725 Charles Burney: *The Present State of Music in France and Italy*, T. Becket and Co., 1771 (2nd edition 1773)

Fleet Marriages, London 1735 Anon (Grub Street Journal): *Chambers Book of Days*, ed. R. Chambers, W&R Chambers Ltd

The End of the Battle of Culloden, Scotland 1746 Chevalier Johnstone: *A Memoir of the 'Forty-Five'*, (Johnstone), ed. Brian Rawson, Folio Society 1958

The Charms of Handel, London c. 1750 Charles Burney: *An Account of the Musical Performances in Westminster Abbey and the Pantheon ... in Commemoration of Handel*, London 1785

First Experience of a Slave-Ship, c. 1755 Olaudah Equiano: *Equiano's Travels*, ed. Paul Edwards, Heinemann 1989

The Lisbon Earthquake, Portugal 1755 Mr Braddock: *Marquis of Pombal*, John Athelstane Smith, Longmans Green Reader and Dyer 1871

Coalminers Brush with Death, Cumberland, England 1759 John Wesley: *Pandaemonium 1660–1886: the coming of the machine as seen by contemporary observers*, ed. Mary-Lou Jennings and Charles Madge, Papermac 1995

A Rake in London, England 1763 James Boswell: *Boswell's London Journal 1762–1763*, Frederick A. Pottle, William Heinemann Ltd 1951

Attack on Fort Michillimackinac, Great Lakes, America 1763 Alexander Henry: *Travels and Adventures in Canada and the Indian Territories between the years 1760 and 1776*, I. Riley 1809

A Vestry Meeting, Sussex, England 1763 Thomas Turner: *The Diary of Thomas Turner*, ed. David Vaisey, Oxford University Press 1985

James Watt's Improved Steam Engine, England 1765 John Robinson: *Pandaemonium 1660–1886: the coming of the machine as seen by contemporary observers*, ed. Mary-Lou Jennings and Charles Madge, Papermac 1995

Prodigious Ability of Mozart, England 1765 Daines Barrington: *Miscellanies of Various Subjects*, J. Nichols 1781

Ball Room Rules, Bath, England 1766 Revd John Penrose: *Letters from Bath 1766–1767*, ed. Brigitte Mitchell and Hubert Penrose, Alan Sutton 1983

Tahitian Funeral Ceremony, 1769 Sir Joseph Banks: *Journal of the Right Hon. Sir Joseph Banks*, ed. Sir Joseph D. Hooker, Macmillan and Co Ltd 1896

A Duel Between Two Cadets, Comoro Islands 1769 William Hickey: *Memoirs of William Hickey*, ed. Peter Quennell, Century Publishing 1984

Dealing with a Smuggler, England 1770 William Hickey: *Memoirs of William Hickey*, ed. Peter Quennell, Century Publishing 1984

Cannibalism and Human Trophies, New Zealand 1770 Sir Joseph Banks: *Journal of the Right Hon. Sir Joseph Banks*, ed. Sir Joseph D. Hooker, Macmillan and Co Ltd 1896

A Feast with Musquito Indians, South America 1773 Olaudah Equiano: *Equiano's Travels*, ed. Paul Edwards, Heinemann 1989

Dr Johnson in the Highlands, Scotland 1773 James Boswell: *Everybody's Boswell*, G. Bell and Sons Ltd 1956

Treatment of Slaves, Surinam 1773 John Stedman: *Expedition to Surinam*, Folio Society 1963

Publication of Edward Gibbon's Decline and Fall, London 1776 Edward Gibbon: *Gibbon's Autobiography*, ed. MM. Reese, Routledge and Kegan Paul 1971

A Skirmish in the American Revolution, 1776 Joseph Martin: *Private Yankee Doodle*, ed. George E. Scheer, Eastern Acorn Press 1995

A Tahitian Massage, Tahiti 1777 Captain James Cook: *Captain Cook's Voyages of Discovery*, JM. Dent, Reprinted by permission of Everyman's Library, David Campbell Publishers Ltd

The Death of Captain Cook, Hawaii 1779 Captain James King: *Captain Cook's Voyages of Discovery*, JM. Dent Reprinted by permission of Everyman's Library, David Campbell Publishers Ltd

The Gordon Riots, London 1780 George Crabbe: *The London Anthology*, ed. Hugh and Pauline Massingham, Spring Books circa 1955

Surrender at Yorktown, Virginia, America 1781 Johann Conrad Döhla: *A Hessian Diary of the American Revolution*, ed. and trans. Bruce E. Burgoyne, University of Oklahoma Press 1990

A Captive of the Shawnee, Ohio, America 1782 John Glover: *The World of Adventure*, Cassell and Co Ltd 1891

Lunardi's Balloon Voyage, London, 1784 Vincent Lunardi: *Pandaemonium 1660–1886: the coming of the machine as seen by contemporary observers*, ed. Mary-Lou Jennings and Charles Madge, Papermac 1995

Flight from Mad King George III, Kew Gardens, London 1789 Fanny Burney: *The Diary of Fanney Burney* ed. Lewis Gibbs, Dent 1971, Reprinted by permission of Everyman's Library, David Campbell Publishers Ltd

Mutiny on HMS Bounty, South Pacific 1789 William Bligh: *Narrative of the Mutiny of the Bounty*, William Smith 1838

A Description of Australian Aboriginals, New South Wales, c. 1791 George Barrington: *A Voyage to Botany Bay*, The Brummell Press 1969

The September Massacres, Paris 1792 Restif de la Bretonne: *Paris in the Revolution – a collection of eyewitness accounts*, ed. Ray Tannahill, The Folio Society 1966

Dalton Discovers his Colour Blindness, Manchester, England 1792 John Dalton: *Dalton and the Contribution of Self-Observation to Scientific Discovery*, Roseneath Scientific Publications 1992

Jenner's Vaccination Experiments, Gloucestershire, England c. 1796 Edward Jenner: *On the Origine of the Vaccine Inoculation*, DN. Shury 1801

A Navel Surgeon at the Battle of Camperdown, off the Dutch Coast, 1797 Robert Young: *St. Vincent and Comperdown*, Christopher Lloyd, BT. Batsford 1963

First Impressions of a Press Tender, London c. 1798 Jack Nastyface (pseudonym): *The British Sailor*, Peter Kemp, JM. Dent and Sons 1970

Lake District Scene, England 1800 Dorothy Wordsworth: *Dove Cottage: the Wordsworths at Grasmere 1799–1803*, ed. Kingsley Hart, Folio Society 1966

Petticoat Lane, the Jewish East End, London c. 1800 Israel Zangwill: *Children of the Ghetto*, William Heinemann 1893, reproduced courtesy of the Estate of Israel Zangwill

The Battle of Trafalgar, Coast of Spain 1805 Captain Pierre Servaux: *Eyewitnesses to Nelson's Battles*, James Hewitt, Osprey Publishing Ltd 1972

Seized by the Press Gang, London 1811 Robert Hay: *Landsman Hay – the memoirs of Robert Hay 1789–1847*, ed. MD. Hay, Rupert Hart-Davis 1953

Beethoven: 'the poor deaf maestro', Vienna, Austria 1814 Louis Spohr: *Autobiography*, Longman, Green, Longman, Roberts and Green 1865

An Infantry Square at Waterloo, Belgium 1815 Captain Gronow: *The Reminiscences of Captain Gronow*, ed. Nicholas Bentley, The Folio Society 1977

Laennec and the Birth of the Stethoscope, Brittany, France 1816 Rene-Theophile-Hyacinthe Laennec: *Laennec: his life and times*, Roger Kervran, trans. DC. Abrahams-Curiel, Pergamon Press 1960

A Visit to a Fortune-Teller, Paris c. 1819 Captain Gronow: *The Reminiscenses of Captain Gronow*, ed. Nicholas Bentley, The Folio Society 1977

Berlioz Discovers his Musical Vocation, Paris 1822 Hector Berlioz: *The Life of Hector Berlioz*, trans. Katherine F. Boult, JM. Dent 1912, Reprinted by permission of Everyman's Library, David Campbell Publishers Ltd

A Hindu Widow Commits Suttee, India c. 1826 Captain Burnes: *Cutch*, Mrs. Postans, Smith Elder and Co. 1839

The Embarrassments of Travel, Hampshire, England 1826 William Cobbett: *Rural Rides*, ed. George Woodcock, Penguin 1985

Social Conditions Among Redundant Cloth Workers, Wiltshire, England 1826 William Cobbett: *Rural Rides*, ed. George Woodcock, Penguin 1985

Life On Board a Slave-Ship, West Africa 1827 Theodore Canot: *Memoirs of a Slave Trader*, ed. AW. Lawrance, Jonathan Cape 1929

A Fundamentalist Prayer Meeting, America 1827 Frances Trollope: *The Domestic Manners of the Americans*, ed. Herbert Van Thal, Folio Society 1974

An Encounter with a Virtuoso, Paris 1828 Wilhelm von Lenz: *The Great Piano Virtuosos of our Time*, trans. Philip Reder, Regency Press 1971

A Thug Foray, India 1831 Khaimraj: *Thug or a Million Murders*, Col. James L. Sleeman, Sampson Low Marston and Co Ltd

Delacroix Visits Morocco, 1832 Eugene Delacroix: *The Journal of Eugene Delacroix*, trans. Lucy Norton, Phaidon Press Ltd 1951

Body-Snatchers, England c. 1834 'Lord' George Sanger: *Seventy Years a Showman*, JM. Dent and sons 1952

Darwin in the Galapagos Islands, 1835 Charles Darwin: *Journal of Researches into the Natural History and Geology of the Countries Visited During the Voyage of HMS Beagle Around the World*, Ward Lock and co. 1890

Premiere of Berlioz's Requiem, Les Invalides, Paris 1837 Hector Berlioz: *A Life of Love and Music: the memoirs of Hector Berlioz 1803–1865*, trans and ed. David Cairns, The Folio Society 1987

Chartist Riots, Newport, Wales 1839 'Lord' George Sanger: *Seventy Years a Showman*, JM. Dent and sons 1952

Spanish Gypsies, 1840 George Borrow: *The Gypsies of Spain*, John Murray 1907

Sioux Sun-Dance, Great Plains, America c. 1843 George Catlin: *Illustrations of the Manners, Customs and Condition of the North American Indians*, Henry G. Bohn 1848

Borneo Pirates, Sarawak 1845 Surgeon Edward Cree: *The Cree Journals*, ed. Edward Levien, Webb and Bowen 1981

A Buffalo Hunt, Great Plains, America 1846 Francis Parkman: *The Oregon Trail*, The Folio Society 1973

An Eviction in the Great Famine, Ireland 1847 Henry Tuke: *The Irish Famine (quoting Tuke, 'A Visit to Connaught in the Autumn of 1847')*, Thames and Hudson 1995

A Duel in a Bedroom, Mexico 1847 Samuel Chamberlain: *Recollections of a Rogue*, Museum Press Ltd 1957

The Amazonian Rain Forest, 1848 Alfred Russel Wallace: *Narrative of Travels on the Amazon and Rio Negro*, Ward Lock and co 1864

Gay Sex in a Cairo Bathhouse, Egypt 1849 Gustav Flaubert: *Flaubert in Egypt*, ed. Francis Steegmuller, Penguin 1996

Sims Perfects a Gynaecological Treatment, America 1849 James Marion Sims: *Sims and the Treatment of Vesico-Vaginal Fistual*, Roseneath Scientific Publications 1992

Problems of Photography, Egypt 1850 Maxime DuCamp: *Flaubert in Egypt*, Francis Steegmuller, Penguin 1996

A Mob Murder in Lancashire, England 1850 'Lord' George Sanger: *Seventy Years a Showman*, JM. Dent and Sons Ltd 1952

The Charge of the Light Brigade, Crimea 1854 George Loy Smith: *A Victorian RSM*, Costello 1987

Charlotte Bronte's Honeymoon, Ireland 1854 Charlotte Bronte: *An Account of Her Honeymoon*, The Brotherton Library 1930

Florence Nightingale in the Crimean War, Balaclava 1855 Florence Nightingale: *Florence Nightingale: Letters from the Crimea*, ed. Sue M. Goldie Mandolin (an imprint of Manchester University Press) 1997

An English Lady at the Siege of Lucknow, India 1857 Mrs G. Harris: *A Lady's Diary of the Siege of Lucknow*, John Murray 1858

A Sewer-Hunter, London 1861 Henry Mayhew: *The London Anthology (quoting Henry Mayhew's London Labour and the London Poor)*, ed. Hugh and Pauline Massingham, Spring Books circa 1955

Tothill Fields Prison, London 1862 Henry Mayhew: *The London Anthology (quoting Henry Mayhew's London Labour and the London Poor)*, ed. Hugh and Pauline Massingham, Spring Books circa 1955

A Confederate Soldier in Battle, Virginia, America 1864 William H. Morgan: *Personal Reminiscences of the War of 1861–5*, Books for Libraries Press 1971

A Visit to Brigham Young, Utah, America 1865 Albert D. Richardson: *Beyond the Mississippi*, American Publishing Company 1867 ·

The Assassination of Lincoln, Washington, America 1865 Daniel Dean Beekman: *We Saw Lincoln Shot – one hundred eyewitness accounts*, Timothy S. Good, University Press of Mississippi 1995

A Victorian Picnic, Snodhill Castle, England 1879 Revd Francis Kilvert: *Kilvert's Diary 1870–1879*, ed. William Plomer, Penguin 1977

An Awkward Funeral, Worcester, England 1879 Revd Francis Kilvert: *Kilvert's Diary 1870–1879*, ed. William Plomer, Jonathan Cape 1977, Reproduced courtesy of the Estate of William Plomer

Chinese Punishment of Criminals, 1870 Revd E.D.G. Prime: *Around the World*, Harper and Brothers 1876

The Paris Commune, 1871 Edmond de Goncourt: *Pages from the Goncourt Journal*, ed. and trans. Robert Baldick, Oxford University Press 1962

Lister Operating with Carbolic Acid, Edinburgh, Scotland 1874 John Rudd Leeson: *Lister As I Knew Him*, Balliere, Tindall and Cox 1927

An Indian Account of the Battle of the Little Big Horn, Montana, America 1876 Two Moon: *The Penguin Book of Interviews*, McClure's Magazine 1989, Christopher Silvester, Penguin 1993

Pasteur's Public Demonstration of the Germ Theory, Pouilly le Fort, France 1881 Louis Pasteur: *The Life of Pasteur*, Rene Vallery-Radot, trans. Mrs R.L. Devonshire Constable and Company Ltd 1920

Eruption of Mount Krakatoa, East Indies 1883 Seaman Dalby: *Krakatoa*, Rupert Furneaux, Secker and Warburg 1965

Death of General Gordon, Khartoum, Sudan 1885 Rudolph C. Slatin Pasha: *Fire and Sword in the Sudan*, Rudolf C. Slatin (Pasha), Edward Arnold 1896

Tchaikovsky Meets Brahms, Leipzig, Germany 1888 Anna Lvovna Brodsky: *Recollections of a Russian Home*, Sherratt And Hughes 1904

Despair of Vincent Van Gogh, Arles, France 1889 Vincent van Gogh: *Dear Theo – an autobiography of Vincent Van Gogh from his letters*, ed. Irving Stone, Constable and Company Ltd 1937

Prison Conditions in a Russian Penal Colony, 1890 Anton Chekhov: *The Island – a journey to Sakhalin*, Century Hutchinson Ltd 1987

A Description of the Ainu Sakhalin, Russia 1890 Anton Chekhov: *The Island – a journey to Sakhalin*, Century Hutchinson Ltd 1987

A Japanese Childhood, Tokyo c. 1890 Junichiro Tanizaki: *Childhood Years – a memoir*, trans P. McCarthy, Flamingo 1991

An Anarchist Attempts to Murder Henry Clay Frick, Pennsylvania, America 1892 Alexander Berkman: *The Essential Works of Anarchism (quoting Prison Memoirs of an Anarchist)*, Bantam Books 1971

An Encounter with the Ona, Tierra del Fuego, South America, 1894 E. Lucas Bridges: *Uttermost Part of the Earth*, Readers Union 1951

Queen Victoria's Diamond Jubilee, London 1897 Ernest H. Shepard: *Drawn from Life*, Methuen 1961

Cavalry Charge at Omdurman, Sudan 1898 Winston Churchill: *Frontiers and Wars*, Penguin 1972

Winston Churchill is Captured by Boers, South Africa 1899 Winston Churchill: *Frontiers and Wars*, Penguin 1972

An Incident in the Boxer Rebellion, China 1900 Frank Richards: *Old Soldier Sahib*, Faber and Faber 1965

Breaking Through the Blockhouse Line, South Africa 1902 Deneys Reitz: *Commando*, Charles Boni Paper Books 1930

Renoir Battles with Arthritis, Essoyes, France 1902 Jean Renoir: *Renoir my Father*, William Collins Sons and Co Ltd 1962

At the Opera, Covent Garden, London 1905 George Bernard Shaw: *letter to The Times, 3 July 1905*

Dreyfus is Honoured at the Ecole Militaire, Paris, 1906 Alfred Dreyfus: *Dreyfus: his life and letters*, trans. Dr. Betty Morgan, Hutchinson and Co. Ltd 1937

The San Francisco Earthquake, America 1906 John Barrymore: *Confessions of an Actor*, Robert Holden and Co. Ltd. 1926

Force-feeding a Suffragette, Liverpool, England 1910 Constance Lytton: *Prisons and Prisoners*, Heinemann, 1914

Escape from the Titanic, North Atlantic 1912 Colonel Archibald Gracie: *Titanic* Alan Sutton Publishing Ltd 1985

Scandalous Premiere of Stravinsky's Rite of Spring, Paris 1913 Igor Stravinsky: *Conversations with Igor Stravinsky*, Robert Craft, Faber and Faber 1959

Shackleton and his Crew Abandon Ship, Weddell Sea, Antarctic 1915 Sir Ernest Shackleton *South: the Story of Shackleton's Last Expedition*, Century 1983

A Day in the Trenches, France 1915 Robert Graves: *Goodbye to All That*, Penguin 1960

A Zeppelin is Shot Down, London 1916 Charles Ricketts: *The London Anthology (quoting Charles Ricketts – self portrait)*, eds. Huch and Pauline Massingham, Spring Books

The First Day of the Somme, an Aerial View, France 1916 Cecil Lewis: *Sagittarius Rising*, Peter Davies 1936

Storming of the Winter Palace, St Petersburg, Russia 1917 John Reed: *Ten Days That Shook The World*, Penguin 1977

Ambush at Kilmichael, Ireland 1920 Tom Barry: *Guerilla Days in Ireland*, The Mercier Press Ltd 1955

Fighting the Riffs, Spanish Morocco 1921 Arturo Barea: *The Track*, Fontana 1984

A Chinese Wedding, 1922 Nora Waln: *The House of Exile*, Penguin 1939

Howard Carter Discovers Tutankhamun's Tomb, Egypt 1922 Howard Carter: *The Face of Tutankhamun*, Christopher Frayling, Faber and Faber 1992

An Execution by Guillotine, French Giana c. 1925 Krarup Nielson: *Hell Beyond the Seas*, John Lane 1935

Howling Dervishes, Syria 1927 W.B. Seabrook: *Adventures in Arabia*, WB Seabrook, George G. Harrap and Co Ltd 1936

Lingbergh Flies the Atlantic, Crossing the French Coast 1927 Charles A. Lindbergh: *The Spirit of St. Louis*, John Murray 1953

Lynching of a Black Prisoner, Indiana, America 1930 James Cameron: *A Time of Terror*, Writers and Readers Ltd 1995

Pierrepoint's First Hanging, Ireland 1931 Albert Pierrepoint: *Executioner Pierrepoint*, Coronet Books 1977

An Air Crash in the Libyan Desert, 1936 Antoine de Saint-Exupery: *Wind Sand and Stars*, Penguin Books 1995

George Orwell is Wounded, Spain 1937 George Orwell (pen name of Eric Blair): *Homage to Catalonia*, Penguin 1966

One of Stalin's Executioners, Russia c. 1938 Lev Razgon: *True Stories – the memoirs of Lev Razgon*, trans. John Crowfoot, Ardis Publishers 1997

The Holocaust, Mass Arrests in Nazi-occupied Lodz, Poland 1939 Dawid Sierakowiak: *The Diary of Dawid Seriakowiak*, trans. Kamil Turowski, Bloomsbury 1996

The Holocaust, On the Run from Nazi Terror, Poland 1942 Chaim Prinzental: *Final Letters from the Yad Vashem archive*, eds. Reuven Dafni and Yehudit Kleiman, Weidenfeld and Nicolson 1991

Amon Goeth's Birthday Party, Plaszow Concentration Camp, Poland 1943 Natalia Karpf: *The War After: living with the holocaust*, Heinemann 1996

A Secret Hiding Place, Holland 1942 Anne Frank: *The Diary of Anne Frank*, eds. Otto H. Frank and Mirjam Pressler, trans. Susan Massotty, Penguin 1995

Working on the Burma Railway, Thailand 1943 Alfred Allbury: *Bamboo and Bushido*, Robert Hale Ltd 1955

A German Account of 'D' Day, Normandy, France 1944 Joseph Haeger: *Nothing Less Than Victory*, Russell Miller, Penguin Books 1994

V.E. Day, London 1945 Countess of Ranfurly: *To War With Whitaker*, Mandarin 1995

Bomb-devastated Hiroshima, Japan 1945 Kenneth Harrison: *Road to Hiroshima*, Rigby Publishers 1983

A Turkish Brothel, Istanbul c. 1952 J.A. Cuddon: *The Owl's Watchsong*, Century Hutchinson Ltd 1960

An Indian Hunter, Amazonia, South America 1958 Adrian Cowell: *The Decade of Destruction*, Hodder and Stoughton 1990

A Polish Immigrant Arrives in Montreal, Canada 1959 Eva Hoffman: *Lost in Translation*, Minerva 1991

The Cuban Missiles Crisis, Washington, America 1962 Robert F. Kennedy: *13 Days: the Cuban missiles crisis October 1962*, Macmillan and Co. Ltd 1969

Jim Garrison Learns of the Assassination of President Kennedy, New Orleans, America 1963 Jim Garrison: *On The Trail of the Assassins: my investigation and prosecution of the murder of President Kennedy,* Sheridan Square Press 1988

First Arrival on Robben Island, South Africa 1964 Nelson Mandela: *Long Walk to Freedom,* Abacus 1995

An Incident in the Cultural Revolution, China 1967 Jung Chang: *Wild Swans,* Flamingo 1993, Harpercollins 1993

Massacre at My Lai, Vietnam 1968 Pham Thi Thuam: *Sunday Times Magazine –23rd April 1989,* © Michael Bilton/TheSunday Times Magazine, 1989

Flight of Apollo 11: First Men on the Moon 1969 Edwin E Aldrin: *First On The Moon: a voyage with Neil Armstrong, Michael Colling and Edwin E. Aldrin Jr.,* Written with Gene Farmer and Dora Jane Hamblin, Michael Joseph 1970

Ted Bundy on Death Row, Florida State Prison, America 1980 Stephen G. Michaud: *The Only Living Witness,* Stephen G. Michaud and Hugh Aynesworth, Signet 1993

The Falklands War, the Liberation of Goose Green, Falkland Islands Robert Fox: *Eyewitness Falklands – a personal account of the Falklands,* Methuen 1982

The Meeting of the Beirut Hostages, Lebanon 1986 Brian Keenan: *An Evil Cradling,*Hutchinson 1992

A Day in Sarajevo, Yugoslavia 1992 Zlata Filipovic: *Zlata's Diary,* Puffin Books 1995

The End of an Empire, Hong Kong 1997 Chris Patten: Chris Patten's Speech at the Handover Ceremony of Hong Kong

The Funeral of Diana, Princess of Wales 1997 Extract from a feature by Carol Simpson talking to Lorraine Fraser originally published in The Mail on Sunday on September 7, 1997. Reproduced courtesy of Solo Syndications/The Mail on Sunday.

PICTURE CREDITS

p.1 A Viking long-ship reaches North America; Corbis-Bettmann

p.4 William's invasion as shown in the Bayeux Tapestry; reproduced from a woodcut taken from the Bayeux Tapestry

p.10 A skirmish between Saracens and Crusaders; from a contemporary woodcut

p.21 Kublai Khan 1216-94; e.t. archive, National Palace Museum Taiwan

p.30 King Charles VI of France; Popperfoto

p.31 A prison inside the Tower of London; reproduced from *The Tower of London* by William Harrison Ainsworth, illustrations by George Cruikshank; Routledge, London, 1897

p.33 The Battle of Agincourt; e.t. archive, Bibliotheque Nationale Paris

p.38 Leonardo da Vinci, self-portrait; e.t. archive, engraving from an original drawing by Da Vinci

p.52 The burning of Archbishop Cranmer; e.t. archive

p.58 A head and shoulder engraving of Martin Frobisher; Corbis-Bettmann

p.62 A typical English galleon from the time of the Armada; *The Table Book*

p.63 The Tower of London; reproduced from *The Tower of London* by William Harrison Ainsworth, illustrations by George Cruikshank; Routledge, London, 1897

p.66 The Gunpowder Plotters; e.t. archive

p.70 The landing of the Pilgrims; Corbis-Bettmann

p.82 Fleeing from the Great Plague; reproduced from *A Looking-glass for Town and Country*; a broadside in the collection on the Society of Antiquaries

p.88 The Great Frost Fair on the Thames; reproduced from a broadside in the British Museum

p.95 Lady Mary Wortley-Montagu; *The Omnibus Two Hundred Years Ago*. March 18. Introduction of Inoculation.

p.108 James Watt studies the improvement of the steam engine; Corbis-Bettman, French woodcut.

p.115 Dr Samuel Johnson; from an engraving by Finden

p.120. The Gordon Riots at Newgate, 1780; e.t. archive

p.123. Lunardi's Balloon; Barnaby's Picture Library (Fotomax index)

p.125 Lt. Bligh and officers cast adrift from the *Bounty*; e.t. archive, the National Maritime Museum, Aquatint by Robert Dodd

p.141 Hector Berlioz; from a lithograph by Baugniet

p.145 Diagram of the lower deck of a slave ship; e.t. archive

p.150 Darwin testing the speed of an elephant tortoise in the Galapagos Islands; Corbis-Bettmann

p.166 Florence Nightingale; e.t. archive, RAMC Historical Museum

p.179 General Custer's death struggle at the Battle of Little Big Horn; Corbis-Bettmann

p.185 Anton Chekhov; Corbis-Bettman

p.193 A typical Boer War block house; Malby and sons Lithograph

p.198 Sketches of the sinking of the Titanic made by a survivor while he was on one of the vessel's collapsible rescue boats.

p.208 Howard Carter discovers the Tomb of King Tutankhamun; e.t. archive

p.211 Charles Lindbergh and his plane, *The Spirit of St Louis;* e.t. archive

p.214 George Orwell (Eric Blair); Corbis-Bettmann

p.217 Anne Frank; Corbis-Bettmann

p.223 Hiroshima after the first atomic bomb; Barnaby's Picture Library

p.229 Nelson Mandela leaving prison, 1990; Corbis-Bettmann

p.232 Buzz Aldrin; e.t. archive

Opposite p.147: Floral Tributes for Diana, Princess of Wales, September 1997. Picture reproduced courtesy of Rex Features Ltd.

All colour illustrations excepting that opposite p.147 courtesy of e.t. archive